[redacted]

INTERPRETATIONS OF THE *BHAGAVAD-GĪTĀ* AND IMAGES OF THE HINDU TRADITION

The *Bhagavad-Gītā* is probably the most popular – and certainly the most frequently quoted and widely studied – work of Hindu sacred literature. This book investigates the *Bhagavad-Gītā*'s rise to prominence in the nineteenth and twentieth centuries, and its relationship with the Hindu tradition in the modern era.

It features a range of influential Indian and Western thinkers to illustrate trends in writing about the *Bhagavad-Gītā*, including Western academic, Indian activist, Christian theological, Hindu universalist, perennialist mystical and contemporary experiential accounts. Examining the ideas of such influential figures as F. Max Müller, M.K. Gandhi, Bede Griffiths, Swami Vivekananda, Aldous Huxley and Swami Bhaktivedanta, this book demonstrates the inextricable link between different interpretations of the *Bhagavad-Gītā* and images of the Hindu tradition.

This accessible book aptly demonstrates the relevance of the *Bhagavad-Gītā* for an understanding of Hinduism as a modern phenomenon.

Catherine A. Robinson is Senior Lecturer in the Study of Religions at Bath Spa University; she is the author of *Tradition and Liberation: The Hindu Tradition in the Indian Women's Movement* (RoutledgeCurzon, 1999).

INTERPRETATIONS OF THE *BHAGAVAD-GĪTĀ* AND IMAGES OF THE HINDU TRADITION

The song of the Lord

Catherine A. Robinson

Routledge
Taylor & Francis Group
LONDON AND NEW YORK

First published 2006
by Routledge
2 Park Square, Milton Park, Abingdon, Oxon OX14 4RN

Simultaneously published in the USA and Canada
by Routledge
270 Madison Ave, New York, NY 10016

Transferred to Digital Printing 2006

Routledge is an imprint of the Taylor & Francis Group

Typeset in Times New Roman by
Newgen Imaging Systems (P) Ltd, Chennai, India
Printed and bound in Great Britain by
Antony Rowe Ltd, Chippenham, Wiltshire

British Library Cataloguing in Publication Data
A catalogue record for this book is available
from the British Library

Library of Congress Cataloging in Publication Data
Robinson, Catherine A.
Interpretations of the Bhagavad-Gita and images of the Hindu tradition:
the Song of the Lord / by Catherine A. Robinson.
p. cm.
Includes bibliographical references.
1. Bhagavadgītā – Commentaries – History and criticism.
2. Bhagavadgītā – Influence – Modern civilization. 3. Hinduism. I. Title.

BL1138.66.R63 2005
294.5′924046′09–dc22 2005001998

ISBN10: 0–415–34671–1
ISBN13: 978-0-415-34671-9

TO CHRIS AND ERIC ROBINSON
FOR EVERYTHING

CONTENTS

PREFACE

For some years, I have been teaching an undergraduate course on the Hindu tradition explored through the *Bhagavad-Gītā*. Initially, the concentration on the text was purely as an organizational principle in order to structure a survey course which, with limited time, could not hope to cover all aspects of the tradition. In teaching this course, though, I began to think that there might indeed be something more to be said about the connection between text and tradition. For example, I read at the close of Eric Sharpe's *The Universal Gītā: Western Images of the Bhagavadgītā* that 'in an important sense Hinduism itself has been recreated on the Gita's foundations' (Sharpe 1985: 175). Observations such as this prompted me to reflect further, especially in the light of new perspectives on the nature and provenance of 'Hinduism' as a modern phenomenon: could the *Bhagavad-Gītā* be central to this process? This study is thus an exploration of the thesis that there is a strong relationship between the prominence of the *Bhagavad-Gītā* and the construction of the Hindu tradition.

Certainly a cursory review of comments found in general works on the Hindu tradition would support the claim that the *Bhagavad-Gītā* has a special status. For instance, Gerald Larson who has made a significant contribution to the understanding of the text writes in an essay on 'Hinduism in India and in America' that '[t]he *Bhagavad Gita* is known and beloved by all Hindus', adding that '[i]f there is any one text that comes near to the totality of what it is to be a Hindu, it would be the *Bhagavad Gita*' (Larson 2000: 132). Similar statements abound in single volume introductions, among them Gavin Flood's description of the *Bhagavad-Gītā* as 'perhaps the most famous of the Hindu scriptures' that 'has touched the hearts of millions of people both in South Asia and throughout the world' (Flood 1996: 124) and Klaus Klostermaier's description of the *Bhagavad-Gītā* as the 'one book... that virtually all Hindus know and recite daily by heart' that 'has become a classic also in the West' (Klostermaier 1994: 14). Yet it is increasingly recognized that the part now played by the *Bhagavad-Gītā* in the West and in India too is a feature of the modern period. That this is pertinent to the construction of the Hindu tradition is suggested by the tendency to ascribe to the *Bhagavad-Gītā* a foundational role in religion, frequently by likening it to Christian scripture. Accordingly, this study takes as its starting-point the claim that the *Bhagavad-Gītā*'s rise to greatness is an important aspect of the reification of the Hindu tradition.

However, at the outset it must be acknowledged that texts other than the *Bhagavad-Gītā* have been promoted as epitomizing Hindu beliefs and practices, while factors other than the focus on scripture have been involved in the representation of the Hindu tradition as a religion. Moreover, to take this line obviously entails a sample that in crucial respects is far from complete, excluding as it does a wealth of material that does not offer an ideological exposition of the *Bhagavad-Gītā* or refer to a textual norm for the Hindu tradition. Nevertheless, the *Bhagavad-Gītā* has largely eclipsed its rivals, chiefly the *Vedas* and the *Upaniṣads*, and scripture continues to be the basis of many versions of the Hindu tradition. Of course, the dominance of the *Bhagavad-Gītā* in the context of the dominance of scripture holds true only for particular levels of discourse, those associated with official or formal pronouncements addressed to a wider educated audience in India and beyond, but it has been very influential for all that. This is why this study has been written – to demonstrate how interpretations of the *Bhagavad-Gītā* have had their impact on images of the Hindu tradition.

ACKNOWLEDGEMENTS

I would like to begin by thanking everyone who gave me the help and encouragement that enabled me to complete the project. In particular, I am grateful to Prof. Denise Cush and Ms Ann Siswell for their comments on the draft, Mrs Kay Millard who read the manuscript for style and clarity and Mrs Jan Sumner who word-processed the result. Mark Annand provided invaluable technical advice and assistance. Special thanks are due to Prof. John Brockington for his constructive criticism of the introduction. Special thanks are also due to Prof. Alexis Sanderson for providing me with a copy of his forthcoming work, *Śaivism: Development and Impact*, and for permitting me to cite it here and to Dr Grevel Lindop for sending me his work in progress, 'The Indian Influence on Blake', to which I have referred in the conclusion. If any copyright has been unwittingly infringed, the author offers her sincere apologies and will make restitution accordingly. Last, but not least, I am indebted to the National Centre for English Cultural Tradition, Sheffield, and the Wellcome Library, London, for allowing me access to rare material as well as to library staff at Bath Spa University for their ingenuity and tenacity in obtaining elusive books and articles.

Note

References to the *Bhagavad-Gītā* (both the text and associated commentary) are generally given in round brackets. Where only one figure is given, this refers to a chapter, e.g. (15). Where two or more figures are given separated by a full stop, these refer to a chapter and, after the full stop, the verse or verses, e.g. (18.64). Multiple references employ a semi-colon to divide chapters, e.g. (15; 18) and (1.28; 3.12). Successive verses are linked by a hyphen, e.g. (4.7–8). Verses from the same chapter are divided by a comma, e.g. (2.39, 49).

References to other Hindu texts include their full titles but are presented in the same style, e.g. (*Ṛg Veda* 1.164.46).

INTRODUCTION

The *Bhagavad-Gītā* and modernity – the construction of 'Hinduism', 'religion' and 'scripture'

In a now famous article, Gerald Larson remarks:

> What the *Gītā* is, finally, is inseparable from its many contextual environments, ancient and modern, Eastern and Western, scholarly and popular, corporate and personal, secular and sacred – contextual environments that have emerged in an on-going historical process and will continue to emerge as that historical process unfolds.
>
> (Larson 1975: 666)

This article refers to the work of Milton Singer (Larson 1975: 654) who identifies what he calls a 'cleavage between the textual and contextual studies of religion', the former – Indological studies of sacred literature – being connected with the humanities, and the latter – anthropological studies of religious communities – being connected with the social sciences (Singer 1972: 40). Singer's approach, advocating an interdisciplinary method, influences Larson's 'socio-analytic criticism' or 'praxis-analysis' that proposes to conduct literary research in such a way as to take account of its social setting (Larson 1975: 658). Indeed, it is noteworthy that when Singer insists upon the value of contextual knowledge for the understanding of specific texts, he cites the example of the *Bhagavad-Gītā* as 'a sectarian text [that] has become widely popular' where its study both as text and in context 'may suggest "dominant ideas" in Hinduism' (Singer 1972: 49).

This book takes Larson's statement as a starting point for an investigation into nineteenth- and twentieth-century interpretations of the *Bhagavad-Gītā*. In so doing, it follows Singer's lead, especially by extending the scope of the enquiry to include the relationship between these interpretations and images of the Hindu tradition. It examines commentaries on the *Bhagavad-Gītā* (defined very broadly to encompass brief comments on the text as well as full-length commentaries) by important figures and associated with influential movements as a means of examining various representations of the Hindu tradition.[1] It will emphasize that, just as there are multiple interpretations of the *Bhagavad-Gītā*, there are multiple images of the Hindu tradition and that these are inextricably linked. That is, it focuses upon the *Bhagavad-Gītā* as text but, by viewing the text in the light of instances of its commentatorial corpus, reads it in a series of different contexts, historically, culturally and spiritually, in order to analyse the Hindu tradition as a modern concept.[2]

The *Bhagavad-Gītā*

The *Bhagavad-Gītā* (*Song of the Lord*), traditionally attributed to Vyāsa ('arranger' or 'compiler'), legendary composer of the *Mahābhārata* in the mists of antiquity, comprises 700 verses arranged in 18 chapters. The magisterial work, *The New Encyclopaedia Britannica*, describes it as 'one of the greatest and most beautiful of the Hindu scriptures' which 'gives a synopsis of the religious thought and experience of India through the ages' (Encyclopaedia Britannica 1998: 2.183). It is found in the *Bhīṣmaparvan* (the sixth of 18 sub-divisions) of the *Mahābhārata*,[3] an epic that describes the conflict between the Pāṇḍavas and the Kauravas over the succession to the throne of the Kurus. The *Bhagavad-Gītā* occurs at the point in the narrative where this conflict has come to a climax and the two great armies are ranged on the plains of Kurukṣetra with battle about to commence.

Briefly, the rivalry between the Pāṇḍavas and the Kauravas arises in the context of the chequered history of the royal brothers, Pāṇḍu, the younger brother and father of the Pāṇḍavas, and Dhṛtarāṣtra, the elder brother and father of the Kauravas. Dhṛtarāṣtra is blind and has therefore been passed over in favour of Pāṇḍu. However, Pāṇḍu goes into exile and later dies, leaving Dhṛtarāṣṭra as king. As the Pāṇḍavas and Kauravas grow up, Dhṛtarāṣṭra attempts to settle their competing claims by dividing the kingdom between the Pāṇḍavas led by Yudhiṣṭhira and the Kauravas led by Duryodhana. Yet this does not end the bitter feud and in due course Duryodhana challenges Yudhiṣṭhira to a game of dice, a game in which Yudhiṣṭhira loses everything he has, his kingdom, his brothers, himself, and memorably Draupadī, their joint wife. Gambling and losing once more when the stake is 12 years' exile in the forest and a further year living anonymously, Yudhiṣṭhira takes the Pāṇḍavas into exile. Even when the Pāṇḍavas have fulfilled these conditions and accordingly return to reclaim their kingdom, Duryodhana angrily refuses to abide by his side of the agreement and the antagonists prepare for battle. Kṛṣṇa, a leading figure of the Yādava clan, sends his soldiers to fight for the Kauravas but himself serves as charioteer to Arjuna, the third of the five sons of Pāṇḍu and a hero renowned for his martial courage and prowess. It is in the *Bhagavad-Gītā* that Kṛṣṇa reveals himself as God while Arjuna is portrayed as a warrior, paralysed by a moral dilemma, unwilling to make war.[4]

The *Bhagavad-Gītā*, reported by the royal bard, Saṃjaya, to Dhṛtarāṣṭra, relates the crisis of conscience experienced by Arjuna as he contemplates the battle. Facing the awful prospect of killing his teachers and members of his own family, a dejected Arjuna slumps down in his war chariot, his bow falling from his hand. Foreseeing evil consequences in the light of which both victory and kingship lose their appeal, he declares to Kṛṣṇa that in such circumstances it would be better to die than to kill. In response to Kṛṣṇa's admonition, Arjuna requests instruction and what follows largely consists of this instruction concerning the divine, the self and the world, as well as liberation and the means to its attainment. All these arguments, and indeed the theophany in which Kṛṣṇa reveals his true nature to Arjuna, are intended to persuade Arjuna to do his duty as a warrior and fight. In this, Kṛṣṇa is successful and Arjuna resolves to engage in the battle. Once Arjuna has reached this decision, the *Bhagavad-Gītā* comes to its close with Saṃjaya's praise for the dialogue. The battle which lasts 18 days then begins and, with Kṛṣṇa's help and Arjuna's skilful generalship, the Pāṇḍavas triumph.

At the outset, it should be acknowledged that there are some literary-critical issues that have proved contentious, notably the authorship, date, provenance and unity of the *Bhagavad-Gītā*. Scholarly opinion tends to differ from traditional views and, in many significant respects, is itself divided on these interrelated topics. Debate has centred principally on four areas. First, it addresses whether the text is the work of one or more authors and editors, their identities and affiliations (Feuerstein 1983: 41; cf. Edgerton 1972: 107). Second, it addresses whether the text originates from some centuries before or after the start of the Common Era, in whole or in part (Radhakrishnan 1989a: 14; cf. van Buitenen 1981: 6; cf. Zaehner 1973: 7). Third, it addresses whether the text is an essentially independent composition or from the outset has been an integral part of the *Mahābhārata* (Edgerton 1972: 105–6; cf. van Buitenen 1981: 5; cf. Zaehner 1973: 7). Finally, it addresses whether the text is an intentionally syncretic composition or has passed through distinct stages of compilation (Feuerstein 1983: 39; cf. Johnston 1937: 6–7). These are interesting questions in their own right, albeit associated mainly with the Western canons of critical scholarship. Nevertheless, detailed discussion of these questions lies outside the scope of this study except insofar as they have a bearing on specific interpretations of the *Bhagavad-Gītā* associated with specific images of the Hindu tradition.[5] More important for present purposes is an initial brief consideration of the status and role of the *Bhagavad-Gītā* in the pre-modern period.

The *Bhagavad-Gītā* in the pre-modern period

Hindu sacred literature is conventionally divided into two categories designated śruti, heard or revealed literature, and smṛti, remembered or traditional literature. Although these categories and their contents tend to be represented as static and straightforward – śruti as earlier, superior and exclusive; smṛti as later, inferior and inclusive – this is far from the case as the *Bhagavad-Gītā* demonstrates. The *Mahābhārata*, as an epic and an example of itihāsa (tales and legends), is classified as smṛti. Since the *Bhagavad-Gītā* is located within the *Mahābhārata*, some scholars have concluded that its classification as smṛti is unambiguous (e.g. Bharati 1980: 131; Larson 1975: 661). However, other scholars have argued that the *Bhagavad-Gītā* has been regarded almost as if it was śruti (e.g. Coburn 1984: 449; van Buitenen 1981: 12). Evidence cited by Thomas Coburn in support of this view is both internal and external to the text, such as the comparatively low number of variant forms of the text, a characteristic attributed to śruti, the claim made in the colophons of the chapters to be Upaniṣadic, and the text's inclusion in an index to the *Upaniṣads* on the grounds that it is associated with this śruti literature (Coburn 1984: 448–9).[6] J.A.B. van Buitenen provides additional evidence including Bhāskara's commentary prohibiting women and low class men, those traditionally barred access to śruti, from listening to sections of the *Mahābhārata*, such as the *Bhagavad-Gītā*, which expound the Vedānta, and also the existence of quotations from the *Bhagavad-Gītā* in the *Vedānta Sūtra* indicating its śruti-style eminence at an early period (van Buitenen 1981: 10–12).[7] This qualifies, if it does not contradict, Aghenanda Bharati's suggestion that the 'suppression of the traditional distinction between *śruti* and *smṛti*' is a feature of modernity, giving as his example the way in which 'the *Bhagavadgītā* has tacitly been given *śruti* status' (Bharati 1971: 84–5).

Despite some protestations to the contrary, there is, then, no doubt of the prestige enjoyed by the *Bhagavad-Gītā* in the pre-modern period, as testified by the wealth of commentaries it has generated and the number of texts called '*Gītā*' that it has inspired (cf. Coburn 1984: 452–3). The *Bhagavad-Gītā* has been prized by Vedāntins as a constituent of the prasthāna-trayā (threefold canon or triple foundation) along with the *Upaniṣads* and the *Vedānta Sūtra*. Hence Vedāntic philosophers and theologians, among them Śaṅkara, Rāmānuja and Madhva, have produced commentaries on the *Bhagavad-Gītā* in accordance with Advaita (non-dualist), Viśiṣṭādvaita (qualified non-dualist) and Dvaita (dualist) Vedānta respectively. Even Śaivites composed commentaries on the *Bhagavad-Gītā*. Abhinavagupta's *Gītārthasaṃgraha*, for instance, purported to present the text's secret meaning, portraying Kṛṣṇa as the preacher of the path to a liberation defined in terms of union with Śiva (Sharma 1983: 10, 21–2, 57–9, cf. 101, 129–30, 213–15).

In addition to the commentatorial literature on the *Bhagavad-Gītā*, there are many other *Gītās*. There is the *Anu-Gītā*, also in the *Mahābhārata* but after the war has been won, when Arjuna again requests Kṛṣṇa's instruction and Kṛṣṇa responds, not by repeating his earlier discourse, but by telling him an ancient story (Telang 1908). There is the *Uddhava-Gītā* in the *Bhāgavata Purāṇa*, where Uddhava, another friend of Kṛṣṇa, having pleaded unsuccessfully to be allowed to accompany him, receives guidance about ultimate truths and their implications for true religiosity (Saraswati 2000). There is the *Śiva-Gītā* in the *Padma Purāṇa* in which Śiva, like Kṛṣṇa in the *Bhagavad-Gītā*, offers spiritual counsel albeit to Rāma who, like Arjuna in the *Bhagavad-Gītā*, is a warrior reluctant to join battle (Deutsch and Siegel 1987: 2.127). There is the *Devī-Gītā* in the *Devī Bhāgavata Purāṇa* in which Bhuvaneśvarī, the World Mother, teaches her devotee, the Mountain King Himālaya, expounding different disciplines and revealing her divine nature, themes with clear counterparts in the *Bhagavad-Gītā*'s account of knowledge, action and devotion and its theophany of Kṛṣṇa as God (Brown, C.M. 1998). These and many other texts ally themselves with the *Bhagavad-Gītā*, all of which, however different from the original, seek to benefit from its exalted reputation.

It is thus possible to conclude that the *Bhagavad-Gītā* was important in the pre-modern period, even without considering the vast vernacular literature also associated with the text, most famously the Marathi version of Jñāneśvara, the *Bhāvārtha-dīpika* (better known as the *Jñāneśvarī*). What is also apparent is that the *Bhagavad-Gītā*'s importance was limited in its scope, at least in comparison with the text's pre-eminence in the modern period.

The construction of 'Hinduism' in the modern period

In the first half of the nineteenth century, Raja Ram Mohan Roy variously described the *Bhagavad-Gītā* as 'the essence of all the Smritis, Puranas, and Itihasas' and 'the essence of all Sastras' while he argued that its 'authority is considered the most sacred by Hindus of all persuasions' (Roy, R.M. 1945: 93, 105, 134). Perhaps these statements reflect the pre-modern status of the text, perhaps they anticipate its modern status. In any case, it is increasingly recognized by scholars that the extraordinary prominence of the *Bhagavad-Gītā* is a feature of modernity despite disagreement over the date at which it became dominant.

Eric Sharpe, observing that '[t]raditionally the Gita had been accessible to the learned, to the *pandits*', contends that the change occurred from the 1880s onwards but especially after 1900, whereupon the *Bhagavad-Gītā* 'came to occupy a position (which in the popular mind it has since that day never lost) as the undisputed statement of all that is most central and most important in the Hindu world of ideas' (Sharpe 1985: 67, 69). However, Arvind Sharma, allowing that the *Bhagavad-Gītā* 'was always an important scripture', suggests that its special role can be traced to the 1920s, since when 'it has grown in stature to acquire the rank of the most significant text of modern Hinduism, with the consequence that any Hindu leader or scholar worth his or her salt has felt compelled to comment on it in one manner or another' (Sharma 1993: 33). In order to understand how the *Bhagavad-Gītā* attained such significance, it is necessary to locate it in the context of the construction of 'Hinduism' on a model of 'religion' derived from the Western cultural heritage with an emphasis upon 'scripture'.

Origins and development of 'Hinduism'

Although not without forthright and trenchant criticisms from dissenting views, a consensus has now emerged in which 'Hinduism' is understood to be a modern Western concept, adopted and adapted by 'Hindus' yet nevertheless based on the modern Western concept of 'religion' that accords undue significance to 'scripture'.[8] This deconstructionist and anti-essentialist consensus informed by post-colonial and other perspectives, not only marks a decisive break from earlier academic studies that accepted that 'Hinduism' was the one ancient indigenous 'religion' of the subcontinent founded upon 'scripture', but also contrasts with the common portrayal of 'Hinduism' as unproblematic despite its complex and contested nature. As Friedhelm Hardy observes, '[a]lthough in popular writing the alleged content of "Hinduism" is rapidly developing a monolithic and stereotyped character, this is no more than a fairly arbitrary abstraction from a random set of facts' (Hardy 1990: 145). Consequently, it is important to differentiate between 'Hinduism' as a contemporary phenomenon with ideological power and practical implications and the historical process that produced it, imbuing it with an appropriate past and aura of antiquity (cf. Davis 1995: 5).

Influential in challenging assumptions about 'Hinduism' as an age-old notion has been the work of Wilfred Cantwell Smith who represents 'Hinduism' as a recent invention, declaring that it is 'a particularly false conceptualization, one that is conspicuously incompatible with any adequate understanding of the religious outlook of Hindus' (Smith, W.C. 1978: 63). His impact has been such that few, if any, discussions of the nature of 'Hinduism' fail to mention his ideas about the modernity of both term and concept. Certainly he has drawn attention to the provenance of 'Hinduism' and, related to it, the history of the word 'Hindu'.

In order to appreciate how 'Hinduism' came into being, it is thus important to investigate the changing meaning of 'Hindu' whereby an original ethnic and cultural meaning was much later superseded by a religious meaning. This was initially promoted by a negative criterion – non-adherence to Islam whether expressed in ethnic, cultural or even religious terms – that arose out of the dichotomy between indigenous and exogenous civilizations, and latterly by a positive construction – adherence to the 'Hindu religion' on the part of the indigenous population not otherwise affiliated – that involved an abstraction from, and a homogenization of, diverse beliefs and practices.

The word 'Hindu' was derived from the Sanskrit 'Sindhu', meaning river in general and the River Indus in particular, which passed into foreign use as the Persian 'Hindu' and cognate terms in other languages such as the Greek 'Indos' (Jackson 1996: 88). By extension, the word was employed to denote the people of the area around the river and their way of life. Opinion differs as to whether 'Hindu' was essentially an alien term (Smith, W.C. 1978: 256 n.46) or whether it drew upon native precedent and parallel (Lipner 1994: 8). In either case, 'Hindu' referred to an inhabitant of the subcontinent who participated in the indigenous civilization, related to the geographic and linguistic senses of 'Hindustan' and 'Hindustani' respectively. 'Hindu' did not designate religious affiliation nor did it distinguish among affiliations to what are now regarded as different 'religions'. This conclusion is supported by the common origin of 'Hindu' and 'Indian' in the Sanskrit 'Sindhu', suggesting that the distinction between the former as a term for religious identity and the latter as a term for national identity owes something to happenstance (von Stietencron 1991: 12).

The change in the meaning of 'Hindu' from the ethnic and cultural to the religious occurred in two important phases during which 'Hindu' was defined negatively through the exclusion of Muslims and then positively through the association of those identified as 'Hindu' with a single unified 'religion'. In the medieval period, in Islamic usage, 'Hindu' tended to denote an Indian who was not a Muslim but who might have belonged to any of a number of movements, none of which corresponded with the concept of the 'Hindu religion' either individually or altogether. In the modern period, in Western usage, 'Hindu' tended to denote an Indian who was neither a Muslim nor a member of another movement recognized as a 'religion' and who, by virtue of this, was deemed to belong to the 'Hindu religion'. Of course, the meaning of 'Hindu' did not change in clear, self-contained stages – there is some evidence to suggest that later Islamic sources regarded 'Hindu' as a religious identity associated with the 'Hindu religion' and similarly that earlier Western sources regarded 'Hindu' as an ethnic and cultural identity associated with the indigenous civilization of India. Even so, there is a striking difference between the tendency to refer to the existence of many 'religions' among the 'Hindus' typical of Islamic usage and the existence of one 'Hindu religion' typical of Western usage.

As for 'Hindus', in pre-modern India they saw themselves as belonging to a particular tradition, be it Vaiṣṇava, Śaiva or some other group or school, so that it was only in modern India, to some extent as a result of Western influence, that they came to identify themselves and their fellows as 'Hindus' in the sense of being members of the 'Hindu religion'. Of course, this does not entail a denial of commonalities between what are now categorized as components of 'Hinduism', shared features not found in Buddhist or Jain belief or practice (Sanderson forthcoming: 7), nor does it involve a rejection of unifying factors, including pilgrimage to sacred sites, famous regional temples, worship of images, devotion to the divine and the conduct of textual scholarship (Flood 2003: 4). Certainly this does not detract from the importance of medieval India in the development of 'Hindu' identity, not least the response to, and reaction against, the Muslim presence, albeit not initially or exclusively presented in religious terms.[9]

Studies of India were produced by Muslim scholars, who ranged widely across religious subjects as well as other themes. A famous example is Al-Birūnī's *Kitāb fī tahqiq mā li'l-hind*, which set up an opposition between 'Hindus' and Muslims, stating at the outset 'the Hindus entirely differ from us in every respect' (Sachau 1910: 1.17). These differences included those of 'religion' – 'they totally differ from us in religion' – alongside those of more general cultural characteristics including language and custom (Sachau 1910: 1.19). His portrayal of religious attitudes, the comparative absence of controversy about religious issues combined with a strong sense of exclusivity when it came to foreign influence, was thus an integral, if significant, part of a broader cultural clash (Sachau 1910: 1.19–20). Insofar as studies such as his discussed 'Hindu religion', what matters most is whether they identified one 'religion' of the 'Hindus' and whether any one 'religion' was the 'Hindu religion'.[10]

Many Muslim scholars mentioned a plurality of 'Hindu religions' (Lawrence 1976: 13–32; von Stietencron 1991: 12, 1995: 77). For instance, al-Idrīsī, writing in the mid-twelfth century though following the example set by Ibn Khurradādhbih some three centuries earlier, is credited with having enumerated

42 'religions' (Larson 1993: 181; cf. Thapar 1985: 17). The assumptions underlying this type of approach can be illustrated by considering another work from the twelfth century, Shahrastānī's *Kitāb al-milal waṇ nihal*, especially his *'Ārā' al-hind* (*The Views of the Indians*), which, within an overarching theological framework ordering other 'religions' by criteria derived from their closeness to Islam, ranks lowest those religious groups without a revealed book or fixed laws (Lawrence 1976: 16–17). In addition to the sheer diversity that he described, his discussion of '[t]he Barāhima/Brahmans' and 'Indian Philosophers' demonstrates a very different conceptualization of 'religions' – the former category containing '[t]he Followers of the Buddhas' on the same basis as '[t]he Proponents of Meditation' and '[t]he Proponents of Metempsychosis' – with no unified vision of the 'Hindu religion' – the origins of the former category as a rational system are traced to 'Barhām' and that of the latter category as an intellectual tradition to 'Braḥmanan' without establishing any relationship between the two (Lawrence 1976: 38–47, 56–62, 266). Accordingly, the medieval Islamic view of 'Hindu', though establishing a clear line of demarcation between the Muslim and the 'Hindu', did not extend to describing the 'Hindu' in terms of allegiance to a 'religion' but instead frequently referred to a multiplicity of 'cults' and 'sects'.

This pattern was replicated in the indigenous usage of 'Hindu' to denote non-Muslims that, though later, indicates that for indigenous authors too what united 'Hindus' and differentiated them from Muslims were general cultural ideas and observances rather than particular religious beliefs and practices. Joseph O'Connell, for instance, in his survey of the use of the word 'Hindu' in sixteenth to eighteenth century Gauḍīya Vaiṣṇava texts allows that its usage did extend to the religious – his examples include '"ghost (or idol) of the Hindu(s)" (*hindura bhūta*), "god of the Hindu(s)" (*hindura debatāra*), "God of the Hindu(s)" (*hindura īśvara*) and "Hindu scripture" (*hindu śāstre*)' – but insists that its primary sense was to designate a people and hence their way of life (O'Connell 1973: 341–2). Evidence such as this suggests that the conflict in medieval India was principally conceived in cultural terms; from the point of view of the Gauḍīya Vaiṣṇava authors, a distinction was made between 'the more native and cultivated people, the Hindus, and the more foreign and barbarous people, the Yavanas or Mlecchas, not thought of primarily as a religious group' (O'Connell 1973: 342).

O'Connell's interpretation of Vaiṣṇava sources and their use of the word 'Hindu' is supported by Alexis Sanderson's analysis of Śaiva sources. Sanderson's study of the development and impact of Śaivism poses the question whether the Vaidika (Veda-related), the Vaiṣṇava, the Śaiva and the Saura (Sūrya-related) traditions were regarded as parts of one 'religion' distinguished from both Buddhism and Jainism (Sanderson forthcoming: 4). In answering this question in the negative, he does point out that the word 'Hindu' was used to differentiate between Muslims and non-Muslims, for example, by the fifteenth-century Śaiva historian, Śrīvara (Sanderson forthcoming: 4). However, while acknowledging that the heading 'Hindu' included Śaivas, Vaiṣṇavas and Vaidikas, he adds that 'there is no reason to think that it did so with the sense that these were coreligionists rather than sharers of certain cultural or socio-religious practices that distinguished them from Muslims, such as the cremation of the dead and an abhorrence of cow-slaughter, even if, and this is by no means certain, it was intended to exclude the Buddhists and Jainas' (Sanderson forthcoming: 4–5). Thus, from a Śaiva perspective too, medieval India was divided along cultural rather than religious lines, the indigenous and the exogenous cultures rather than 'Hinduism' and Islam, a view confirmed by the pronouncements of Śaiva, Vaiṣṇava and Vaidika authorities who upheld the independence of their religious traditions and rejected any idea of their unity (Sanderson forthcoming: 5). Consequently, this substantiates the claim that it would be anachronistic to assume that indigenous usage of 'Hindu' connoted a common religious identity.[11] On the contrary, the decisive shift from a number of 'Hindu religions' to the 'Hindu religion' was associated with modern Western ideas though appropriated by 'Hindus' for their own purposes.

A complicating factor in this account is the existence of alternative terminology in the modern West, notably 'Gentoo' which the *Oxford English Dictionary* defines as 'a pagan inhabitant of Hindustan, opposed to Mohammedan' while citing instances of its use from the seventeenth through the nineteenth centuries (Simpson and Weiner 1989: VI.454–5). *Hobson-Jobson*, citing instances from as early as the sixteenth century, explains that the term 'is a corruption of the Portuguese *Gentio*, "a gentile" or heathen, which they applied to the Hindus in contra-distinction to the *Moros* or "Moors," *i.e.* Mahommedans' (Yule and Burrell 1996: 367–9).[12] This derivation from the concept of 'Heathen' explicitly links it with the Christian world view, which classified the world's population in accordance with '*lex christiana, lex iudaica, lex mahometana* and *lex gentilium*', that is, Christians, Jews, Muslims and 'Heathens' (von Stietencron 1995: 74).

Such a fourfold classification, with the fourth category labelled 'Idolaters', is found in Edward Brerewood's 1614 treatise, *Enquiries Touching the Diversity of Languages and Religions through the Chiefe Parts of the World*, which referred to 'Christians', 'Mahometans', 'Jews' and 'Idolaters' and estimated 'the proportion with respect to the whole earth, that each one of the forementioned religions, have to the other', concluding that 'Idolaters' possessed nearly two-thirds of the world (Brerewood 1614: 118; cf. Smith, J.Z. 1998: 271). All 'Heathens' were believed to be under the power of the Devil and hence to belong to one 'religion' where the varieties of *lex gentilium* were differentiated only by region of the globe (von Stietencron 1991: 12, 1995: 74). Thus in J. Newton Brown's 1835 work, *Encyclopedia of Religious Knowledge, or, Dictionary... Containing Definitions of All Religious Terms*, 'Idolatry' was treated as a fundamentally unitary phenomenon with the same character and constitution. Any variety in its manifestations in specific societies was relegated in importance by suggesting 'that all the idolatrous systems of religion, which have ever existed in the world, have had a common origin, and have been modified by the different fancies and corruptions of different nations' (quoted in Smith, J.Z. 1998: 276). The application of this to India can be seen as late as the early eighteenth century when Bartholomäus

Ziegenbalg, replicating the fourfold religious classification of humanity into Jews, Christians, Muslims and 'Heathens', relied upon a geographical referent to distinguish the particular 'Heathens' about whom he was writing from 'Heathens' in general, hence the title *Malabarisches Heidenthum* (*Malabarian Heathenism*) (von Stietencron 1991: 12).[13]

The obvious implication was that all Indian 'Heathens' belonged to one 'religion' but this was only because all 'Heathens' everywhere, irrespective of any differences between them, belonged to the same 'religion' (von Stietencron 1991: 13). In such circumstances, it is possible to find mention of 'the religion of the Gentoos' in an Indian context (King, R. 1999: 100). However, in the light of new knowledge and understanding, the insistence upon there being but one 'religion' of the 'Heathens' became increasingly difficult to defend (von Stietencron 1995: 75). Along with the idea that the Indian 'Heathen' had their own 'religion' came a preference for the term 'Hindu' over 'Gentoo' so that references to 'the religion of the Hindus' tended to displace those to 'the religion of the Gentoos' (King, R. 1999: 100).[14] Indeed the way in which 'Hindus' were thought to be co-religionists can be regarded as a consequence of Christian ideas and experience in areas other than the classification of 'Heathenism'; for instance, Christianity's exclusive truth claims and powerful ecclesiastical authorities led to the expectation of conflict between 'religions', hence the absence of such conflict among 'Hindus' could not be reconciled with a situation of religious pluralism (von Steitencron 1991: 13–14, 1995: 75–6).

Consequently, the concept of the 'Hindu religion', that is 'an Indian religion with a coherent system of beliefs and practices that could be compared with other religious systems' (Jackson 1996: 88), was well established in the latter half of the eighteenth century, whereas the word 'Hinduism' was in common currency in the early nineteenth century when it was 'interpreted as being the primal and ancient religion of the subcontinent' (Omvedt 1995: 9). The forces contributing towards this construction of 'Hinduism', however, require a more detailed analysis.

The impact of empire

British imperialism played a leading part in the construction of 'Hinduism', not least in the priority attached to 'religion' and especially to the 'Hindu religion' as the basis of Indian civilization (e.g. Ludden 1993: 259). British involvement was both direct and indirect, including the enforcement of 'Hindu' personal law and the administration of 'Hindu' religious institutions as well as official use of certain categories to classify 'religion'. This led to the reification of 'Hinduism' whereby this abstract idea was turned into a practical reality alongside similar processes in respect of other 'religions' in India, invoking the notion of different 'religions' as discrete entities with definite lines of demarcation.

In his Judicial Plan of 1772, the then Governor-General of Bengal, Warren Hastings, declared that 'in all suits regarding inheritance, marriage, caste, and other religious usages, or institutions, the laws… of the *Shaster* with respect to

Gentoos shall be invariably adhered to' (quoted in Acharrya 1914: 153). Embedded in this declaration was a series of crucial judgements (Rocher 1993: 220–1): first, that indigenous law would be administered to Indians in order to conform as closely as possible to their own norms and values (Cohn 1994: 289); second, that the competence of indigenous law would extend only to those areas regarded as religious by the British in accordance with the jurisdiction of canon law administered in ecclesiastical courts (Derrett 1968: 233–5); and third, that books would be designated as the source of indigenous law despite the fact that this and other related decisions entailed a significant shift in jurisprudential principles and procedures where British legal standards were substituted for Indian ones (Levy 1973: 90).

What this meant was that it was necessary to come to some conclusions about 'the *Shaster*', that is *dharmaśāstra*, and so Hastings commissioned a panel of paṇḍits to compile a digest of 'Hindu' legal literature under the supervision of Nathaniel Halhed. Hastings' concern was to ensure that the people of India were ruled in a manner consistent with that which 'time and religion had rendered familiar to their understandings and sacred to their affections' (quoted in Feiling 1954: 103). The completed digest, *A Code of Gentoo Laws, or, Ordinations of the Pundits*, as Halhed explained, was to serve as a source for 'the legal accomplishment of a new system of government in Bengal, wherein the British laws may, in some degree, be softened by a moderate attention to the peculiar and national prejudices of the Hindoo' (Halhed 1777: xi). Consequently, a concept of 'Hindu' personal law emerged based on Brāhmaṇic sources that was to supplant local and regional legal traditions and supersede customary standards and context-sensitive criteria for legal judgements. This concept, associated with a unitary view of 'Hindu' identity and authority, was thus in reality a British contrivance, albeit unrecognized as such.

These early events were decisive in establishing the context in which later developments were located. Although there were changes (e.g. Edwardes 1967: 302), these only consolidated the literary bias of 'Hindu' personal law and in so doing reinforced its hybrid quality given the extent of British intervention. Of course, British impact on the nature, and role in the implementation, of 'Hindu' personal law existed in some tension with an ostensible policy of non-interference in religious matters, under which heading the British themselves had placed personal law. In any case, this policy was at odds with the guarantee of equal protection under the law that allowed for the possibility of ameliorative legislation (e.g. Heimsath 1964: 172). Certainly various legal measures, whether prescriptive or permissive in character, were taken to modify 'Hindu' personal law as it had been defined under British rule. Thus the British were responsible for overt as well as covert changes in 'Hindu' personal law, while this process of definition and redefinition of familial and societal norms, characterized as religious in nature, promoted the reification of 'Hinduism'.

British administration of 'Hindu' religious institutions had the same effect. Such involvement was both continuous with pre-modern practice, where the ruler had a relationship with religious institutions, and discontinuous, where this relationship developed in new directions. In pre-modern India, the ruler exercised special responsibilities towards, and derived special privileges from, temples – providing protection for the deity in return for acknowledgement of the authority of his kingship (Appadurai 1981: 214). Some modification of this intimate relationship between ruler and temple was surely inevitable under British rule, yet it did not exclude efforts at establishing connections with indigenous religious institutions to which patronage was offered and from which legitimacy was gained.

Even so, Regulation VII of 1817, the Madras Endowments and Escheats Regulation, was of great importance. Although its origins may have lain in an ambition to safeguard India's rich cultural and religious heritage, its outcome was more transformative than conservative (Frykenberg 1991: 35–6). Under this regulation, the Government of Madras made it its duty to administer all the religious institutions in the presidency, a duty that ranged from managing revenue and maintaining buildings to participation in ritual activities (Frykenberg 2000: 7). This situation was not allowed to continue without challenge for long as British opinion, antipathetic towards the East India Company's support for native religious institutions amounting to a 'Hindu' establishment, favoured the adoption of a policy consonant with Christian faith and witness as championed by the Anti-Idolatry Connexion League (Frykenberg 1991: 37, 2000: 14–17). What was perhaps intended only to ensure the perpetuation of indigenous custom and practice, however far-reaching its consequences, was increasingly criticized as an explicit endorsement and active affirmation of a non-Christian creed (Frykenberg 1991: 37). Here also, the much-vaunted notion of non-interference took centre-stage though it was not clear what non-interference might mean in this context (Frykenberg 2000: 15).

In 1843, the Government of Madras finally bowed to pressure by ending its participation in ritual activities while preserving its role in respect of religious endowments (Frykenberg 2000: 17). Eventually, in 1863, this power over endowments was surrendered too (Frykenberg 2000: 18). Yet it is doubtful whether either of these acts actually brought about a reversal in the course of events set in train by Regulation VII of 1817 by which all 'Hindu' religious institutions had been unified under the East India Company's control (Frykenberg 1991: 37). On the contrary, if the policy of withdrawal was intended to detract from the empire's 'Hindu' character or disestablish 'Hinduism' as a state 'religion', in actuality it served to reinforce these very tendencies (Frykenberg 2000: 19). 'Hinduism' gained a reality through litigation in the courts (producing a body of case law) and additional legislative provisions (specifying under what conditions and with what effect the state could take control of a temple) as well as through the rise of new pressure groups (to meet a perceived threat to 'religion') and civil campaigns (to influence the direction of government policy) (Frykenberg 2000: 18–23). In this way, British administration of 'Hindu' religious institutions promoted the reification of 'Hinduism' as a legal entity and a public cause, notwithstanding subsequent events that also inadvertently advanced the same process.

Another factor in the reification of 'Hinduism' was the official use of certain categories to classify 'religion'. This was most evident in the Indian census that, far from simply supplying objective statistical information for the government, objectified the concepts it used to compile the data collected (Cohn 1987). As a result, these concepts – one of which was 'religion' on the assumption that India was particularly religious – acquired a reality and a relevance beyond census reports, bureaucratic record-keeping and administrative efficiency.

The 1871 census, the first to be conducted on an all-India basis, set out to gather data on 'religion' that was then employed to analyse and interpret data discussed under other headings (Jones 1981: 80). This inclusion of 'religion' in the Indian census, indeed, the fundamental position assigned to 'religion' as a pervasive feature of Indian life and a principal element in the account given of the population of the subcontinent, was the most obvious way in which it was different from its British counterpart (Jones 1981: 78). Moreover, the inclusion of 'religion' and the role accorded to it posed particular problems for enumerators and analysts, arguably at their most intractable when it came to identifying 'Hindus' and hence 'Hinduism' (Jones 1981: 79). This is evident in the Punjab census report of 1881, where it was noted that anyone who was unable to define their religious affiliation or who did so but not in terms of a recognized 'religion' had been entered as a 'Hindu' (Jones 1981: 92).

Certainly a number of questions were involved in determining who was a 'Hindu' (Jones 1981: 79). Among them was the availability of alternative religious rubrics such as Sikh, raising other issues such as the status of Sikhs with cut hair when Khalsa membership was the normative definition of Sikh identity (Jones 1981: 92). Another was the appropriateness of including tribal peoples and low castes in the 'Hindu' community, when the former were often described as animists and the latter frequently barred access to places of worship (Jones 1981: 79–80, 89, 98). There was also the relationship of 'Hinduism' with specific movements, where these movements could be classified either as 'Hindu sects' or as independent groups (Jones 1981: 87, 89, 98). This emphasizes that, when the census produced knowledge about 'religion', it transformed what it claimed merely to report and represent (Jones 1981: 84). Not only did census reports accord increasing importance to 'religion' both as a subject in its own right and in relation to other subjects, but they also offered a conceptualization of 'religion' in terms of a community, membership of which could be established by reference to specific criteria and counted and hence compared with the membership of other such communities (Jones 1981: 84). When enumerating 'Hindus', the census made judgements about the limits of 'Hinduism' that, in turn, became the focus of controversy, thereby establishing how official use of certain categories to classify 'religion' promoted the reification of 'Hinduism'.

The role of missionaries

If British imperialism played a leading part in the construction of 'Hinduism', the Christian missionary presence was also important. It was not in fact unrelated to British imperialism (Frykenberg 1991: 39) though European missionaries had lived and worked in India long before this period, arguably as agents of European states' expansionist ambitions as well as representatives of their respective churches. However interesting the ideas of these early European missionaries, their influence on later missionary thinking and impact on wider Indian society appear to have been minimal. In some respects, then, missionary activity under British rule was different in both content and context. Christianity was the religion of Britain as the 'Mother Country', the 'religion' espoused by India's rulers. Moreover, a close alliance was forged between the proselytizing effort of the Christian missionaries and the British Empire's exercise of power. Thus missionaries could preach the Gospel under the protective canopy provided by the raj while the empire could be justified as an instrument of divine providence in bringing salvation to India.

Some pioneers had been active earlier, often engaged in an effort to establish their own legitimacy since there were tensions between their objectives and those of officials. However, it was only in 1813 that missionaries were formally admitted to the territories under East India Company control (Jackson 1996: 94). Considering the strength of their convictions and their confidence in the superiority of Christianity, missionaries' portrayals of 'Hinduism' inevitably displayed a marked tendency towards censure and condemnation. Christianity as an ethical monotheism was contrasted with the idolatrous superstition of polytheistic 'Hinduism' (Dalmia 1995: 179–82).

Even more important than the specific criticisms levelled against 'Hinduism' was the way in which these criticisms were directed against another 'religion'. For example, the Scottish Calvinist missionary, Alexander Duff, devoted a chapter in his book on missions in India to 'the grand theory of Hinduism' intended 'to show how the varied parts of so incongruous and multifarious a scheme are made to hang together' (Duff 1840: vi–vii). Denouncing 'Hinduism' as a compound of error, corruption and exaggeration, he wrote that '[o]f all systems of false religion it is that which seems to embody the largest amount and variety of semblances and counterfeits of divinely revealed facts and doctrines' (Duff 1840: 204). His description of 'Hinduism' as 'false religion', contrasted with Christianity as 'true religion', not only presented an unfavourable account of 'Hinduism' but also helped to define it as an entity. In this and other instances, the Christian missionary presence, through positing the existence of a non- or anti-Christian alternative, was a further step in the reification of 'Hinduism'.

The influence of Orientalist scholarship

Orientalist scholarship was similarly significant in the construction of 'Hinduism', though it was influenced both by a British imperial and a Christian missionary agenda. The imperial agenda of Orientalist scholarship was expressed in unambiguous terms by Lord Curzon, previously Viceroy of India, during a House of Lords debate on Oriental languages. Insisting upon the vital importance for the empire of proper funding for Oriental studies, he declared that 'familiarity, not merely with the languages of the peoples of the East, but with their customs, their feelings, their traditions, their history and religion' was essential to secure the future of empire (Curzon 1909).

Similarly, the missionary agenda of Orientalist scholarship was clearly articulated in the bequest of Lieutenant-Colonel Boden of the Bombay Native Infantry that endowed a Chair of Sanskrit at the University of Oxford. Sir Monier Monier-Williams, the second incumbent of the Boden Professorship, explained his decision to concentrate on lexicography by reference to the role of dictionaries in facilitating translation of the Bible. After all, as he indicated, Lieutenant-Colonel Boden's will specified the furtherance of the translation of the Bible into Sanskrit in order 'to enable his countrymen to proceed in the conversion of the natives of India to the Christian Religion' (Monier-Williams 1976: ix). Evidence such as this demonstrates that the Orientalist scholarship that informed the construction of 'Hinduism' was itself informed by broader social and political trends, including notions of imperialism and the missionary impulse.[15]

'Hindus' and 'Hinduism'

Yet, though it is necessary to acknowledge the Western contribution towards the construction of 'Hinduism', members of the Indian elite were also actively involved, not only as assistants, informants or agents serving Western purposes, but also as advocates of, and apologists for, 'Hinduism' in their own right. 'Hindus' played an important part in shaping Western perceptions of 'Hinduism' itself, hence gaining for their particular beliefs and values a more general currency. Further, 'Hindus' agitated for and against changes in personal law; they used the resources provided by the state to vie for control of religious institutions while mobilizing to protect 'Hindu' interests perceived to be under threat from powerful alien forces; and they organized to influence census returns in favour of community size and solidarity. Moreover, 'Hindus' responded to Christian missionary polemic by espousing a similar style of propagandizing to reject, through redrawing its boundaries, the adverse properties ascribed to 'Hinduism', or to revalue those properties so that, with their revised meanings, they became a source of pride. Or again, they drew upon Orientalist scholarship both to bear out and cast doubts upon its conclusions in the course of furthering their own ends. Although not going so far as to suggest that ' "Hinduism" *qua* "religion" was the *creation* of nineteenth century Indians' (Laine 1983: 165–6), a response on their part to the confrontation with Western ideas in the modern period, it is clear that the construction of 'Hinduism' arose out of encounter and interaction and consequently owed much to the Indian elite.

Some of the ways in which 'Hindus' shaped and reshaped 'Hinduism' were obviously religious, others were associated with social and political campaigns. In religious terms, Ram Mohan Roy and the Brahmo Samaj proposed a contrast between contemporary practice, considered corrupt and degenerate, and the pure theological and moral principles of the past, the unity of the divine and an ethic of service vested in the *Upaniṣads* (Kopf 1979). Dayananda Saraswati's vision of iconoclastic monotheism, however, was attributed to the *Vedas*, and the Ten Principles of the Arya Samaj, proclaiming the foundational role of these texts, grounded the organization's programme in the primacy of Vedic knowledge and the onus on all Aryas to study and teach the *Vedas* (Jones 1989). Ramakrishna, a mystic, called on his own varied experience when declaring the oneness of truth and hence an inclusive view of 'Hinduism' and a universalist view of 'religions' as different routes directed towards the same God (Nikhilananda 1942). There was also the emergence of a popular 'Hinduism' in modern India, at least in part a reaction against movements of reform and revival, constituted by shared norms and values in spite of the wide range of ideas and observances still in existence (Pennington 2001). In any case, the diversity of such formulations should not obscure the fact that they were part of the process of reifying 'Hinduism'.

In social terms, an early example of how 'Hindus' shaped 'Hinduism' is demonstrated in the controversy over sati (a woman's self-immolation on her husband's funeral pyre) that culminated in its legal prohibition by Lord William Bentinck in 1829. 'Hindu' involvement occurred in a number of capacities: paṇḍits who were consulted by British officials concerning the status of sati; reforming 'Hindus' who campaigned for the abolition of sati; and orthodox 'Hindus' who campaigned against its abolition (Mani 1987: 130–43). Yet the official discourse to which the paṇḍits contributed, the progressive discourse of the reformers and the conservative discourse of the orthodox had much in common, at least insofar as the mode of argument and type of evidence were concerned (Mani 1987: 143–53). Thus Lata Mani refers to a 'conception of tradition . . . that is specifically "colonial"' though she also presents a persuasive argument for treating the 'Woman Question' as a special case since '[w]omen become emblematic of tradition, and the reworking of tradition is conducted largely through debating their rights and status in society' (Mani 1987: 121–2). In this way, debate about the position of women contributed towards the reification of 'Hinduism'.

In political terms, a later instance of how 'Hindus' shaped 'Hinduism' is demonstrated in the articulation of nationalist ambitions by many organizations. In various ways, such organizations linked the land of India ('Hindustan') as the holy motherland, the people of India ('Hindus') as descended from the Aryans and unified by Vedic culture, and the religion of India ('Hinduism') as the spiritual aspect of Indian civilization (cf. Jaffrelot 1996: 25–31). For example, the Hindu Mahasabha (Great Hindu Association), founded in 1909, was based on the 'Hindutva' (Hinduness) ideology of Vir Savarkar with his call to 'Hinduize Politics and Militarize Hinduism' (quoted in Klostermaier 1994: 463).

Accordingly, Savarkar exhorted members to fight 'heroically to defend and consolidate Hinduism in such wise as…to herald the resurrection of a Hindu nation' (quoted in McLane 1970: 124). Although the Hindu Mahasabha soon fell into decline, the Rashtriya Svayamsevak Sangh (RSS) (National Volunteer Association), established in 1925, developed into the leading force in 'Hindu' nationalism (Jaffrelot 1996: 33), its mission being 'to unite and rejuvenate our nation on the sound foundation of Dharma' (RSS 2003). One of its offshoots, the Bharatiya Jana Sangh (BJS) (Indian People's Party) (Jaffrelot 1996: 116–19), thus determined that 'it is the duty of the Hindu society to make concerted efforts to Indianize those sections of the Indian society which have been cut off from the national mainstream because of the influence of foreign invaders and foreign missionaries' (quoted in Chatterji 1984: 316). The Vishva Hindu Parishad (VHP) (World Hindu Council) too was initiated by the RSS, specifically in an effort to meet the challenge posed by Christianity and advance the cause of 'Hindu' unity among the different 'sects' (Jaffrelot 1996: 194–202). Dating from 1964, it was inaugurated with three aims, the first two of which were '[t]o consolidate and strengthen the Hindu Society' and '[t]o protect, promote [and] propagate Hindu values of life, the ethical and spiritual in the context of modern times' (VHP 2003). These movements also contributed towards the reification of 'Hinduism', whereby 'Hinduism', broadly defined, was associated with a conception of nationhood and a radical political project.[16]

'Hinduism' and 'Hinduisms'

Variously conceived, 'Hinduism' has generally been regarded as 'the essential religion of India' (Inden 1990: 4) yet views differ as to the essence of 'Hinduism'. It has been adjudged to be one, though often its unity has been asserted in the face of a plurality of perspectives and an immense variety of beliefs and practices (von Stietencron 1991: 14). It has been adjudged to be ancient, but frequently its remote origins have been contrasted with more recent developments where the former have been idealized and the latter have been relegated or marginalized (Zavos 2000: 32–3). It has also been adjudged to be indigenous, indeed, its credentials as an authentic expression of Indian religiosity have been accepted very widely at the cost, and to the exclusion, of other traditions (Thapar 1985: 21). Thus there has been a tendency towards treating 'Hinduism' as a separate and coherent entity, identifying it with a particular version of history and equating it with the subcontinent.

Moreover, it is possible to suggest certain influential interpretations of 'Hinduism' producing different versions of 'Hinduism'; in effect, different 'Hinduisms'. For instance, there is the predominance of neo-Vedānta, an activist re-working of Śaṇkara's non-dualism, as a philosophy of 'Hinduism' that offers an attractive means of reconciling apparently conflicting stances within 'Hinduism' as a single system (Fitzgerald 1990: 101). Or again, there is the predominance of Vaiṣṇavism as a theology of 'Hinduism', centred on devotion to one God and traced to the Vedic period, that represents itself as the principal constituent and true form of 'Hinduism' (Dalmia 1995: 179). Further, there is the juxtaposition of supposedly foreign faiths, such as Christianity, Islam and Zoroastrianism, with 'Hinduism', and a degree of ambivalence towards other native 'religions' such as Buddhism, Jainism and Sikhism (Dalmia and von Stietencron 1995: 20–1).

These portrayals of 'Hinduism' have often been framed by a concentration on certain sources, themes and traditions – Sanskrit literature, philosophical schools and the renunciant ideal – rather than others – vernacular texts, folk practice and this-worldly ritual (Erndl 1993: 7–8; Narayanan 2000: 763). Nevertheless, efforts have been made to locate unifying factors, providing competing and conflicting accounts of what defines and demarcates 'Hinduism'. However, these efforts, albeit articulating an aspiration towards unity, may unwittingly reproduce some of the dichotomies that made the enterprise of locating a basis for unity both imperative and, arguably, implausible.

This is evident in the emphasis upon the Veda: the acceptance of its authority has been taken as a fundamental principle of 'Hinduism' notwithstanding both the Sanskritic literary bias of this criterion that discounts the extendibility and flexibility of Veda as a category and the inadequacy of this criterion as a means of incorporating many movements that either reject entirely or only nominally accept the authority of the Veda. A comparable drive for unity is seen in the history of scholarship where previous differentiation between 'Vedism' (the 'religion' of the Vedic hymns), 'Brahmanism' (the 'religion' of the priestly elite) and 'Hinduism' (the 'religion' of the people), has given way to the use of the term 'Hinduism' to cover all this material (von Stietencron 1991: 13). Parallel to this, the 'Hindu' claim to adherence to a unified 'religion' has been advanced by adopting a Sanskrit term, 'Sanātan(a) Dharm(a)' (Eternal Law or Way), as an ostensibly indigenous equivalent to 'Hinduism' (Vertovec 2000: 12), whether directed against Christianity as a historical 'religion', where it equated to Vaidika Dharma, or linked with the Western concept of the Perennial Philosophy, where it offered the basis for the unification of 'religions' (Halbfass 1988: 345–6). This is in spite of the fact that the meaning of dharma is far wider than 'religion' since its application to religious subjects does not distinguish 'religion', such as Bauddha Dharma, from 'sect', such as Vaiṣṇava or Śaiva Dharma (von Stietencron 1991: 15). In any case, one important usage of 'Sanātan(a) Dharm(a)' in modern India was to signify orthodoxy as opposed to reform and revival as types of 'Hinduism' (Zavos 2001: 111).

These portrayals of 'Hinduism' have frequently also been framed by the centrality of brāhmans who exerted a decisive influence over the development of 'Hinduism' as self-proclaimed leaders of native society in the modern era (Frykenberg 1991: 34) and whose self-image as custodians of sacred order and timeless truth received endorsement from Western commentators in terms of representing true 'Hindu' beliefs and values (Metcalf 1995: 134). Inextricably bound up with their dominance is the question of texts, both because the primacy of the brāhmans is attested in Sanskrit literature and because the nature of Brāhmaṇic learning included expertise in the interpretation of such literature. The accuracy of this account is doubtful, however, even while acknowledging that Sanskrit literature was important for, and Brāhmaṇic learning prestigious in, sections of pre-modern Indian society. It is doubtful as it involves an uncritical acceptance of textual authority and, its corollary, the superior status of exegetes as widely, if not universally, valid. Yet these notions, despite being selective even in respect of Sanskrit sources and contested not least by anti-Brāhmaṇic movements, have proved extraordinarily persistent and powerful (Apffel-Marglin and Simon 1994: 28–9). The impact of Brāhmaṇic ideology on 'Hinduism' and the allied importance assigned to Brāhmaṇic texts, therefore, exemplify the interplay and mutual reinforcement of Brāhmaṇic norms and Western ideas in the process of reification (Cohn 1994: 288).

Considerations such as these lead many scholars to stress that 'Hinduism' is a recent construct, irrespective of its air of antiquity and one that arises out of specific historical conditions in modern India.[17] This is the opinion eloquently expressed by Robert Frykenberg who insists that it is impossible to identify one comprehensive 'religion' with its origins in the *Vedas* but instead points to the product of a reification process occurring over the last 200 years (Frykenberg 1991: 33). Moreover, the 'Hinduism' so created possesses certain characteristics associated with 'religion' and 'scripture', characteristics that reflect Western assumptions but that also serve the interests of 'Hindus' who find a shared identity and a basis for common action in 'Hinduism'. For example, Romila Thapar's description of '[t]he new Hinduism' sets out some of its most significant aspects, citing advocacy of belief in a holy book along with insistence on the historicity of divine incarnations, appeal to a monotheistic ethos, recognition of the authority of specific 'sects' and pursuit of a proselytizing agenda (Thapar 1989: 228). Clearly, then, 'Hinduism' as it came into being was formed 'by an implicit (and sometimes explicit) tendency to define Indian religion in terms of a normative paradigm based upon contemporary Western understandings of the Judaeo-Christian traditions' as well as 'by locating the core of Indian religiosity in certain Sanskrit texts' (King, R. 1999: 101). The way in which 'Hinduism' was constructed as a 'religion' with 'scripture' has obvious implications for an understanding of the *Bhagavad-Gītā*'s modern dominance.

'Hinduism' and theories of 'religion'

Any discussion of the construction of 'Hinduism' as a 'religion' has to take account of growing scepticism about the objective reality and universal applicability of 'religion'. Scholars no longer tend to assume that 'religion' has an independent or autonomous existence. For example, Russell McCutcheon rejects 'religion' when regarded 'as an ontologically distinct category, an irreducible aspect of human experience or consciousness', in other words, 'religion' as *sui generis* (McCutcheon 1997: 19). Consequently, scholars now tend to take a more critical attitude towards 'religions' in terms of their having certain inherent and intrinsic properties. For instance, Philip Almond refers to 'religions' as 'fictive entities' and on these grounds explains that 'the attempt to discern the essence of any religion "behind" its socio-cultural expressions across space and time is a meaningless one' (Almond 1992: 54).

A theorist who has argued convincingly against the once prevalent essentialist view in favour of the reification thesis is Jonathan Z. Smith.[18] He suggests that 'religion' is an act of imagination, reasoning that 'man [*sic*] has had his entire history in which to imagine deities and modes of interaction with them' though 'man, more precisely western man, has had only the last few centuries in which to imagine religion' (Smith, J.Z. 1982: xi). It is significant that there is a historical and cultural specificity to this act of imagination, yet paradoxically 'religion' has been imagined to be present in all human societies, in all places and at all times. Such specificity – the recognition that, as Talal Asad points out, 'definition is itself the historical product of discursive processes' (Asad 1993: 29) – means that attention must be paid to the history of ideas concerning 'religion' with particular emphasis upon the meanings attributed to 'religion' in the modern West. This is because the concept of 'religion' arises out of modern Western ways of thinking while modern Western global hegemony has facilitated its exportation and imposition worldwide.[19]

Even the etymology of 'religion' is unclear. The derivation of the Latin '*religio*' has been traced to '*relegere*' meaning 'to read over again' but also to '*religare*' meaning 'to bind', and it is this second meaning that is generally preferred (Simpson and Weiner 1989: XIII.568).[20] Whatever its origins, it is certainly the case that its connotations have changed over the centuries. This has been demonstrated by Wilfred Cantwell Smith in his historical survey of Western usage of the word 'religion'.[21] This survey begins with an analysis of Roman usage before noting early and later Christian usage (Smith, W.C. 1978: 19–32). Roman usage was cultic and ritual, a usage maintained in early Christianity where it was associated, among other things, with martyrdom for the refusal to participate in traditional ceremonies on the grounds that they were false forms of worship (Smith, W.C. 1978: 21, 25–7). Although also a development from cultic and ritual norms, later Christian usage was more distinctive, relating as it did to the monastic life and hence the various monastic orders and rules (Smith, W.C. 1978: 31–2).[22] However, it was only in the modern period that 'religion' acquired great significance (Smith, W.C. 1978: 32). Having discussed developments from the Renaissance and Reformation as well as the impact of Enlightenment rationalism and Romantic sensibilities, Wilfred Cantwell Smith summarizes the range of meanings ascribed to 'religion' in the Western heritage (Smith, W.C. 1978: 32–48). He refers to the following senses of 'religion': 'a personal piety'; 'an overt system whether of beliefs, practices, values, or whatever'; and 'a generic summation' (Smith, W.C. 1978: 48–9). These are important as they distinguish 'religion in a man's life from indifference (or rebellion) [,] . . . one religion from another [, and] . . . religion from other aspects of human life' respectively (Smith, W.C. 1978: 49).

Such a survey establishes that even in the modern West the word 'religion' has been used in a number of ways and emphasizes the need for an awareness of its complicated development and disputed character – one sense, 'religion' as a system, is particularly important because it is associated with the plural 'religions' that emerges 'when one contemplates from the outside, and abstracts, depersonalizes, and reifies, the various systems of other people' (Smith, W.C. 1978: 43). Wilfred Cantwell Smith's account of the reification of 'religion', the process of 'gradually coming to conceive it as an objective systematic entity', thus relates 'religion' and the 'religions', explaining that the reification of 'religion' has been fostered by 'the rise into Western consciousness in relatively recently [*sic*] times of several so conceived entities, constituting a series: the religions of the world' (Smith, W.C. 1978: 51). This leads him to question whether there was a concept analogous to 'religion' as a system in other cultures, answering this question in the negative with reference to a range of cultures including that of India; he then explores how the 'religions' received their names, culminating in the addition of the suffix '-ism' to the name given to a tradition's followers where it was necessary to differentiate the religious from the social group as was the case for 'Hinduism' (Smith, W.C. 1978: 51–62).[23]

Inasmuch as this has a bearing on the so-called Eastern 'religions', then the invention of Eastern 'religions' through the superimposition of a Western concept onto Eastern beliefs and practices can be considered an example of Orientalism. Where previously Orientalism denoted expertise in Eastern language and literature or, in India especially, differentiated advocacy of an ostensibly indigenous-style administration from the overtly Westernizing approach known as Anglicism, Edward Said has been responsible for extending and changing its meaning. In his famous study of the same name, he defines Orientalism as an academic title related to specialization in the Orient, a mode of thought predicated upon the division between the Orient and the Occident and as a 'corporate institution for dealing with the Orient' by which he means 'a Western style for dominating, restructuring, and having authority over the Orient' (Said 1995: 2–3).[24] His study is ambitious in its scope, including but extending far beyond 'religion', yet, however provocative and insightful his analysis, it offers very little by way of comment on India and hence its importance for 'Hinduism' has to be inferred from its general tenor. Accordingly, 'Hinduism' has to be re-examined in the light of the history of imperialism and the complicity of scholarship with the imperial project, stressing the ideological loading of conventional categories and the social situatedness of all narratives. The recognition of the Western provenance of the concept of 'religion' and the realization of the part this has played in the construction of Eastern 'religions', including 'Hinduism', can for these reasons be regarded, at least in part, as inspired by Said.[25]

Frits Staal takes the view that 'Hinduism does not merely fail to be a religion; it is not even a meaningful unit of discourse' (Staal 1989: 397). This is because he is among those who argue that the concept of 'religion' is Western and, on the basis of '[t]he inapplicability of Western notions of religion to the traditions of Asia', explains 'the *creation* of so-called religions' (Staal 1989: 393). The significance of this is Staal's claim that the concept of 'religion' is alien, on the grounds that the object so designated in the West has no counterpart in Asian cultures. He bases his account on 'the notion of exclusive truth', which he regards as a defining characteristic of Western 'religions' (Staal 1989: 393). Insisting that 'such religions do not exist' in Asia, he relates that this has not discouraged the effort to discover them and, where they are not discovered, the endeavour to transpose terms for indigenous concepts and transform them into terms for such 'religions' (Staal 1989: 393). He lists the 'religions' so created while representing them as false creations when compared with 'ancestors and teachers – hence lineages, traditions, affiliations, cults, eligibility, and initiation – concepts with ritual rather than truth-functional overtones' (Staal 1989: 393). This indicates one of Staal's central concerns, the mismatch between Eastern phenomena and Western categories, as well as one of his major preoccupations, the role of ritual.

In seeking to clarify and resolve the issues associated with Eastern 'religions', Staal adopts two approaches, evaluating the usefulness of a concept of 'religion' modelled on the Western monotheistic 'religions' and proposing another more open concept of 'religion' (Staal 1989: 397). In respect of the former, he works with three features derived from Judaism, Christianity and Islam, these being 'a belief in God, a holy book, and (at least in two cases out of these three) a historic founder' (Staal 1989: 398). Taking various examples of Eastern 'religions', he concludes that Asian traditions do not conform to the Western model (Staal 1989: 398). In respect of the latter, he turns to what he calls an ' "extended Durkheim" concept of religion, which incorporates the categories of doctrine (belief), ritual, mystical experience and meditation', though he regards ritual as primary because he deems it to be independent in nature with its form preserved both within and outside religious traditions (Staal 1989: 401, cf. 388). Moreover, the importance he attaches to ritual stands in contrast to the Western concentration on belief over practice, justified as consistent with the Eastern priority of orthopraxy over orthodoxy (Staal 1989: 389).

Subsequently, the role of ritual has been taken up by S.N. Balagangadhara in an even more radical account. Staal prioritizes ritual, criticizing the Western concept of 'religion' constituted by doctrine and the consequent imbalance in the study of 'religion' (Staal 1989: 399–401, 415–16, 418–19). Balagangadhara, arguing that Staal is still in some sense committed to 'religion' as a cultural universal, advocates its replacement by an alternative 'configuration of learning' appropriate to Asia, ritual, that is, 'a culturally specific way of going-about in the world' described as '[p]erformative or practical knowledge' (Balagangadhara 1994: 315–16, 465). He labels 'Hinduism' as 'an imaginary entity', the creation of Western scholars, adding that 'there could simply be no "religion" in India' because Indian traditions do not deal with cosmogonic questions (Balagangadhara 1994: 138, 298, 394, 398). Be that as it may, he identifies some serious problems with the concept of 'religion', both by stressing its dependence on Christianity and its extension to Judaism and Islam, and by drawing out its implications for treating other traditions as 'religions' (Balagangadhara 1994: 19–25, 301–6).

The issue Balagangadhara raises is what makes Judaism, Christianity and Islam 'religions' and whether this holds true for other traditions, pointing to features such as articles of faith, ideas of God, holy books and religious institutions that are fundamental to Judaism, Christianity and Islam but are not significant for other traditions (Balagangadhara 1994: 22–4). He summarizes the resulting difficulty in these terms – 'if the Semitic religions are what religions are, other cultures do not have religions' whereas '[i]f other cultures have religions, then the Semitic religions are not religions' (Balagangadhara 1994: 24–5). In his judgement, then, certain features are necessary to Judaism, Christianity and Islam as 'religions' but, as they are not found in other cultures, presumably these cultures do not have 'religions'. On the other hand, if without satisfying these criteria, other cultures have 'religions', then this casts doubt on whether Judaism, Christianity and Islam are 'religions' (Balagangadhara 1994: 24–5). Thus Balagangadhara problematizes what makes a tradition a 'religion' and questions the existence of 'religion' in all cultures.[26]

This conundrum is a familiar one to students of 'Hinduism' who regularly read statements to the effect that 'Hinduism' is a 'religion' albeit not a 'religion' as conventionally understood (cf. Balagangadhara 1994: 15–16). Lacking a founder and a prophet, a unified theological and ethical system and a centralized organization, as well as not being based on a creed, a belief in God or a holy book and possessing no distinctive or defining principle or practice, it is nevertheless averred that 'Hinduism' is a 'religion' on the basis perhaps of a common history and heritage or a shared sense of identity (e.g. Dandekar 1971: 237; Weightman 1997: 261; cf. Balagangadhara 1994: 15–16). Yet an increasingly common approach to the defence of 'Hinduism' as a 'religion' is to appeal to Ludwig Wittgenstein's model of 'family resemblance', looking less for common features and clear boundaries than for multiple strands of similarity interwoven with, and overlaid on, one another (Ferro-Luzzi 1991: 187; cf. Knott 1998: 113–14; Lipner 1994: 6–7). The attraction of this approach rests on its reconciliation of heterogeneity with unity. However, in addition to a tendency towards circularity in the selection and evaluation of those characteristics by which 'family resemblance' is determined, there is an issue of comparability since other 'religions' are not generally described or discussed in this way. Thus the status of 'Hinduism' as a 'religion' has been questioned, especially in terms of its existence as one 'religion' entailing the categorization of distinct systems as 'sects' within a diverse whole, but also in terms of its classification as a 'world religion' alongside some other traditions though modelled on Christianity.

If the concept of 'religion' is retained, and arguably to do so is an error that reinscribes Western cultural assumptions and forecloses the possibility of genuine encounter with indigenous ideas, it can be concluded that Vaiṣṇavism, Śaivism and Śāktism, not 'Hinduism', are 'religions' on the grounds that '[t]hey each have a different theology, rely on different holy scriptures, follow the teaching of a different line of teachers . . . and worship a different supreme deity reciting different prayers' (von Stietencron 1995: 51). The consequence of seeing them as 'sects' and not 'religions' in their own right, according to Heinrich von Stietencron, is comparable to seeing Judaism, Christianity and Islam as 'sects' of a single 'religion' (von Stietencron 1991: 16–17). 'Hinduism', in his view, should be considered as a group of 'religions' – Vaiṣṇavism, Śaivism and Śāktism, on a par with Judaism, Christianity and Islam, regarded as 'religions' in their own right (von Stietencron 1991: 21). His proposed solution to the difficulty of defining 'Hinduism' as a 'religion', a difficulty with which, he stresses, scholars have struggled for so long, is thus to take ' "Hinduism" to denote a socio-cultural unit or civilization which contains a plurality of distinct religions' (von Stietencron 1991: 11). Distinguishing between 'Hinduism' and what he calls 'its distinct religious entities', characterizing the former in terms of variety and contradiction but the latter in terms of unity and coherence, von Stietencron's approach is an attempt to establish equity between 'Hindu religions', rather than 'Hinduism', and other 'religions' (von Stietencron 1991: 20).[27]

Further, even if the concept of 'Hinduism' as one 'religion' is retained, another issue arises, whether it is a 'world religion' like other 'religions' with a global presence or at least a global ambition. The category of 'world religion' arose in the nineteenth century as part of a taxonomy of types of 'religion'. A notable contribution was made by Cornelius Petrus Tiele who divided 'religion' into two main types, one being 'ethical religions', subdivided into 'nomistic or nomothetic communities' and 'universal or world religions' (Tiele 1886: 20.368). He defended the use of the term 'world religions' for those 'religions' that had reached many peoples with an expansion inspired by 'the intention to conquer the world' and to distinguish these 'religions' from others that had remained the property of one people where any expansion occurred 'only in the train of, and in connexion with, a superior civilization' (Tiele 1886: 20.368). Classifying 'Brahmanism, with its various ancient and modern sects' in the category of '[n]ational [n]omistic ([n]omothetic) religious communities', he classified only Islam, Buddhism and Christianity as '[u]niversalistic religious communities' (Tiele 1886: 20.370).[28] Nevertheless, he privileged Christianity, considering Islam to be 'not original, . . . but rather a wild offshoot of Judaism and Christianity' and Buddhism to be 'infected by the most fantastic mythology and the most childish superstitions' (Tiele 1886: 20.369). For Tiele, therefore, 'Hinduism' (or its nearest equivalent) was not a 'world religion' whereas Christianity, by virtue of its superior moral and spiritual qualities, seemed destined to be the only 'world religion'. Later, Tiele's distinction between the national, which had included 'Hinduism', and the universalistic, which had been epitomized by Christianity, was dissolved and 'Hinduism' was classified as a 'world religion' (Smith, J.Z. 1998: 280). Clearly, this inclusion of 'Hinduism' entailed a revision of the criteria defining a 'world religion' but at the same time other forces were at work shaping 'Hinduism' so that it approximated more nearly to the standard set for a 'world religion'.

Robert Frykenberg among others chronicles the way in which 'Hinduism' has acquired some characteristics consistent with a 'world religion' though he emphasizes that 'Hinduism' is only 'a simulated "world religion" ', expressing reservations about any such simplistic identification (Frykenberg 1991: 34, 40). His misgivings about the compatibility of 'Hinduism' with the category 'world religion' are common (e.g. Lopez 2000: 834). Of course, one source of scholarly misgivings is the category 'world religion' itself which does have a decided textual bias (Bowie 2000: 26–7). Loaded with Christian assumptions, among them a preference for 'scripture', this category has been influential.[29] Certainly 'Hinduism' has been constructed as a 'religion' with 'scripture', in line with the primacy accorded 'scripture' in the construction of 'religion'. This literary tendency was part of the process of reification which produced 'Hinduism', making it necessary to select a 'Hindu scripture'. The *Bhagavad-Gītā* was one of the candidates to be this 'scripture'.

'Hinduism' and 'scripture'

The construction of 'Hinduism' as a 'religion' involves considering the concept of 'scripture' as well as the concept of 'religion' with which it is inextricably connected.[30] 'Scripture', like 'religion', has both a Christian context and Christian connotations, in this case with two consequences: first, the assumption that 'scripture' is foundational to other 'religions'; and second, the assumption that the 'scriptures' of other 'religions' play the same part in these 'religions' as Christian 'scripture' plays in Christianity. Both of these assumptions about 'scripture' – that other 'religions' possess 'a book, or canon of books, that serve as the locus of authoritative doctrine' and that in these other 'religions' 'such books are read, used and thought about in much the way Protestants read, use and think about scripture' – are dubious with, as Miriam Levering comments, an adverse influence on the understanding of 'religions' (Levering 1989: 3). This Christian bias has proved problematic due to the incommensurability of the model of 'scripture' in 'religion' derived from Christianity with the evidence of actual belief and practice in other 'religions'. Making the point 'that the practitioners of South Asian traditions did not, by and large, understand their holy books in a manner analogous to the Christian West', Jeffrey Timm observes that this Christian bias obscures, rather than reveals, the nature and function of texts in other 'religions' (Timm 1992: 2). It is clear that, though other 'religions' may have texts, their importance has been over-emphasized and their role misinterpreted.

Associated with this, and comparable with developments in the concept of 'religion' and 'religions', 'scripture' as a concept has changed in meaning and implications, notably in relation to the 'scriptures' of the 'religions'. Wilfred Cantwell Smith charts these developments: commencing with the word 'scriptures' as a term used for those texts approved by the Church as conveying God's word to humanity; continuing with the word 'scripture' as a term used for the item that included those texts or the totality that together those texts comprised; and culminating with the word 'scriptures' but 'this time designating the mundane series of the world's collection of texts' (Smith, W.C. 1993: 14). The first transition, from plural to singular, is explained with reference to the supercession of the Greek by the Latin '*Biblia*' but particularly to the Reformation, where the many books in the canon came to be seen as constituting one book called the Bible (Smith, W.C. 1993: 13–14). The second transition, from singular to plural, is explained with reference to the encounter with other 'religions', where the Bible as the Christian 'scripture' is but one 'scripture' among many (Smith, W.C. 1993: 12). This second transition, he argues, is significant in that it reflects 'a shift from a transcendent to a positive, even to a positivist, meaning', that is, a relativization of the authority of 'scripture' in which its prime position is relative to a 'religion' and not absolute as divine revelation (Smith, W.C. 1993: 10, 12).[31]

A famous expression of the idea that the 'religions' have 'scriptures', an idea associated with both the priority of 'scripture' in the construction of 'religion' and the resort to a community-centred criterion of canonical status, was F. Max Müller's *The Sacred Books of the East*. This series, edited by Müller and published between 1879 and 1910, provided translations of the 'scriptures' of the Eastern 'religions'. The rationale for this extraordinary enterprise reflected the prevailing view that 'scripture' was primary.[32] Thus the justification for the series was that 'a comparative study of the religions of the East' required first and foremost 'complete and thoroughly faithful translations of their sacred books' (Müller 1879: xi–xii). Further, when considering on what grounds texts were to be chosen for inclusion in the series, divine revelation was set aside as too limiting since few of the books under consideration declared themselves to be revealed, albeit that frequently such a declaration was made on their behalf by later adherents (Levering 1989: 16 n.4; cf. Müller 1873: 127–8).[33] Thus the decision was made to choose for inclusion those texts 'formally recognized by religious communities', choosing them for a status likened to canonicity and hence a role in settling religious, ethical and ritual questions (quoted in Levering 1989: 16 n.4). Moreover, the selection made was determined by a notion of the East and thus which were the 'religions' of the East, as well as which 'religions' possessed 'scriptures'.[34]

Excluding Judaism and Christianity, Müller argued that the 'six Eastern religions' – '[t]he religion of the Brahmans', '[t]he religion of the followers of Buddha', '[t]he religion of the followers of Zarathustra', '[t]he religion of the followers of Khung-fû-tze', '[t]he religion of the followers of Laô-tze' and '[t]he religion of the followers of Mohammed' – were 'the only great and original religions which profess to be founded on Sacred Books' (Müller 1879: xli). Thus this pioneering work not only attached significance to 'scripture' but also assigned superior status to certain 'religions' on the grounds of their association with 'scripture'. As Müller remarked, 'how few are the religions which possess a sacred canon, how small is the aristocracy of real book religions in the history of the world!' (Müller 1873: 103). Apart from Judaism and Christianity, these 'real book religions' comprised in effect only Buddhism, Zoroastrianism, Confucianism, Taoism and Islam together with 'Hinduism', though his terminology was rather different in some cases (Müller 1873: 103–7). This meant that *The Sacred Books of the East* covered most of the eight 'real book religions' of which 'Hinduism', in his terminology 'Brahmanism', was only one example.[35]

In respect of '[t]he religion of the Brahmans' or 'Hinduism', Müller's initial plan was to provide a translation of the *Ṛg Veda*, possibly another collection of Vedic hymns, selected *Brāhmaṇas* and the major *Upaniṣads*. He added that '[t]here [was] every prospect of an early appearance of the Bhagavad-gîtâ', and also samples of legal literature and mythological works (Müller 1879: xliv). Although there were some differences between the proposed and actual contents of the series – the number of volumes produced, the range of 'religions' covered and, insofar as it relates to 'Hinduism', the specific 'scriptures' translated – this was not the case with the *Bhagavad-Gītā* (Müller 1879: xliii–xlvi; cf. Winternitz 1910: xv–xvi). Translated by K.T. Telang, along with the *Sanatsujātīya* and *Anu-Gītā* (also from the *Mahābhārata*), it became the eighth volume in the series, first published in 1882 (Müller 1879: xliv–xlvi; Winternitz 1910: xv–xvi).[36] Its publication and the publication of the other 'Hindu scriptures' in the series – in all, 21 volumes were classified under the heading 'Vedic–Brāhmanic Religion' (Winternitz 1910: xv–xvi) – must also have served to reinforce the notion that 'Hinduism' had 'scriptures'. However, while acknowledging that 'Hinduism' has been constructed as a 'religion' with 'scripture', whether the concept of 'scripture' has either validity or utility in this context is highly debatable.

Memorably, it has been declared that '[s]trictly speaking, there are no books in Hinduism' (Staal 1979: 123). Although this overstates and oversimplifies the situation, it indicates the bias towards writing implicit in the concept of 'scripture' whereas orality is arguably the primary characteristic of 'Hindu' texts (text here being understood as oral as well as written).[37] The etymology of the word 'scripture' is from the Latin '*scriptura*' or 'writing', related to the verb '*scrībere*' meaning 'to write' (Simpson and Weiner 1989: XIV.742), and there are strong reasons for regarding this as problematic since '[t]he fundamentally oral nature of Hindu sacred texts... has been noted and commented on by most students of the Hindu tradition' (Graham 1987: 69). This oral emphasis can be demonstrated negatively in terms of an antipathy towards writing and positively in terms of the supremacy of the spoken word.

The antipathy towards writing is demonstrated by evidence including: textual injunctions such as the ruling of the *Aitareya Āraṇyaka* 5.5.3 that equated writing with eating meat, seeing a corpse and having intercourse; the low status of scribes as mere copyists; and the perishability of writing materials necessitating frequent re-copying (Coburn 1984: 437; Coward 1988: 120–1; Graham 1987: 74; Staal 1979: 121–2). Explanations for this differ. Frits Staal suggests that this antipathy towards writing may have arisen from its foreign origins disqualifying it as a medium for the sacred (Staal 1979: 121). Maurice Winternitz attributes it to a desire to preserve the purity of the *Vedas* from the polluting influence of low castes and C. Mackenzie Brown focuses on the way in which Vedic knowledge was transmitted from guru to disciple in a personal relationship (Brown, C.M. 1986: 72–3). It has even been claimed that this antipathy was only overcome in medieval India when Muslim incursions were posing a threat to the future of oral culture (Losty 1982: 15).

Factors identified as upholding the supremacy of the spoken word include: language being a manifestation of the divine as timeless reality; the divinity of speech, Vāc, as the support of the gods; the special property of sound or word, Śabda, as channelling divine energy associated with the power of mantras; the obligation on a brāhman to recite Vedic verses, even if only the *Gāyatrī Mantra*, every morning and evening; and the prominence of grammar, phonetics and the philosophy of language as religious disciplines (Coward 1988: 112–13; Graham 1987: 70–1, 73; Levering 1989: 1; Staal 1979: 121). However, it would be misleading to omit significant developments whereby a written text emerged and was highly valued.

These developments are associated with the rise of the devotional movement and with the *Purāṇas*, leading to a cult of the book (Brown, C.M. 1986). The *Devī Bhāgavata Purāṇa* promises wealth and learning to the house in which it is kept and worshipped. The *Agni Purāṇa* promises freedom from misfortune to the house in which it is transcribed. The *Kūrma Purāṇa* offers earthly and heavenly rewards to the person who copies the text and gives it to a brāhman. The *Matsya* and *Agni Purāṇas* include statements about the benefits accruing to those who produce and bestow copies of the *Purāṇas*. Thus there is the notion of the *Purāṇas* as books, the possession, transcription and donation of which are pious and meritorious (Brown, C.M. 1986: 77–8). What lies behind this cult of the book is the identification of the book with the divine where the *Purāṇa* is regarded as the visible form of God, an identification symbolized in the representation of Sarasvatī, goddess of learning and wisdom, as both goddess of speech and the alphabet holding both a string of prayer beads and a book (Brown, C.M. 1986: 81–3).

The *Mahābhārata*'s frame narrative portrays it as an oral work, Ugraśravas telling the assembled brāhmans that he had recently returned from a sacrifice where he had heard Vaiśaṃpāyana tell the tales that he had heard from Vyāsa himself, stressing the centrality of both bard and audience to the epic (Brockington 1998: 2, 28). A very late story associated with the *Mahābhārata*, however, relates that Vyāsa was visited by the god Brahmā to whom he complained that there was no scribe to write down the work, leading Brahmā to recommend that he avail himself of the god Gaṇeśa's services (Brockington 1998: 2–3; Brown, C.M. 1986: 76).[38] Other passages refer to the merits of reading the *Mahābhārata* and procedures for worshipping a copy of the text (Brockington 1998: 3; Brown, C.M. 1986: 80). Insofar as the *Bhagavad-Gītā* is concerned, while the epic as a whole passed through stages of oral composition, there is sufficient evidence to suggest that it at least originated in written form. There is also historical evidence of hand-written copies of the *Bhagavad-Gītā* being prepared and offered to brāhmans (Priolkar 1958: 34). That said, its written form does not detract from its oral nature. This is because the oral transmission of the *Vedas* sets the pattern for the oral presentation of works like the *Bhagavad-Gītā*, the recitation and hearing of which are deemed to be auspicious spiritual activities (Graham 1987: 75; cf. Coward 1988: 110).

Another related issue raised by the concept of 'scripture' is that of its intelligibility or comprehensibility, the idea that 'scripture' has a didactic or instructional purpose (Coburn 1984: 445). Although this assumption is one that makes sense in a Christian context where the Bible is widely studied in order to determine its meaning and so discern God's will for humanity, it makes less sense when 'Hindu' texts are considered since their significance need not lie in their being understood or, indeed, understandable. Instead, sanctity is inherent to the text as recited and heard – what matters is realizing its significance, not determining its meaning (Coburn 1984: 445–7). Again, though, this can be exaggerated because the production of commentaries is an example of the efforts made to explain the meaning of texts (Coburn 1984: 452). The *Bhagavad-Gītā* is an example of a text that has attracted a number of commentaries seeking to set forth its teaching.

Perhaps, then, it might be proposed that the *Bhagavad-Gītā* more nearly approaches the Christian concept of 'scripture' than other 'Hindu' texts. Possibly this may account for the way in which '[i]n modern times it is sometimes said that this work has come closer than any other in the whole of Indian literature and thought to functioning formally as an instance of the imported concept "scripture"' (Smith, W.C. 1993: 128). Certainly there was an imperative to identify a 'Hindu scripture' for 'Hinduism' as a 'religion' (Laine 1983: 167–8). The *Bhagavad-Gītā* was among the texts vying to be such a 'Hindu scripture'.

The *Bhagavad-Gītā* as 'Hindu scripture'

Why it was that the *Bhagavad-Gītā* became dominant has been the subject of some debate (see, especially, Sharpe 1985).[39] An important measure of the popularity of the *Bhagavad-Gītā* is the publishing phenomenon associated with it (King, U. 1982: 152). Print technology had been imported to India facilitating the mass production of books on the subcontinent as in Europe and North America. This revolution in typography made it possible to supply a large quantity of cheap publications. Although this is obviously of much wider application, the comparative brevity of the *Bhagavad-Gītā* must have played a part as it could be turned into a small book.

However, other texts were also promoted as 'Hindu scripture' (King, R. 1999: 105). This makes it necessary to consider other points. For example, the *Bhagavad-Gītā*'s official status as smṛti meant that it was more accessible than texts classified as śruti, such as the *Vedas* and *Upaniṣads*, which were hedged about with traditional restrictions prohibiting their dissemination beyond the ranks of twice-born men eligible for a Vedic education. More speculatively, and arguably promoting the *Bhagavad-Gītā* over the *Purāṇas*, the *Bhagavad-Gītā*'s multivalence enabled it to be interpreted as a religious testament controverting Christian propaganda and as a social and political manifesto advancing an activist ethic. Thus the *Bhagavad-Gītā*'s vision of divine incarnation, faith in a personal God and salvation through God's grace offered an equivalent to Christian theology. Notwithstanding some Christian claims that Kṛṣṇa bhakti was the product of Christian influence, the *Bhagavad-Gītā* could be used to assert an indigenous monotheism (indeed, to claim priority over, and not just independence of, Christianity) (cf. Dalmia 1995). Or again, the *Bhagavad-Gītā*'s emphasis on karma-yoga (the path of action) offered a religious rationale for social and political engagement. In the face of the stereotypical portrayals of 'Hinduism' in terms of world-denying asceticism and passive fatalism, the *Bhagavad-Gītā* could be used to underwrite an indigenous sense of individual moral responsibility, social conscience and political awareness (cf. Minor 1991). There was also a tendency on the part of some commentators to praise the *Bhagavad-Gītā* as a philosophic or mystic work that contained the pure spiritual intuitions of the past and/or conveyed vital truths of relevance for humanity as a whole.

Yet, whatever the reason, the *Bhagavad-Gītā* has been hailed 'as the Hindu scripture *par excellence*' (Sharpe 1985: 83). Although not necessarily dominant in the initial stages of the construction of 'Hinduism' as a 'religion', the *Bhagavad-Gītā* has come to eclipse other texts. Accordingly, it has been idealized as an encyclopedia or compendium of 'Hindu' belief and practice and identified as the 'Hindu' Gospel (e.g. Roy, S.C. 1941: 3–5), New Testament or Bible (e.g. Edgerton 1972: ix, 105).

The prominence of the *Bhagavad-Gītā* in the modern period can be illustrated by reference to India and the wider world. Insofar as India was concerned, contemporary observers noted its special status. For example, Bernard Lucas, a Christian missionary, commented on the worship of Kṛṣṇa, which he explained as arising out of contact with Christianity and described as being the most popular form of 'Hindu' devotion, attributing its appeal to the intimacy between the divine and the human (Lucas 1907: 98–100). Although he acknowledged that '[a]mongst the common people it is the Krishna of the Puranas who holds sway over the heart', he added that 'amongst the more thoughtful classes it is the Krishna of the Bhagavadgita who embodies the highest thought and the most profound wisdom' (Lucas 1907: 100). Hence he concluded that India was confronted with a choice between Kṛṣṇa and Christ, though in his view the ultimate triumph of Christ was assured whereupon the Gospel of John and the Letters of Paul would supplant the *Bhagavad-Gītā* (Lucas 1907: 100).

Charles Andrews, another Christian missionary, made a similar observation about the importance of the *Bhagavad-Gītā* for the Indian elite when he commented that 'the chief scripture of educated Hindus is undoubtedly the Bhagavad Gītā' (Andrews 1912: 103). In his book, he discussed the rise of reform movements in response to Western norms and values, especially the influence of Christianity (Andrews 1912: 145–7). Relating nevertheless that the reform of

'Hinduism' had been effected by reference to her own resources, he cited the *Bhagavad-Gītā* as a case in point (Andrews 1912: 145–6). Noting that copies of the text could then be purchased for small change, he contrasted the *Bhagavad-Gītā's* present with its past status, a hundred years previously when it was largely the preserve of the paṇḍits (Andrews 1912: 146). He reported that within living memory, the *Bhagavad-Gītā* had been promoted 'from a position of comparative obscurity to that of a common and well-read scripture for the whole of educated India' (Andrews 1912: 146).

Lucas' and Andrews' remarks, whether located in the context of a confident assertion of Christianity's superiority over 'Hinduism' or a historical account of 'Hinduism's' reaction to Christianity, are particularly instructive in that they identify the constituency that adopted the *Bhagavad-Gītā* most enthusiastically. In so doing, they indicate the significance of the rise in literacy that created a new readership for religious works, a new readership produced by Western-style English-medium education that needed to read the text in translation. It was members of this elite who were instrumental in advancing a new religious, social and political outlook in modern India, which they did in part by appealing to the *Bhagavad-Gītā*.

Other evidence for its prominence include the formation of a Society for the Printing and Distribution of the *Bhagavad-Gītā* supported by voluntary subscriptions (Smith, W.C. 1993: 202) and the provision of Sarvepalli Radhakrishnan's English translation of the *Bhagavad-Gītā* in Indian hotel rooms (Rocher 1993: 228).[40] Most famously, perhaps, there is the Gītā Press. According to the banner on its web page, the Gītā Press was '[f]ounded in 1923 by Divine Inspiration to propagate the Gita' (Gītā Press 2003a). Its mission statement is set out as follows – 'to promote and spread the principles of *Sanatana Dharma*, the Hindu religion, amongst the general public' (Gītā Press 2003a). This mission is to be fulfilled by producing affordable versions of various Sanskrit texts as well as a range of other books and magazines of a devotional or moral character (Horstmann 1995: 295). The *Bhagavad-Gītā* does have pride of place, however, since it is the *Bhagavad-Gītā* that is regarded as inculcating standards of conduct that tend towards the welfare and improvement of humanity (Gītā Press 2003a). This preference for the *Bhagavad-Gītā* is also attributed to the influential Jay Dayal Goyandka's admiration for the text as a remedy for all ills (Gītā Press 2003a).[41] Although initially its publishing output was in Hindi and Sanskrit as the 'national' and 'classical' languages respectively, subsequently it has branched out into English and Indian regional languages, with editions of the *Bhagavad-Gītā* comprising 46.5 million of the nearly 296 million copies of books sold by March 2000 (Gītā Press 2003b).

A book written by a Western author and published in the early years of the twentieth century referred to the *Bhagavad-Gītā* as '[t]he Chief Scripture of India' (Wilmshurst 1906). Yet the text had achieved a special status in and for the West too, whether as an object of study or a guide to spirituality. The *Bhagavad-Gītā* began its career in the West in 1785 with Charles Wilkins' translation of the text. For Wilkins, the translation was part of a project to translate the *Mahābhārata* as a whole (Hastings 1784: 11; cf. Brockington 1989: 96), describing the *Bhagavad-Gītā* as 'a dialogue supposed to have passed between *Krěěshnă*, an incarnation of the Deity, and his pupil and favourite *Arjŏŏn*' and explaining that '[t]he *Brāhmăns* esteem this work to contain all the grand mysteries of their religion' (Wilkins 1785: 23). Wilkins, a Senior Merchant of the East India Company, was encouraged in his endeavours by Warren Hastings whose patronage of pioneering works of Indological scholarship bequeathed a valuable legacy to later generations.

In his letter of commendation addressed to Nathaniel Smith, Chairman of the East India Company, Hastings called the *Bhagavad-Gītā* 'a very curious specimen of the Literature, the Mythology, and Morality of the ancient Hindoos' and asserted that it was 'a performance of great originality; of a sublimity of conception, reasoning, and diction, almost unequalled' (Hastings 1784: 5, 10). As well as suggesting that Indological scholarship served a practical purpose by promoting mutual respect and good will between ruler and ruled, he made an insightful prediction that texts such as the *Bhagavad-Gītā* would endure 'when the British dominion in India shall have long ceased to exist, and when the sources which it once yielded of wealth and power are lost to remembrance' (Hastings 1784: 13). Indeed, at least in part for political reasons, the East India Company was persuaded to fund the publication of Wilkins' translation (Sharpe 1985: 45) while the translation itself was later to prove significant in terms of stimulating academic study and spiritual reflection (Sharpe 2003: 27).

A century later came Edwin Arnold's verse translation entitled *The Song Celestial*, probably far more influential and important than earlier efforts. Arnold's version was not a verbatim translation but a verse paraphrase, nor was it an independent undertaking but one that relied on translations of the text already produced by scholars (Arnold 1989: ix–xi; cf. Sharpe 1985: 61). His contribution was to present the text in an attractive and artistic manner that won praise for its literary beauty and faithfulness to the original. He portrayed the *Bhagavad-Gītā* as a 'famous and marvelous Sanskrit poem', adding that it had 'immense popularity and authority in India' and adducing evidence of Western admiration for the text '[s]o lofty are many of its declarations, so sublime its aspirations, so pure and tender its piety' (Arnold 1989: vii). He advocated his translation on the grounds that 'English literature would certainly be incomplete without possessing in popular form a poetical and philosophical work so dear to India' (Arnold 1989: x). In this way, he offered a literary rationale for his translation that was distinguished by its aesthetic qualities.

For whatever reason, the *Bhagavad-Gītā* constituted innumerable separate studies and figured in many collections of 'scriptures' and in more broadly conceived series of world 'classics', variously inspired by some sense of the value and importance of the text such that all should read it and profit from it. Two relatively recent examples are translations of the *Bhagavad-Gītā* in the Penguin Classics and Oxford World's Classics series.[42]

Penguin Classics began with the publication of a translation of Homer's *Odyssey*, its translator, E.V. Rieu, becoming the first editor of a series that has sought to make available 'the best literature of several thousand years and countless cultures' (Penguin Classics 2003). The *Bhagavad-Gītā* translated by Juan Mascaró was published as a Penguin Classic in 1962 for a general rather than a specialist readership. Mascaró's poetic rendition of the text, aiming to give 'the spiritual message of the *Bhagavad Gita* in pure English', acknowledges that the translation takes a distinctive line on the rendition of technical terminology involving the substitution of generic, sometimes Christian, ideas and words for specific 'Hindu' concepts and vocabulary (Mascaró 1962: 37). Prioritizing the resonance and cadence of the translation, the poetic over the prose meaning, Mascaró took as his model the 'music' of the Authorized Version of the Bible (Mascaró 1962: 38). He termed the *Bhagavad-Gītā* as 'above all, a spiritual poem', associated with a universal vision that '[g]reat poems in different languages have different values but they are all poetry, and the spiritual visions of man [*sic*] come all from One Light' (Mascaró 1962: 23, 35). This universal vision with its experiential emphasis is articulated clearly in his statement that '[i]f we read the scriptures and books of wisdom of the world, if we consider the many spiritual experiences recorded in the writings of the past, we find one spiritual faith' (Mascaró 1962: 35). By locating the *Bhagavad-Gītā* in this context he claims for it the widest interest and relevance as a poem accessible to all in its evocation of a single shared reality and, at the same time, presents a perennialist perspective on mysticism (Mascaró 1962: 36, cf. 1961).[43]

In like manner, a translation of the *Bhagavad-Gītā* has been published in the Oxford World's Classics series, which prides itself on bringing 'readers closer to the world's finest writers and their works', similarly offering numerous titles produced in very different eras and by very different societies to a non-specialist readership (Oxford World's Classics 2003). Will Johnson's translation of the text was published in 1994, giving explicit recognition to the *Bhagavad-Gītā*'s status as 'the archetype of that necessarily modern phenomenon, the classic of world spirituality' (Johnson 1994: vii). Yet, whereas Mascaró is committed to the essential unity of the religious insights conveyed by seers and mystics through the ages and is convinced that the *Bhagavad-Gītā* is one of many formulations of the same truth, Johnson specifically excludes consideration of the text 'having some universally valid spiritual or religious value' (Johnson 1994: ix). Far from expounding the *Bhagavad-Gītā* by reference to literature from diverse cultures and civilizations as does Mascaró, Johnson warns the modern Western reader 'not to assume that she or he is using, understanding, or valuing the text in ways that are necessarily similar to those employed in the tradition from which it derives' (Johnson 1994: ix). Indeed, this contrast can be related to broader trends in the publication of versions of the *Bhagavad-Gītā* with universal verities, contemporary relevance and ease of expression on the one hand, and an emphasis on the text's unique properties and ancient origins as well as the requirement for academic precision on the other.

There are many examples of the former trend. The front cover of Stephen Mitchell's version bears the legend 'a major new translation of one of the world's spiritual classics'. The *Bhagavad-Gītā*, he writes in his introduction, 'presents some of the most important truths of human existence in a language that is clear, memorable, and charged with emotion' (Mitchell 2000: 18). He stresses its openness and relevance to everyone, an approach exemplified in his advocacy of developing an appreciation of the *Bhagavad-Gītā* through the tribute paid to it by the Americans, Emerson and Thoreau (Mitchell 2000: 13–14). He explains that what these Transcendentalist writers and thinkers discovered in the text were 'truths that are vital to them and to us all' (Mitchell 2000: 14). Thus standing in Arjuna's place, in a state of turmoil and in need of guidance, 'its purpose is to transform your life' (Mitchell 2000: 18). Accordingly, he locates the text in the context of spiritual wisdom that transcends the particularities of tradition and as such invites the reader to make a personal response to its truths (Mitchell 2000: 13–30). This is certainly how the translation is positioned for the market – according to the back cover, it is both 'the essence of Hindu spirituality' and 'among the finest works of world literature', recommended to both 'contemporary spiritual seekers' and 'students of Vedic literature'.

Another example is the new edition of Shri Purohit Swami's translation of the *Bhagavad-Gītā* (Purohit 2001). This edition has been produced by SkyLight Paths Publishing, a publishing house with the maxim '*walking together, finding the way*', in a series entitled SkyLight Illuminations, a series of 'the great classic texts of the world's spiritual traditions', which sets out to prepare 'readers of all backgrounds to experience and understand classic spiritual texts directly, and to make them a part of their lives'. The series editor, Andrew Harvey, contributes a foreword to the translation in which he recalls his introduction to the *Bhagavad-Gītā* in an ashram when he was told 'that... although it is considered the spiritual masterpiece of Hinduism, its message is timeless and universal and transcends all religion' (Harvey, A. 2001: ix). For him, the *Bhagavad-Gītā* teaches the union of mysticism and activism as 'a handbook of spiritual warriorhood and divine realization' (Harvey, A. 2001: xii). Kendra Crossen Burroughs, responsible for the introductory material and textual annotations, similarly suggests that the *Bhagavad-Gītā* addresses itself to all aspirants, despite originating at a specific time and in a specific place (Burroughs 2001: xxi). In common with Harvey, she is clear that '[t]he essential message speaks to each of us today' (Burroughs 2001: xxi). Her hope is that, just as others have been moved by reading the *Bhagavad-Gītā* 'only once with openness to the transforming power of the words of Lord Krishna', those reading this book may be blessed in the same way (Burroughs 2001: xx). It is noteworthy that the front cover includes an endorsement by Transpersonal Psychologist and New Age Guru, Ken Wilbur, recommending this version to those new to the *Bhagavad-Gītā*.

Yet another example is Alan Jacobs' version of the *Bhagavad-Gītā*, a version he is at pains to point out is not a translation but a 'transcreation' by which he means both updated in style and Advaitic in orientation (Jacobs 2003: xiii, xv–xix).

Himself a disciple of Ramana Maharshi, having pursued a variety of spiritual paths in the course of his life, Jacobs dedicates the volume to all those 'who are seeking Truth' (Jacobs 2003: xxi–xxiii). Underlining this universality of the *Bhagavad-Gītā* is his description of it as 'an inspired revelation, a perennial message to humanity, the foundation of the Hindu religion, and a wonderful gift to us all to alleviate the suffering and confusion of our perplexed humanity' (Jacobs 2003: xiv). He interprets the purpose of the text as being to promote self-realization through spiritual practice, with a progressive structure and a transformative potential (Jacobs 2003: xvi, xix). However, though acknowledging its ancient Indian origins, he insists on its relevance for the modern West and, consistent with this, he reads the text in the light of commentaries, ancient and modern, Indian and Western, as well as his own ideas and experiences (Jacobs 2003: xviii–xix). Reviews, quoted on the back cover, acclaim Jacobs' success in presenting the poetry and philosophy of what Ramesh Balsekar calls 'the Indian classic' and Mira Pagal-Decoux 'this universal text of wisdom'.

That popular and scholarly versions of the *Bhagavad-Gītā* abound can be seen in the number of translations of the text into English. Winand Callewaert and Shilanand Hemraj's 1982 survey, for instance, enumerates 273 translations into English since 1785, alongside 28 into German, 25 into French, 19 into Italian, etc. (Callewaert and Hemraj 1982: 114–15). Literature on the *Bhagavad-Gītā* in English includes both translations and commentaries and, if both are considered, the number of works increases markedly. For example, Jagdish Chander Kapoor's survey of imprints between 1785 and 1979 lists 887 publications, though this total does tally re-issues and new editions (Kapoor 1983: 3–98). However, taking Wilkins' and Arnold's versions of the *Bhagavad-Gītā* as convenient points of reference, a pattern emerges of comparatively few works being produced during the first century and many more during the second century, especially latterly. This differential publishing output is evident in the history of English translations with Callewaert and Hemraj indicating that only six volumes were produced in the period 1785–1884, whereas 117 were produced in the period 1950–1980 (Callewaert and Hemraj 1982: 118–20). This is also evident in Kapoor's listing which gives a figure of just over 40 volumes for the years 1785–1884 and just over 400 volumes for 1950 onwards (Kapoor 1983: 3–9, 56–98).[44] Popular and scholarly versions of the *Bhagavad-Gītā* have continued to appear. Bookshops often stock different editions, furnishing choice for seekers and students alike. An academic journal devoted to the *Bhagavad-Gītā* published by the Department of Religious Studies, University of Sydney, was founded in 1981. There was also a minor boom in studies on the text coinciding with the bicentennial of the first English translation of the *Bhagavad-Gītā* (Eder 2003: 169).

One consequence of this publishing phenomenon is that the *Bhagavad-Gītā*, previously the province of a particular section of a faith community, has become far more widely disseminated among the Indian population and thus distanced from traditional religious specialists and their hermeneutical principles and practices. Inevitably, this has entailed the text being approached in the light of new experiences by new interpreters whose accounts of the meaning and import of the *Bhagavad-Gītā* not only differ from historical expositions of the text but are also diverse in themselves. The distancing of the text from traditional interpreters and interpretive paradigms is even more evident in the history of the *Bhagavad-Gītā* outside India where it has been read by those at ever greater remove from the text's traditional constituency, leading to an extraordinary variety of views (cf. Sharpe 1985: xi–xiii).

This means that the sophisticated arguments about exegetical and epistemological issues advanced by schools of thought such as Purva Mīmāṃsā, which created a theory of language, or Nyāya, which specialized in logic as a way to liberation, and especially the works of linguistics associated with vyākaraṇa (grammar) as a Vedāṅga (auxiliary Vedic science), are largely alien to the *Bhagavad-Gītā*'s modern interpreters, both Indian and Western. Of course, the modern era has given rise to its own theories about the interpretation of texts, their presuppositions and purposes often at extreme variance with those informing traditional hermeneutics. In any event, what the modern period offers is a vast array of interpretations of the *Bhagavad-Gītā* based on a range of beliefs and values. Certainly the *Bhagavad-Gītā* has become the 'Hindu scripture' and, because it has attained special status in 'Hinduism' as a 'religion', it has also transcended its specific context and become one of the 'scriptures' of and for the world – read out of intellectual curiosity and out of deep personal interest, read to gain an insight into 'Hinduism' or into the history of 'religions', read as a source of spiritual inspiration and instruction for all seekers after truth.

This book explores the *Bhagavad-Gītā*'s commentatorial corpus produced in the modern period and its relevance for an understanding of the Hindu tradition as a modern phenomenon. Indeed, even if the modernity of 'Hinduism' as a 'religion' with 'scripture' is set aside, this book can be read as an exploration of what modern commentaries on the *Bhagavad-Gītā* reveal about modern views of the Hindu tradition. Each chapter will consider questions about the meaning and importance of the *Bhagavad-Gītā* for a given commentator, the view of the Hindu tradition and the relationship between the text and the tradition for that commentator, and the impact of a particular interpretation of the *Bhagavad-Gītā* on images of the Hindu tradition.

1

ACADEMIC AND SCHOLARLY WRITING

Academic and scholarly writing is important for an understanding of the *Bhagavad-Gītā* and Hinduism for two main reasons. The first is that such writing, as well as representing current research, has exercised an ongoing influence over the ideas of generations of students and the content of conventional subject knowledge. The second is that such writing, especially though not exclusively when presented in popularizing or introductory works, has reached a broader audience and in so doing shaped general perceptions of the text and tradition.

Of course, it is far from easy to differentiate academic and scholarly writing from other writing on the *Bhagavad-Gītā* and Hinduism. After all, other writing may satisfy rigorous specialist criteria while having another principal objective such as the Indological expertise evident in some missionary tracts. Similarly, professional writing may not even aspire towards objectivity, however implausible the goal, and, in any case, may be informed by particular ideological presuppositions such as the imperative to compare Hinduism with Christianity, perhaps with an overt proselytizing purpose. Even so, such writing is a useful focus for analysis of the history of ideas and the examples chosen suggest some significant themes, principally the relationship or parallels with the New Testament, but also the nature of religion, types of mysticism and inter-religious relations.

Charles Wilkins' (1749–1836) translation of the *Bhagavad-Gītā*, the first into a Western language, also contained observations about the text's role and status in a wider context. In his preface, Wilkins emphasized the significance of the *Bhagavad-Gītā*, going so far as to claim that '[t]he *Brāhmăns* esteem this work to contain all the grand mysteries of their religion' (Wilkins 1785: 23). In politic manner, he related that his task of translation would have been well nigh impossible had the brāhmans who treasured and guarded the text not been moved to cooperate by their experience of benevolent British rule and generous patronage of traditional learning (Wilkins 1785: 23–4). With the brāhmans' aid and assistance, he was able to translate the text and was emboldened to venture some comments on its monotheistic and iconoclastic message. He defined the purpose of the *Bhagavad-Gītā* as being 'to unite all the prevailing modes of worship of those days', upholding divine unity against the idolatrous ritual of the *Vedas* (Wilkins 1785: 24). His view was that the author of the *Bhagavad-Gītā* had sought to subvert polytheism by promising only a lesser reward for devotees of other gods, and image-worship by indicating that the same divine spirit indwelt the various icons. In this way, he argued, the author of the *Bhagavad-Gītā* was able to undermine, without directly challenging, both the people's attitudes and the *Vedas*' authority (Wilkins 1785: 24).

Although Wilkins admitted that he had not himself read the *Vedas*, which he acknowledged were the oldest Hindu scriptures, he was clear that they were the basis of a sacrificial cult and a priestly elite (Wilkins 1785: 24–6). This was the foundation for his twofold model of religious belief and practice, contrasting the philosophical beliefs of the brāhmans with the superstitious practices of the people. As he explained, though the wisest brāhmans were 'Unitarians according to the doctrines of *Krĕĕshnă*', they conformed with popular expectations in the provision of ceremonies as prescribed by the *Vedas* (Wilkins 1785: 24). This dichotomy between the high ideals held by the brāhmans and the ceremonial duties they were prepared to discharge on behalf of the people was explained as arising out of the brāhmans' self-interest and popular ignorance in opposition to 'the dictates of *Krĕĕshnă*' (Wilkins 1785: 24). Consequently, for Wilkins, the *Bhagavad-Gītā* taught a pure monotheism and unaffected iconoclasm that stood against the ritualism and priestcraft of the *Vedas*. At the same time, the qualities he identified in the text were those that suggested to his Western contemporaries a superior form of religion whereby the *Bhagavad-Gītā* appeared to be an advanced work of some subtlety and sophistication (cf. Sharpe 1985: 10).[1]

In his letter of commendation, Warren Hastings (1732–1818) gave a similarly favourable account of the *Bhagavad-Gītā*, appealing to it to support his positive evaluation of Indian culture. Although he noted the existence of the *Vedas* as 'the only . . . original scriptures of the religion of Brahmâ' in the context of a discussion of Vyāsa's legendary authorship of a range of texts and his historical role as a religious founder or reformer, he concentrated on the *Mahābhārata* and, within it, the *Bhagavad-Gītā* (Hastings 1784: 5–6). Some measure of his admiration for the *Bhagavad-Gītā* was indicated by his praising it as 'a single exception, among all the known religions of mankind, of a theology accurately corresponding with that of the Christian dispensation' (Hastings 1784: 10). Even where critical of the *Bhagavad-Gītā*, as he was about its ascription of physical attributes to the divine, he defended it not only by insisting that it excelled other texts with which it could be compared but also by indicating that it aimed to change opinion for the better (Hastings 1784: 10). Further, texts such as the *Bhagavad-Gītā* were cited as evidence of the achievements of Indians and proof of their worthiness to be treated with respect.

This was important for Hastings as only by establishing the credentials of India as a civilization could he justify his programme to rule India in what he thought of as an Indian fashion. In this way, the publication of an English translation of the *Bhagavad-Gītā* would serve to support the Orientalist policy of his administration against any and all detractors who regarded Indians as barbarous and primitive. Rejecting the prejudice that Indians were inferiors, he welcomed '[e]very instance which brings their real character home to observation' as conducing towards 'a more generous sense of feeling for their natural rights' (Hastings 1784: 13). Whether by associating the *Bhagavad-Gītā* with higher forms of religion in its teaching against polytheism and idolatry (Wilkins 1785: 24) or by equating its teachings alone with those of Christianity (Hastings 1784: 10), Wilkins and Hastings accorded the *Bhagavad-Gītā* a privileged position.

For Wilkins and Hastings, the *Bhagavad-Gītā* was a text of the highest merit and they cited it as a work of pure spirituality contrasted with the venality and corruption of vernacular religiosity and comparable with Christianity. They were typical of the early period in their appreciation of the *Bhagavad-Gītā*, as also in their unfavourable assessment of, or relative lack of interest in, the *Vedas*. However, this attitude towards the *Bhagavad-Gītā* changed when greater importance was attached to the *Vedas* as the most ancient Sanskrit literature and, accordingly, greater attention was paid to them as constituting the fountainhead of Hindu tradition and revealing the origin of religion (cf. Rocher 1993: 226–8).

F. Max Müller (1823–1900), the most famous and prestigious Indologist of his generation, in whose opinion the *Bhagavad-Gītā* was a rather undistinguished latter-day composition, was representative of this later trend. For Muller, the *Bhagavad-Gītā* was far less significant than the *Vedas*, his fascination with which was the foundation of his distinguished career. Thus, though he too subscribed to a twofold model of religion, contrasting a true vision with a degenerate version, in his case this meant upholding the *Vedas* as an authentic insight into the primeval religious instinct and demoting the *Bhagavad-Gītā* to, at best, an attempt to recover something of this greatness in more recent times. Moreover, he went so far as to deprecate the popularity of the *Bhagavad-Gītā* and its influence on ideas about Sanskrit literature.

Müller's major contribution to knowledge of Sanskrit literature was his six volume edition of the *Ṛg Veda* along with Sāyaṇa's commentary (published 1849–73) – a project, like Wilkins' translation of the *Bhagavad-Gītā*, financially supported by the East India Company (Sharpe 1985: 45, 2003: 29). What he found in the *Vedas* were 'only the simplest thoughts that must have passed through the minds of the Rishis [seers] when they began to ponder on the great phenomena of nature' (Müller 1899: 171). This was why study of the *Vedas* was valuable since they revealed how the gods had first emerged as names for natural objects and events that, through linguistic confusion, became deified – a mythological process he labelled a 'disease of language' (Müller 1899: 190).[2] His aim in studying the *Vedas* was to identify their original meaning and true significance as recording a fundamental religious perception so that he treated them as historical documents that testified to a common Aryan past uniting India and Europe (Müller 1899: 190–1). In comparison with the *Vedas*, the *Bhagavad-Gītā* did not capture his interest or arouse his curiosity because, as a historian of religion, he was most concerned to discover how what he called Aryan religion began and developed.

During his lectures on the Science of Religion at the Royal Institution, Müller distinguished between '[m]odern Hinduism' and 'the Veda', describing the latter as 'the highest authority of the religious belief of the Hindus' (Müller 1873: 28). Thus, when itemizing 'the sacred writings of the Brahmans', he gave pride of place to the *Vedas*, especially the *Ṛg Veda* and associated texts, while including other literature such as epic poetry as necessary

> if we wish to gain an insight into the religious belief of millions of human beings, who, though they all acknowledge the Veda as their supreme authority in matters of faith, are yet unable to understand one single line of it, and in their daily life depend entirely for spiritual food on the teaching conveyed to them by these more recent and more popular books.
>
> (Müller 1873: 107–11)

Interestingly, on this occasion, he made no mention of the *Bhagavad-Gītā* but surely he would have classified it in the category of the 'more recent and more popular books'. Further, this division of literature into the older and the newer was consistent with his notion that Hinduism had passed through stages of increasing complexity and obscurity and its corollary, a strong preference for the pristine purity of the past. His developmental model was one that saw in the *Vedas* the childhood of humanity but likened the Indian religion of his day to 'a half-fossilised megatherion walking about in the broad daylight of the nineteenth century' (Müller 1873: 279). It was a moot point whether, in his view, Hinduism could achieve maturity on its own terms and using its own resources – the imagery suggesting an evolutionary oddity, an ancient survival in the modern world.[3]

In another course of lectures, in this instance delivered at the University of Cambridge to candidates for the Indian Civil Service, he described the earlier phase of Sanskrit literature, epitomized by the *Vedas*, as '*ancient* and *natural*', and its later phase, including the *Mahābhārata*, as '*modern* and *artificial*' (Müller 1883: 88). Discussing the literature of this later phase, he allowed that it might embody 'remnants of earlier times' but, though 'full of interesting compositions, and by no means devoid of originality and occasional beauty', he did not attach equivalent importance to it or regard it as possessing the wider implications or interest of the literature of the earlier phase (Müller 1883: 88–9). In contrast to the earlier literature that he believed demanded the serious consideration of many disciplines, in his judgement the later literature would be attractive only to a specialist audience, to Orientalists, and not to historians and philosophers more generally (Müller 1883: 89).

So it was that Müller lamented the fact that the *Bhagavad-Gītā* and other later literature 'belonging to the second, or the Renaissance period' had acquired prominence in the West before the earlier literature that he esteemed far more highly (Müller 1883: 90). This later literature might be intriguing but initially it had appealed to Westerners on the grounds of its supposed great age and its production by a people hitherto presumed to lack literary sophistication. Latterly, however, the dating of this literature had been revised to reflect the texts' more recent origins and Western perceptions of Indians had been changed to acknowledge their learning and artistry. Hence he asserted the prior claim of the *Vedas* beside which no other text seemed of any particular significance (Müller 1883: 97). Without entirely dismissing the *Bhagavad-Gītā*, for him it amounted to 'a rather popular and exoteric exposition of Vedantic doctrines' (Müller 1883: 252); he did not see in it special qualities nor did he see it as central to an account of India's religion. The marginality of the *Bhagavad-Gītā* was further underlined by its omission from *Lectures on the Origin and Growth of Religion* based on his Gifford Lectures. Although he made many references to India's religions and recommended the study of India's sacred books, what he had in mind was Vedic texts as here too he deplored the fact that Indian literature had first become known through later works such as those associated with Vaiṣṇavism (Müller 1891: 149).

Müller's comments on the *Bhagavad-Gītā* and Hinduism, or to use the term he generally preferred, Brahmanism, showed how much ideas had changed since Wilkins' translation appeared. Müller's concentration on the time of origins led him to emphasize the *Vedas*, not the *Bhagavad-Gītā*, and to vest authenticity in the distant past of the *Vedas*, not the more recent period that gave rise to the *Bhagavad-Gītā*. This dichotomy between ancient and modern, if inflected differently, has remained a feature of many accounts of Hinduism. Where Müller's views have proved less influential on scholars is in his according the *Bhagavad-Gītā* a secondary role and status as illustrative of a stage of decline in the history of Hinduism. Müller's focus was on the *Vedas*, texts generally unknown or unfamiliar to scholars of a previous generation, who, even if aware of them, were, in contrast to Müller, neither particularly impressed nor enthusiastic. With his sights set on the *Vedas*, the *Bhagavad-Gītā* was not the centrepiece of Müller's account of Hinduism insofar as that was ever his concern.

Certainly Müller's views were not entirely endorsed by his contemporary and fellow Sanskritist, Monier Monier-Williams (1819–99), partly because Monier-Williams detected in the *Bhagavad-Gītā* similarities with Christian scriptures just as he detected in Hinduism correspondences with Christianity. Unlike Müller, he was full of praise for the *Bhagavad-Gītā* but, despite this, like Müller, he believed that the *Bhagavad-Gītā* was ultimately unsatisfactory, albeit for reasons very different from those that led Müller to deprecate the text. In Monier-Williams' judgement, the *Bhagavad-Gītā* was of considerable significance for Hinduism and, in its proclamation of devotion to Kṛṣṇa, it provided a basis for his claim that there were connections between Hinduism and Christianity upon which the missionary could build. Moreover, his analysis of the *Bhagavad-Gītā* could not be isolated from his general argument about the development of polytheistic Hinduism from pantheistic Brahmanism and its implications for a popularizing project based on devotion to a personal deity, especially one incarnated in human form. As a text inculcating devotion to a personal deity, the *Bhagavad-Gītā* thus represented Hinduism; it was also fundamental to Vaiṣṇavism, an aspect of Hinduism of which he appeared to approve. Yet the significance he attached to pantheism meant that in the end it was not possible to accord full ontological and soteriological status to the worship of the personal saviour. Hence, for all his appeal, the Kṛṣṇa of the *Bhagavad-Gītā* was not truly comparable to the Christ of the Bible since pantheism undermined incarnation. Considering that the doctrine of incarnation featured prominently in his comparison between Hinduism and Christianity, this inevitably entailed the superiority of Christianity and, by extension, the necessity for Christian missionary endeavour.

In an appendix to *Hinduism* which, like many of his other publications, revised and reproduced sections from *Indian Wisdom* (1875), Monier-Williams praised the *Bhagavad-Gītā* for its beauty and profundity. He noted that it was 'supposed to contain the actual utterances of the god' and that it was 'venerated as one of the most sacred portions of Indian literature', observing that its teachings had 'exerted a powerful influence throughout India' (Monier-Williams 1919: 209). Moreover, he described it as the work of a brāhman who, if Vaiṣṇava in name, was in reality a broad-minded philosopher who could not assent to the tenets of one philosophical system or accept the abuses of Brahmanism and so established 'an eclectic school of his own' (Monier-Williams 1919: 207). Explaining what this meant, he wrote that the author of the *Bhagavad-Gītā* had combined Sāṃkhya, Yoga and Vedānta and upheld the importance of fulfilling one's dharma or duty, but also added that love for Kṛṣṇa formed part of the synthesis (Monier-Williams 1919: 208). Indeed, when considering the purpose of the *Bhagavad-Gītā*, he stressed that the text set out to promote devotion to the divine (Monier-Williams 1919: 209).

Monier-Williams' analysis of the *Bhagavad-Gītā* was illustrated by various references to the Bible – 'numerous parallels to passages in our own sacred Scriptures' (Monier-Williams 1919: 220) – among which was the theophany in chapter 11 as comparable with the Gospel accounts of the transfiguration of Jesus (Mt 17.2; Mk 9.3) (Monier-Williams 1919: 214–15). Yet, if this confirmed the high opinion he had of the text, he was not convinced of the case advanced by Franz Lorinser as to Christian influence on the *Bhagavad-Gītā* that would account for such parallels. Against Lorinser's idea that the *Bhagavad-Gītā* was indebted to the New Testament and even that there were links between the names Christ and Kṛṣṇa, Monier-Williams was critical of the failure to recognize both that some truth could be found even in false religions and that the Bible had an Oriental character when it came to human thought and expression (Monier-Williams 1919: 212 n.1). Overall, he concluded that there was insufficient evidence for Christian influence on Hinduism, suggesting that coincidence could explain away many of Lorinser's examples, without entirely excluding such influence as a possibility (Monier-Williams 1919: 221).[4]

Certainly, when he compared the religions of India with Christianity, it was in Hinduism that Monier-Williams identified most similarities. These similarities, outlined in *Modern India and the Indians*, included a recognition of human fallibility and iniquity, the need for sacrifice, the importance of revelation, the possession of a canon of scripture, the offering of prayer, the futility of worldly existence and the belief in a supreme deity (Monier-Williams 1878: 100–1).

Significantly, he also indicated that Hindus were acquainted with the concepts of the trinity and incarnation as well as being aware of the need for a personal saviour 'however perverted these ideas may be' (Monier-Williams 1878: 100). These similarities did not, of course, detract from the superiority of Christianity or his hopes for the ultimate conversion of Hindus to what he regarded as the true faith (Monier-Williams 1878: 218). Yet his picture of Hinduism was complicated by the distinction he drew between Brahmanism and Hinduism. Brahmanism he defined as denoting the pantheistic system of the brāhmans based on the *Vedas* (Monier-Williams 1878: 89). Hinduism, however, was a degenerate polytheistic form of Brahmanism, produced by contact with Buddhist, Dravidian and Aboriginal traditions, based on a wide range of Hindu texts (Monier-Williams 1878: 90). Consequently, Hinduism was different from Brahmanism though derivative of it (Monier-Williams 1878: 91). Describing Hinduism, he likened it to 'a huge irregular structure which has had no single architect' and 'an ancient overdrawn fabric, with no apparent unity of design' – images of diversity and disorder, yet he insisted that Hinduism had a firm foundation in Brahmanism irrespective of the many influences it had assimilated (Monier-Williams 1878: 91–2).

The process by which Hinduism emerged out of Brahmanism was given detailed attention in *Religious Thought and Life in India* where Monier-Williams explained that it arose from an attempt on the part of the brāhmans to appeal to the people by offering them a more attractive and appropriate form of religion; in short, a form of religion that provided for the people's religious needs by offering a path of devotion to a personal deity (Monier-Williams 1883: 42–3). Hinduism represented the climax of this popularizing project though it had begun earlier: this involved a claim that Brahmanism and Hinduism could be distinguished on the grounds that the former was pantheistic and the latter theistic while acknowledging that the different types of theism were interrelated; this also involved a claim that an intellectual religion with an impersonal object could not command the adherence of the people at large whose spiritual aspirations would only be satisfied by the expression of emotion for a personal figure (Monier-Williams 1883: 54). There was thus a disjunction between what the brāhmans believed concerning knowledge of an impersonal absolute and what the non-brāhmans practised in terms of devotion to a personal deity as a simplified religion for the people. Yet so pervasive and powerful was pantheism that it influenced even 'the most ignorant and bigoted Hindūs' while 'any thoughtful Hindū' would not be prepared to refute its precepts (Monier-Williams 1883: 56–7).

Monier-Williams' insistence that Hinduism was ultimately reducible to Brahmanism meant that devotional theism was relegated to a subordinate position – it was a lower illusory expression of the true knowledge of an impersonal absolute. However, as a popularization of Brahmanism, Hinduism allowed ordinary people to enter into the relationship with the divine that represented the fulfilment of their spiritual aspirations. Among the personal deities to whom worshippers turned, their devotion dependent on the humanity of the divine, he identified Viṣṇu with his many incarnations as the most popular – Viṣṇu being 'the most human, as he is also the most humane' whose incarnations for the welfare of the world ceded Kṛṣṇa pride of place as the full descent of the divine nature (Monier-Williams 1883: 46–7). The significance of this was that the success of popular religion rested upon the divine taking human form to uphold the cause of righteousness and destroy evil. These two themes – the priority of pantheism and the importance of incarnation – ran through his treatment of Hinduism and his account of the *Bhagavad-Gītā*. Moreover, the two were linked in that the fundamentally pantheistic nature of Hinduism as a development of Brahmanism detracted from the reality of incarnation as a manifestation of personal deity.

Certainly the *Bhagavad-Gītā* played an important part in Monier-William's discussion of Hinduism as its declaration of devotion to a personal deity epitomized Hinduism's essential quality. As he explained in *Hinduism*, it was only in the *Bhagavad-Gītā* that the doctrine of devotion to a personal deity reached maturity (Monier-Williams 1919: 115). This occurred in the course of the reconciliation of pantheism and personal deity through the evolution of the impersonal absolute into a multitude of forms (Monier-Williams 1919: 86–7) and the role of incarnations in relation to personal deity as divine interventions in and for the world (Monier-Williams 1919: 108–9). When it came to the *Bhagavad-Gītā*, therefore, his contention that it contained pantheistic elements and centred on Kṛṣṇa as a form of Viṣṇu had to be interpreted in the light of his theories about the nature of personal deity (Monier-Williams 1919: 208, 212). His observation that Kṛṣṇa 'claims adoration as one with the great universal spirit, pervading and constituting the universe' demonstrated the close connections between pantheism and incarnation in the *Bhagavad-Gītā* (Monier-Williams 1919: 212).

If the *Bhagavad-Gītā* typified Hinduism, then for Monier-Williams it was crucial to Vaiṣṇavism, a point he made in an article on Swaminarayan where he called the *Bhagavad-Gītā* one of the 'two chief books' constituting 'the bible of all worshippers of Vishṇu in his most popular manifestation – that of the hero Kṛishṇa' (Monier-Williams 1882: 296–7). Vaiṣṇavism could be pantheistic, he commented, though by the same token it could also be monotheistic and polytheistic – this extraordinary flexibility enabling it to flourish by accepting and absorbing the teachings of other traditions (Monier-Williams 1882: 296). Nevertheless, what characterized Vaiṣṇavism was Viṣṇu's active concern for the world, evident in his incarnations of whom Kṛṣṇa was a popular human form (Monier–Williams 1882: 295). Comparing Vaiṣṇavism with other aspects of Hinduism, he described Brahmanism and Śaivism as 'simply philosophies' and Śāktism as a combination of 'mysticism, licentiousness and demonology', whereas Vaiṣṇavism was 'the only real religion of the Hindūs' (Monier-Williams 1882: 295).[5] Uniquely within Hinduism, Vaiṣṇavism satisfied the criteria for 'a genuine religion' since in his opinion a genuine religion was defined by devotion to a personal deity (Monier-Williams 1882: 296). Such a positive evaluation of Vaiṣṇavism owed much to its similarities to Christianity but, as he made explicit elsewhere, however exalted the Kṛṣṇa of the *Bhagavad-Gītā*, the pantheistic nature of Brahmanism as the basis of Hinduism proved to be a problem.

The heart of the matter for Monier-Williams was that the similarities between Vaiṣṇavism in particular, and more generally Brahmanism or Hinduism, and Christianity were more apparent than real. That is, the common notions of personal deity and incarnation were only superficially similar since the pantheism that was fundamental to Hinduism relegated personal deity to impersonal absolute and reduced incarnation to mere appearance. He made points such as these when comparing Indian religions (Buddhism and Islam as well as Brahmanism or Hinduism) and Christianity in *Modern India and the Indians*. Here too he differentiated between the pantheism of Brahmanism and polytheism of Hinduism but vested their unity in 'emanation' (Monier-Williams 1878: 210). Thus the personal deities were emanations of the impersonal absolute and, in turn, incarnations, notably Rāma and Kṛṣṇa, were emanations of one of those personal deities, Viṣṇu (Monier-Williams 1878: 211). The goal was, then, the return of every emanation to its source, the impersonal absolute (Monier-Williams 1878: 211). This was why Hinduism could not withstand the challenge of Christianity where devotion to a personal deity was established on the primacy of the saviour to whom worship was offered (Monier-Williams 1878: 214).

If, in Christianity, 'the Personal God made man', Christ, redeemed fallen humanity through his atoning death, his resurrection holding out the promise of eternal life in heaven, in Hinduism, the personal nature of the divine and the character of incarnations such as Kṛṣṇa were undermined by the positing of a more fundamental reality, the impersonal absolute (Monier-Williams 1878: 215–17). In Hinduism, the goal of union with the impersonal absolute was 'effected by faith in an apparently personal God' whose 'seeming personality melts on scrutiny into a vague spiritual essence' (Monier-Williams 1878: 216–17). Further, in respect of incarnation, in Hinduism there was but 'a seeming combination of the human and divine – an apparent interchange of action' (Monier-Williams 1878: 217). The choice of words was crucial in Monier-Williams' distancing of Christianity from Hinduism, the reality of the personal God and the divine incarnation in Christianity from the appearance thereof in Hinduism. In the end, despite the description of Kṛṣṇa in the *Bhagavad-Gītā* 'as the source of all life and energy', Monier-Williams was doubtful of the possibility of any real relationship between human and divine when both would merge into the impersonal absolute (Monier-Williams 1878: 217). Hence he concluded that, though Brahmanism or Hinduism had much in common with Christianity, these commonalities did not establish equity between the religions (Monier-Williams 1878: 216–17). Even the *Bhagavad-Gītā*'s message of devotion to Kṛṣṇa was susceptible to the criticism that the focus of worship was only an 'emanation' of an impersonal absolute, its theism undercut by pantheism. Thus the *Bhagavad-Gītā*, whatever its outstanding qualities, was typical of Hinduism in terms of the precedence of pantheistic Brahmanism.

Monier-Williams found much to admire in the *Bhagavad-Gītā*, especially its teaching of devotion so suggestive of the Christian scriptures. More generally, he pointed to the resemblances between Hinduism and Christianity, though these were more apparent than real. The reason for this was that he distinguished Hinduism from Brahmanism, Hinduism constituting a popularized form of the latter centred on personal deity but a form that was only an exoteric and fictive representation of the truths taught by Brahmanism, especially the impersonal absolute. For him, the *Bhagavad-Gītā* was an expression of the pervasive feature of Hinduism – devotion to a personal deity, especially the divine incarnation – and as such the *Bhagavad-Gītā* had to suffer from the fatal flaw that he thought ran through Hinduism – that its inculcation of devotion to a personal deity, including Kṛṣṇa as a human form of Viṣṇu, was subordinated to the knowledge of an impersonal absolute that characterized Brahmanism. In this way, the *Bhagavad-Gītā* could not sustain a Hindu challenge to Christianity because devotion to Kṛṣṇa could not be taken literally, only as a metaphorical version of pantheistic philosophy.

Rudolf Otto (1869–1937) took a very different approach to the *Bhagavad-Gītā*, arguably two different approaches – a fascination with literary critical questions that did not preoccupy Monier-Williams and a concern with common mystical experience rather than the prospects for proselytizing Hindus, though he too was a committed Christian and espoused a theological agenda. Otto, like Monier-Williams, regarded the *Bhagavad-Gītā* as an eclectic work, albeit as the product of different stages of composition, and attached considerable significance to the theophany, albeit as an illustration of the 'mysticism of horror'. Otto cited the *Bhagavad-Gītā* as an example of the literature of the 'numinous' or the 'holy' and an instance of mysticism. His interest in mysticism, particularly in theistic types of mysticism, was pursued in comparative studies of Indian religion and Christianity. By Indian religion he meant Hinduism and, without ignoring its diversity, his portrait of Hinduism was of devotional religion. The *Bhagavad-Gītā*, according to Otto, both articulated the diversity he implicitly attributed to Hinduism and declared the importance of devotion to which he gave pride of place. Likening the *Bhagavad-Gītā* to the New Testament, he made it the basis for a comparison between Indian religion and Christianity and the means of establishing their distinct natures.

Otto's most detailed treatment of the *Bhagavad-Gītā* was in *The Original Gītā: The Song of the Supreme Exalted One*.[6] This has proved particularly controversial in its thesis of an original text, an integral part of the *Mahābhārata*, to which various treatises and glosses had been added. The original *Bhagavad-Gītā*, 'a fragment of most magnificent epic narrative', according to him comprised: 1; 2.1–13, 20, 22, 29–37; 10.1–8; 11.1–6, 8–12, 14, 17, 19–36, 41–51; and 18.58–61, 66, 72–3 (Otto 1939: 15). In describing the original text, he explained that it was

> Krishna's own voice and deed, referring directly to the situation in which Arjuna finds himself; intended, however, not to proclaim to him any transcendent dogma of salvation, but to render him willing to undertake the special service of the Almighty Will of the God Who decides the fate of battles.
>
> (Otto 1939: 14)

The remainder of the current version of the text, he argued, was the result of a series of interpolations, identified as such by their failure to address Arjuna's immediate situation and by their doctrinal nature, included in order to accord divine authority to various ideas (Otto 1939: 134, 236). He understood the diverse nature of these interpolations as producing a composite text which contained significant inconsistencies, insisting that, while the *Bhagavad-Gītā* had a certain unity, the search for uniformity was mistaken (Otto 1939: 133). His account of the perspectives found in the final version of the text included Sāṃkhya and Yoga philosophies, the ethical principles associated with the guṇas or strands of nature, the Vedic cult of sacrifice and Vedāntic thought about Brahman, as well as the Vaiṣṇavite theology of devotion to Kṛṣṇa (Otto 1939: 9–10). The refusal to regard the *Bhagavad-Gītā* as a unitary work and the rejection of its representation as a harmonizing and harmonious work of synthesis gained him many detractors.[7]

Yet Otto's reputation rested chiefly on his book *The Idea of the Holy* where he proposed the now famous concept of the 'numinous' and the sense of awe and wonder that encounter with it inspires (Otto 1950: 12). Here too, though, the *Bhagavad-Gītā* made an appearance. In appendix II, he cited the *Bhagavad-Gītā* as an example of 'numinous poetry' and, in the main text, the same incident – the theophany of Kṛṣṇa – was discussed as an instance of a 'blending of appalling frightfulness and most exalted holiness' (Otto 1950: 62). In Otto's opinion, this 'mysticism of horror', found in both Buddhist and Hindu mysticism, was not to be found in the West (Otto 1950: 105). Indeed, one of his major concerns was the relationship between Eastern and Western forms of religiosity, especially comparative mysticism, where he evinced a particular interest in theistic types. He gave much attention to bhakti or devotion and, without necessarily referring to Hinduism, a significant proportion of his theological reflections related to Hinduism as conventionally defined.

Otto's interest in theistic types of mysticism was evident in his discussion of Śaṅkara's commentary on the *Bhagavad-Gītā* in *Mysticism East and West: A Comparative Analysis of the Nature of Mysticism.* Calling the *Bhagavad-Gītā* 'the great basic text of Indian theistic piety', he sought to redress the balance in perceptions of Indian religion, generally thought of in terms of 'impersonal mysticism' but also encompassing 'personal theism' (Otto 1987: 104–5). In this context, his choice of Śaṅkara, the great non-dualist philosopher, was perhaps surprising since Śaṅkara espoused the view that the personal diety was but an appearance of the impersonal Brahman. Otto justified his choice, however, by commenting that '[t]he impersonal Brahman rests here also on a theistic basis, and this is not unimportant for the conception of Brahman itself' (Otto 1987: 104). His argument was that, at the lower level of truth, Śaṅkara himself was a theist and that this too constituted knowledge (Otto 1987: 107, 111). This affirmation of the lower level of truth associated with the personal deity, an affirmation arising out of a developmental rather than an oppositional model of knowledge of Brahman, meant that he described Śaṅkara's thought as 'super-theism', not 'anti-theism' (Otto 1987: 112). Thus it was that he portrayed

Śaṅkara's commentary on the *Bhagavad-Gītā* as one that conflated the qualities of the personal deity with the impersonal Brahman, and applauded it as an account of the *Bhagavad-Gītā* that did not trivialize the importance of the text with its message of devotion to the divine (Otto 1987: 112–23). On the basis of a comparison between Śaṅkara and the Christian mystic, Meister Eckhart, Otto concluded that theism 'arises out of the deep necessity of mankind in general' (Otto 1987: 123). In this and other works, the examination of theistic types of mysticism interrelated with devotion was combined with a strong comparative element drawing heavily on Indian, mainly Hindu, material for a discussion of similarities and dissimilarities to Christianity.

India's Religion of Grace and Christianity Compared and Contrasted was one such comparative study of bhakti or devotional religion and Christianity. The discussion, some of it relating directly to the *Bhagavad-Gītā* and its commentators, focused upon Hindu belief and practice, seemingly equating the Indian with the Hindu. Contrasting bhakti religion and Christianity, Otto suggested certain significant differences but it was in relation to the doctrine of grace that he declared were found 'the most striking similarities' and simultaneously 'the most profound difference of all' (Otto 1930: 86). This difference consisted in the contrast between grace that releases a soul from sin and guilt, in the case of Christianity, and grace that releases a soul from the bonds of sāṃsara (the wheel of existence), in the case of Indian religion. Such was the basis of his claim that the two religions turned on different axes though he acknowledged that this contrast could be over-stated (Otto 1930: 86–94). Thus he asserted that the Indian notion of sin and related concepts such as repentance and confession were not as developed as they were in Christianity and that conscience was not as central (Otto 1930: 94–104). This led him to emphasize that Christian and Indian theologies accorded God distinctive and different parts to play, contrasting Christ with Kṛṣṇa and Rāma, not in terms of a mediating role or incarnational status, but in terms of Christ's atoning death '[f]or India has no "expiator," no Golgotha, and no Cross' (Otto 1930: 105–8). His summary of the contrasts between bhakti religion and Christianity amounted in effect to a contrast between devotional forms of Hinduism and Christianity. However, though this left an impression of Hinduism that favoured the devotional over other aspects, his interest in devotional religion did not exclude his realization of the variety of Indian, that is, for the most part Hindu, religion.

The relationship between the *Bhagavad-Gītā* and Hinduism, at least to the extent that Otto's understanding of Hinduism gave particular prominence to devotion, was that the *Bhagavad-Gītā* was widely acknowledged both in India and the West 'as the fundamental *Text* of Hindu "*Bhakti* religion"' – an observation he made in his study of the *Bhagavad-Gītā* (Otto 1939: 9). However, here too, the distinction he drew between the first and final forms of the *Bhagavad-Gītā* was relevant. The original version of the *Bhagavad-Gītā*, he declared, was 'not the doctrinal literature of any system nor, again, a catechism attached to any creed, and least of all of syncretistic Hindusim in general' (Otto 1939: 12). Not only did this indicate that the current version of the *Bhagavad-Gītā* had a very different character but it also suggested that he had a notion of syncretic Hinduism, the diverse strands that shaped the final form of the text revealing 'the rich multiplicity of Indian experience and thought' (Otto 1939: 236). Nevertheless, while he acknowledged the diversity of Hinduism, partially reflected in the *Bhagavad-Gītā*, his concern was more with devotion and this too was represented in the *Bhagavad-Gītā*.

Otto's perspective on the role of the *Bhagavad-Gītā* in relation to Hinduism was implied by the comparison he drew with the Christian Bible, explaining that it 'occupies the exalted position that *The New Testament*, and especially *The Gospel of St. John*, holds in the religious world of the West' (Otto 1939: 9). This statement in *The Original Gītā: The Song of the Supreme Exalted One* suggested that the *Bhagavad-Gītā* was constitutive of Hinduism in much the same way that the New Testament was of Christianity, though this could be nothing more than an expression of conventional sentiments about the significance of the text. Certainly, in his comparative study of bhakti religion and Christianity, his emphasis on their distinctive characters meant he did not accept that the relationship between the *Bhagavad-Gītā* and the New Testament was analogous to that between the Old and New Testaments, so rejecting the notions of preparation and fulfilment – 'the religion of India turns upon an altogether different axis from the religion of the Bible' he concluded (Otto 1930: 63–5). Irrespective of certain similarities (including divine incarnation and grace), he insisted that the two religions were different in spirit (Otto 1930: 66). This difference was initially encountered through feeling, not thinking, with the *Bhagavad-Gītā* representing 'the spirit of India' just as the Psalms, Prophets, Gospels and Letters of Paul represented 'the spirit of Palestine' (Otto 1930: 66). In the last analysis, he affirmed Indian religion to be different from that of Christianity.

Otto regarded the *Bhagavad-Gītā* as important but, in his literary critical treatment of the text, though he identified devotion to Kṛṣṇa, he also identified other, in his view, ultimately irreconcilable, standpoints. Such a focus on internal tensions was why his literary critical approach received an unenthusiastic reception. Notwithstanding this issue, the *Bhagavad-Gītā* played its part in his most influential work, *The Idea of the Holy*, where the theophany was adduced as evidence of a particular mystical experience. As for Hinduism, he tended to refer to Indian or bhakti religion. For Indian religion, it was possible to read Hinduism and in this respect he was aware of its diversity. His emphasis on bhakti religion, illustrated by Hindu examples, indicated a concentration on devotional forms of Hinduism consistent with his interest in theistic mysticism and his comparisons between Indian religion and Christianity. In his view, the *Bhagavad-Gītā* replicated the diversity of Hinduism and also embodied the teaching of devotion, its role in his treatment of Hinduism being principally as source material for a comparative survey leading to an analysis of contrasts with Christianity.

R.C. Zaehner (1913–74) accorded similar emphasis to devotion to a personal deity and, in common with Otto, was interested in mysticism, including its theistic forms. In contrast to Otto, he paid scant attention to literary critical questions about the *Bhagavad-Gītā* and, generally, his reputation rested more on his work on Hinduism than was the case with Otto.[8] Zaehner's lengthy exposition of the *Bhagavad-Gītā*, in his textbook on Hinduism and his selection of Hindu scriptures as well as his commentary, was inspired by its devotional message and theistic mysticism, themes he also addressed in *Mysticism: Sacred and Profane* and *Concordant Discord*. In his view, the rise of devotion to a personal deity and the allied form of mysticism were of the greatest importance in Hinduism. Indeed, it was to the *Bhagavad-Gītā* that he attributed the subsequent dominance of devotional Hinduism, appealing to it as proof of the part played by theistic mysticism in the history of Hinduism.

Zaehner's descriptions of the *Bhagavad-Gītā* stress its importance to Hindus. In various books, he compared it with John's Gospel – '[a]mong the Hindu scriptures the Gītā corresponds in a sense to the fourth Gospel in the New Testament canon' (Zaehner 1970: 153) – hailed its popularity – 'Hinduism's best-loved scripture' (Zaehner 1966a: 65) – and remarked on its associated literature – 'the most commented on of all the sacred texts of Hinduism' (Zaehner 1966b: xvi). For his own part, he accorded the *Bhagavad-Gītā* considerable importance since it was the source of a new teaching – loving devotion, the superiority of the personal deity and the hope of eternal communion with that deity. Discussing the way of devotion, he rejected the notion that this was just one of the three paths to liberation along with knowledge and action. He argued that while knowledge and action were differentiated from one another, they were not so clearly differentiated 'from the life of love and devotion to God' that fulfilled them both (Zaehner 1966b: xvii). This emphasis on devotion was accompanied by an emphasis on the personal deity as the spring of saving grace to liberate living beings. Thus he commented that only divine grace could free a living being to 'become Brahman' and thereby 'be in a fit state to draw near to God' (Zaehner 1966a: 96). In his analysis, there was both what he called 'a lower and a higher *bhakti*', the lower being faith in the personal deity, the higher being experience of the personal deity as the quality of the highest spiritual state (Zaehner 1973: 27–8). So it was that he regarded realization of the divine as personal both as superseding realization of the self and as defining the ultimate liberation whereby the self enjoys a blissful relationship with the divine (Zaehner 1973: 31–2). On this basis, he judged Rāmānuja to be the better interpreter of the *Bhagavad-Gītā*, observing that he was 'nearest to the mind of the author of the Gītā', since Rāmānuja's theology of the personal divine was informed by the text (Zaehner 1973: 8–9).

This also meant that for Zaehner the *Bhagavad-Gītā*, which he called one of '[t]he Hindu mystical classics', favoured a theistic type of mysticism (Zaehner 1957: 130). Although he recognized the plurality of perspectives in the text, he insisted that the *Bhagavad-Gītā* went beyond monism in its declaration of the personal divine so that 'the dominant theme is that of theism' (Zaehner 1957: 146). The *Bhagavad-Gītā* thus contained different forms of mysticism, both those to which love was central and those from which love was absent (Zaehner 1973: 2).

What he prized in the *Bhagavad-Gītā* was the combination of these forms of mysticism that permitted their differentiation, upholding theism over monism in his reading of the text whereby the monistic identity with Brahman was deemed preparatory for, and preliminary to, the theistic communion with the divine characterized by love (Zaehner 1973: 2–3). Hence he preferred theistic commentators on the text, including Rāmānuja, over monistic commentators such as Śaṅkara for whom the theistic was a less adequate interpretation of a monistic reality (Zaehner 1973: 3).

Zaehner's account of Hinduism certainly acknowledged the existence of different trends in Hindu thought, meaning that it was 'perfectly possible to be a good Hindu whether one's personal views incline towards monism, monotheism, polytheism, or even atheism' (Zaehner 1966a: 1–2).[9] Part of the explanation he provided for this diversity was a historical analysis of the development of Hinduism (Zaehner 1966a: 6–9). The third, perhaps most significant, of the stages he identified was that which had witnessed the rise of monotheism – devotion to a personal deity as the ultimate reality (Zaehner 1966a: 7). Henceforward, in his view, this devotional religion was the religion of the people (Zaehner 1966a: 7). Here, as elsewhere, the principal role he assigned to devotional religion was in evidence, not least because this religion based on a loving deity was open to all castes, to men and to women (Zaehner 1966a: 12). Moreover, he pointed out that even Śaṅkara, the famous exponent of monistic philosophy, was known as the composer of devotional hymns, albeit as a popular expression of a lesser truth (Zaehner 1957: 175).

Clearly, the diversity he detected in Hinduism was reflected in forms of Hindu mysticism. Calling Hinduism a 'complex mosaic', he insisted that 'Hinduism has its theists as well as monists' (Zaehner 1957: xvii, 205). This led him to be critical of Teilhard de Chardin's assessment of Hindu mysticism since de Chardin's theory was that in Hinduism the 'pantheism of identification' predominated over the 'pantheism of union' (Zaehner 1970: 152). This, Zaehner declared, amounted to 'a . . . generalization and a travesty', ignoring as it did the *Bhagavad-Gītā* and the theistic mysticism to which it gave rise (Zaehner 1970: 153).

Both in terms of devotion and mysticism, the *Bhagavad-Gītā* was a point of reference for Zaehner's account of Hinduism. He claimed that the *Bhagavad-Gītā* was the 'first literary source for *bhakti*, as devotional religion is called in India' (Zaehner 1966a: 93). The reason for labelling the *Bhagavad-Gītā* 'seminal' was thus its role in the growth of devotional religion (Zaehner 1966a: 92). If, on some occasions, he insisted that the *Bhagavad-Gītā* was innovative in introducing 'a totally new element in Hindu spirituality' (Zaehner 1966a: 10), on other occasions, he acknowledged that devotion to God was foreshadowed in Upaniṣadic literature (Zaehner 1966a: 92) and also present in Epic literature (Zaehner 1970: 118). Even so, he explained that the *Bhagavad-Gītā* changed Indian religious history (Zaehner 1970: 118) and initiated the process of transforming Hinduism (Zaehner 1966a: 134), though he acknowledged that the type of devotion it inculcated was not the impassioned self-abandonment later to characterize the bhakti movement but detached dutiful service (Zaehner 1966a: 96).

Zaehner recognized the importance of the *Bhagavad-Gītā* for the West as well as India, noting the frequency of its translation into English (Zaehner 1970: 119). Perhaps this was part of the reason for his according the *Bhagavad-Gītā* a pivotal position, hailing it as 'a religious classic' that was 'by far the best known and by far the most influential text within the Hindu tradition' and also 'the most significant sacred text in the whole history of religion' (Zaehner 1970: 117). Its significance as a work of devotional religion that marked a 'turning-point' in the history of Hinduism (e.g. Zaehner 1966a: 10) was paralleled in its significance for Hindu mysticism where it established the existence of theistic forms.

When discussing mysticism, Zaehner did not seek to deny the monistic element in Indian thought though he stressed that monism was not unique to India and, in any case, was only one aspect of Hinduism, one that was contested and, even if consistent with the tenets of the *Upaniṣads*, 'plainly at variance with the main teachings of the Bhagavad-Gītā' (Zaehner 1957: xvii). This enabled him to claim that in Hinduism, as well as in other religions, there were trends towards both monistic and theistic forms of mysticism (Zaehner 1957: 204–5). In his view, the *Bhagavad-Gītā* held a pivotal position as 'the great divide in Hinduism' and 'the eastern end of the great religious bridge' (Zaehner 1970: 150). In relation to the *Bhagavad-Gītā's* role in Hinduism, he referred to the text as a 'watershed' between Upaniṣadic 'pantheistic monism' and Purāṇic 'pantheistic theism' (Zaehner 1970: 153). In relation to the *Bhagavad-Gītā's* role in religions, he explained that it bestowed on Hinduism a special mediating property as 'the *via media*' between Buddhist 'atheistic mysticism' and Semitic 'theistic mysticism' (Zaehner 1970: 150). Consequently, the text was 'the starting point' for a conversation between Eastern and Western religions with their respective tendencies towards 'immanent pantheism' and 'transcendental . . . monotheism' (Zaehner 1970: 150). Thereby the *Bhagavad-Gītā* was more than a means of redressing the balance in understandings of Hindu mysticism – it was the basis for dialogue between religions (Zaehner 1970: 150).

Zaehner was convinced of the significance of the *Bhagavad-Gītā*. In it he found the teaching of devotion and a theistic type of mysticism, using these to nuance his treatment of Hinduism. He judged that the rise of devotion had transformed Hinduism and regarded as inadequate the prevalent monistic stereotype of Hindu mysticism. He believed that the *Bhagavad-Gītā* initiated a devotional revolution in Hinduism, though in his opinion its influence extended further. Its theistic mysticism similarly had an impact not just on Hinduism, where he saw it as evidence of an unacknowledged or underestimated feature of the tradition, but in a wider context as investing Hinduism with a part to play in inter-religious relations.

The publication of Wilkins' translation first brought the *Bhagavad-Gītā* to a Western audience with Wilkins' preface and Hastings' letter of recommendation together articulating an extremely positive assessment of the text. However, the development of the study of Hinduism, predicated upon the study of Hindu scriptures, meant that over the years the *Bhagavad-Gītā* was subjected to further critical scrutiny and, in the process of their academic work on the text, scholars portrayed Hinduism in a range of ways. That their portraits of the *Bhagavad-Gītā* differed so markedly, and as a result their portraits of Hinduism, underlined the complexity of the text and the tradition as well as an extraordinary diversity of theoretical and methodological positions.

For Müller, the *Bhagavad-Gītā* was a lesser text of a later period and as such it demonstrated something of the degeneracy of post-Vedic Hinduism. For Monier-Williams, the *Bhagavad-Gītā* was an admirable text of devotion to a personal deity, the defining characteristic of his description of Hinduism, yet it was undermined by Brahmanism's teaching of an impersonal absolute, which relegated Hinduism to an inferior status and upheld the superiority of Christianity. For Otto, the *Bhagavad-Gītā* was important as a work of devotion and theistic mysticism, its diversity mirroring that of Hinduism and furnishing the basis for a comparison with Christianity. For Zaehner too, the *Bhagavad-Gītā* was a work of devotion and theistic mysticism, stressing trends in Hinduism that he believed had been given insufficient attention. He also appealed to the *Bhagavad-Gītā* as having global relevance and as giving Hinduism an important place in religious dialogue.

2

SOCIAL AND POLITICAL ACTIVISM

One of the most significant changes in the interpretation of the *Bhagavad-Gītā* associated with the modern period was the emphasis on activism, that is, a focus on karma-yoga as the primary or principal meaning of the text. In the process, Hinduism was recast as an engaged social and political ideology. The *Bhagavad-Gītā*'s message of action in the world for the welfare of others was one that provided a religious justification for modern social and political campaigns and gave Hinduism an activist dimension, often directly opposed to renunciatory views of withdrawal from the world and the quest for personal liberation.

The connection between karma-yoga and social and political action was often overt, even if its contemporary implications were suggested rather than stated. In some instances, the relevance of karma-yoga to current events became evident through personal example and charismatic leadership; in other instances, this teaching had a more generalized impact in inspiring action.

Bal Gangadhar Tilak (1856–1920) was a leading nationalist of the 'extremist' school for whom the *Bhagavad-Gītā* held a special importance. Not only did he hail it as 'one of the most brilliant and pure gems of our ancient sacred books' but he also praised it for ordaining

> a logical and admirable harmony between Devotion (*bhakti*) and Spiritual Knowledge (*jnāna*), and ultimately between these and the duties of ordinary life enjoined by the *Śāstras*, thereby inspiring the mind, bewildered by the vicissitudes of life to calmly and, what is more, desirelessly adhere to the path of duty.
>
> (Tilak 1991: 1–2)

Thus from the beginning of his commentary, the *Śrī Bhagavadgītā Rahasya or Karma-Yoga-Śāstra*, Tilak offered an activist interpretation. This was associated with an account of the *Bhagavad-Gītā* as an exposition of Bhāgavata religion and an accent on the martial setting of the work.

Tilak equated the *Bhagavad-Gītā* with the Bhāgavata religion for a number of reasons: the name of the *Bhagavad-Gītā* recalled the name by which Kṛṣṇa was known in the Bhāgavata religion, Śrī Bhagavān; the reference in the

Bhagavad-Gītā (4.1–3) to its re-disclosure of what had earlier been revealed to Vivasvant and hence to Manu and Ikṣvāku conformed with the chronicle of the Bhāgavata religion in the tretā-yuga (third age); and other references in the *Mahābhārata* linked the *Bhagavad-Gītā* with the Bhāgavata religion (Tilak 1991: 12–13). The importance of this equation was that he understood the Bhāgavata religion in terms of 'Energism' and, accordingly, regarded Kṛṣṇa's instruction of Arjuna as relating 'principally to the Energistic Bhāgavata religion' (Tilak 1991: 13–14). Further, he believed that the *Bhagavad-Gītā* provided the rationale for the activist emphasis in Bhāgavata religion (Tilak 1991: 14).

However, Tilak reminisced about his initial uncertainty concerning the meaning of the *Bhagavad-Gītā*, especially when confronting the commentatorial literature; unsure whether the text did indeed declare only liberation through knowledge or salvation through devotion, it was only when he attempted to read the text for himself that he realized that its message was action (Tilak 1991: xvii–xviii). Thus he insisted that 'the Gītā has propounded the device of performing Action in such a way that one ultimately attains Release without committing sin, namely, the Karma-Yoga founded on Knowledge, in which Devotion is the principal factor' (Tilak 1991: xx). The this-worldly orientation of Tilak's thought was such that action in the sense of selfless or desireless action without expectation of result or hope of reward was enjoined, both because action could not be avoided and because action was necessary for the welfare of the world (Tilak 1991: 499). His ideal was of the person who had achieved the highest spiritual goal but who performed action as duty for the benefit of all (Tilak 1991: 688–9). In general terms, he repeatedly claimed it was better to perform action than to abandon action, counterposing activism (pravṛtti) and renunciation (nivṛtti), karma-yoga and karma-saṃnyāsa (Tilak 1991: 431, 433, 440).

Moreover, Tilak's understanding of the *Bhagavad-Gītā* as a Karma-Yoga-Śāstra[1] was closely related to the martial setting of the discourse. Tilak's uncertainty had been how to reconcile the teachings on knowledge and devotion with the exhortation of Arjuna to fight (Tilak 1991: xvii). In the end, though, he claimed that the chief object of the *Bhagavad-Gītā* was obvious from its context where Arjuna was beset by doubts about the nature of his duty when confronting a conflict in moral imperatives – his duty towards his family and his duty as a warrior – and in urgent need of advice about right action (Tilak 1991: xx). Since Arjuna was faced with the sin of killing members of his own family, if he did fight, and the sin of abnegating his vocation as a warrior, if he did not fight, Tilak asserted that it would have been inappropriate for Kṛṣṇa to have made knowledge or devotion his main theme (Tilak 1991: 34–5). Kṛṣṇa, he concluded, was not seeking to have Arjuna adopt an ascetic discipline in pursuit of knowledge nor worship the Lord with music and dance in a spirit of devotion (Tilak 1991: 35–6). Rather, Kṛṣṇa called Arjuna to act but to do so in a selfless or desireless way as this was the only relevant response to the position in which Arjuna found himself (Tilak 1991: 37). For Tilak, the purpose of the dialogue was to enable a confused Arjuna to identify 'a sinless path of duty' whereby 'the proper preaching in this place would be of Energism'; hence 'the purport of the Gītā religion must also be to support Energism, that is, to support Action' (Tilak 1991: 37–8). On many occasions, Tilak reiterated that Kṛṣṇa's discourse was directed towards Arjuna's present plight, instructing him to fight in a just war with equanimity as to the outcome.

Tilak's view of the *Bhagavad-Gītā*, as he recognized, was at odds with the commentatorial literature that stressed that the text preached release, favouring either knowledge or devotion. His own interpretation involved a repudiation of Śaṅkara's commentary since Śaṅkara focused on release through knowledge, demoting the world to an appearance of Brahman and action to a path for the ignorant (Tilak 1991: 15–21). It also involved a rejection of Rāmānuja's commentary that, like Śaṅkara's, focused on release but through devotion (Tilak 1991: 21–3). He treated Madhva's commentary in much the same way as Rāmānuja's (Tilak 1991: 23). Summing up his analysis of the renunciatory trend, he offered some explanation for the dichotomy between his own interpretation of the text and that provided by other figures (Tilak 1991: 23–8). He suggested that 'the doctrinal method of determining the purport of a book [w]as faulty' (Tilak 1991: 30). The implication was that this was the method that had been adopted by those who regarded the *Bhagavad-Gītā* as a renunciatory work, on the grounds that doctrinal affiliation pre-determined the meaning to be found in the text (Tilak 1991: 33). His belief was that, once 'the doctrinal method' was rejected, the true meaning of the *Bhagavad-Gītā* (in his judgement, activism) would emerge (Tilak 1991: 34).

Clearly, therefore, Tilak was aware of diverse strands in Hinduism, evident in the commentaries on the *Bhagavad-Gītā* and explained in terms of different sectarian stances, though he preferred to refer to Vedic religion (Tilak 1991: 440). At its most fundamental, he drew a distinction between the performance and the abandonment of action. His description of Bhāgavata religion emphasized that action was a lifelong duty that excluded renunciation as a lifestyle, upholding the householder ideal and combining action with knowledge and devotion (Tilak 1991: 475–6). However, this description of Bhāgavata religion was located in the wider context of a chronicle of historical developments in the tradition. He argued that the oldest form of the Vedic religion was based on action but that this was challenged by the rise of renunciation. Nevertheless, he asserted that even in this second phase of Vedic religion there were those who did not advocate the renunciation of action. In the third phase of Vedic religion, action and renunciation were reconciled in terms of the āśramas (stages of life). Yet, at this stage too, he detected different tendencies related to the āśramas as successive stages or alternative ways of life, both extolling the renunciation of the mendicant and the action of the householder. Overall, he claimed that action was an ancient path albeit a path given a new quality in the Bhāgavata religion where the synthesis of action and knowledge was infused with devotion. Subsequent phases had again brought renunciation to the fore though he reiterated the authenticity of action as a Vedic injunction (Tilak 1991: 486–9).

The place of the *Bhagavad-Gītā* in Tilak's scheme was as 'the most important treatise on the science of Karma-Yoga' (Tilak 1991: 489). There was no doubt of the value he attached to the text; after all, he recommended its reading to all those who desired to learn 'the basic principles of the Hindu Religion and Morality', principles applicable to life in the world and harmonizing knowledge, devotion and action (Tilak 1991: xxv). He equated this message proclaimed by the *Bhagavad-Gītā* with the Bhāgavata religion (Tilak 1991: 700). Moreover, he explained that what he called the Gītā religion embodied the essence of the Vedic religion (Tilak 1991: 713). Tilak vested the significance of the *Bhagavad-Gītā* in the accessibility of its spiritual discipline to ordinary people in their day-to-day lives (Tilak 1991: 616–17) and its wide appeal in the combination of the paths (Tilak 1991: 582–3).

Tilak related the *Bhagavad-Gītā* to Hinduism in a speech he made in 1917. On this occasion, he recalled that as a child he had been informed that spiritual progress could not be achieved when caught up in worldly affairs (Tilak 1922: 231). This led him to ask whether his religion required him to renounce the world (Tilak 1922: 231). In answering this question, he turned to the *Bhagavad-Gītā* because he had also been informed that it 'was universally acknowledged to be a book containing all the principles and philosophy of the Hindu religion' (Tilak 1922: 231). He continued with an insistence that the text had to be interpreted without prejudice and with due regard for the reasons for its composition (Tilak 1922: 232). Characteristically dismissive of commentatorial literature, he argued that the composer of the *Bhagavad-Gītā* must have had one objective in mind (Tilak 1922: 232–3). In contrast to other commentators whom he thought had interpreted the text in line with their own ideologies, he thought he had successfully discerned its composer's intentions (Tilak 1922: 233). Claiming that he could do so because he was unprejudiced with no ulterior motive, his summary of the teaching of the *Bhagavad-Gītā* was that it taught action in the world, notwithstanding the achievement of liberation through knowledge or devotion (Tilak 1922: 233). The continued performance of action was necessary to ensure that the world progressed along the lines ordained for it by its creator but such action had to be selfless in character to avoid bondage to the wheel of existence (Tilak 1922: 233).

For Tilak, this constituted 'the lesson of the *Gita*' (Tilak 1922: 233). Without denying the existence of knowledge or devotion, he subordinated them to action on the grounds that '[i]f the *Gita* was preached to desponding Arjuna to make him ready for the fight – for the action – how can it be said that the ultimate lesson of the great book is Bhakti or Gnana alone?' (Tilak 1922: 233–4). This advocacy of action on Tilak's part was exemplified by Kṛṣṇa who acted without thought of himself for the good of the world and, since the aim of the aspirant was union with the divine, it necessarily involved identification with the divine purpose (Tilak 1922: 234–5). Consequently, to act for the world in obedience to God's will was 'the surest way of Salvation' (Tilak 1922: 234–5). Given such a this-worldly emphasis, the relevance of the *Bhagavad-Gītā* and, through the text, Hinduism to the India of his day was obvious. Nevertheless, his commentary had to address a number of exegetical issues in order to make the teaching of Kṛṣṇa to Arjuna binding on modern Indian citizens and to provide Hinduism with an activist ethic.

These issues concerned the nature and scope of duty since, in order to establish public good as an overriding priority and thus its protection as a duty laid upon everyone, Tilak needed to go beyond the requirement for all members of society to do their duty as appropriate to their station in life (Tilak 1991: 689–90, 697).[2] The claim that duty could be chosen by the agent, and not merely determined by one's varṇa (class), was substantiated by citing the example of a brāhman who became a warrior and was commended for abandoning prayer and worship in favour of soldiering (Tilak 1991: 697–8). Yet if it was praiseworthy to adopt a duty other than that incumbent on one's varṇa, despite dire warnings against performing another's duty, it was vital to explain when and why this was the case. In Tilak's view, what justified the general adoption of the warrior's duty to protect society, if necessary through violence, was the perception of a national crisis so long as this was consistent with the guidance offered by the wise (Tilak 1991: 510–65).

Throughout Tilak maintained the intimate connection between the performance of action as part of an integrated spiritual discipline and the prosperity of India since he believed that the leaders of any nation had to be activist in outlook (Tilak 1991: 700). Further, he stressed that sacred literature had ruled against renunciation in the present age of decline, the kali-yuga (Tilak 1991: 701). Moreover, such action by no means excluded violent action, a pacifist misconception that he believed derived from the decline of karma-yoga; instead he insisted, while the *Bhagavad-Gītā* advocated equanimity towards all, it did not advocate non-violence because karma-yoga prioritized the duty to act to secure the welfare of the world (Tilak 1991: 555–6). Indeed, karma-yoga embraced nationalism as an intermediate point in the development of a universal concern, though not rejected on its attainment (Tilak 1991: 556). So it was that Tilak could account for India's past greatness – a time when the Gītā religion was practised and the nation flourished – and its present distress – now that the Gītā religion had fallen into desuetude (Tilak 1991: 713). So too he could look towards a return to activism achieved by a rediscovery of the Gītā religion uniting knowledge, devotion and action (Tilak 1991: 713).

The link between the *Bhagavad-Gītā*, Hinduism and nationalism was often more implied than stated – the *Bhagavad-Gītā* as a call to action associated with the nation's fortunes, activism as a significant aspect of Hinduism with importance for India, and nationalism as a component of the karma-yoga taught in the *Bhagavad-Gītā* and hence an authentic expression of Hindu norms and values. Nevertheless, this link was established in Tilak's championing of Shivaji, a seventeenth-century Maratha leader, as a national hero. This choice was explained in *The Maratta* in terms of Shivaji living at a time when the Indian people were oppressed and his possessing the altruism and bravery to inspire confidence in India's destiny (Tilak 1922: 48).

The significance of the *Bhagavad-Gītā* in Tilak's promotion of Shivaji was stated in 1897 at the celebration of a festival commemorating Shivaji's coronation. During this festival, the conduct of Shivaji was debated and defended by various speakers including Tilak (McLane 1970: 54–6). The events with which they were concerned were those surrounding the death of Afzal Khan, general of the Bijapur army that was laying siege to Shivaji's Pratapgarh fortress (McLane 1970: 52–3). Specifically, controversy centred on Shivaji's assassination of Afzal Khan under the flag of truce on the pretext of agreeing the terms for the Maratha surrender to the superior Muslim forces. *Kesari*'s report of Tilak's speech on this occasion had him set aside historical questions and propose that, even if the conventional account of Shivaji's alleged treachery was accepted, the moral character of his actions had to be assessed in relation to Shivaji's special status (McLane 1970: 56).

In justifying Shivaji's conduct, Tilak appealed to the *Bhagavad-Gītā* – Kṛṣṇa's instruction to Arjuna to kill his preceptors and relatives and the injunction to act without thought of reward – in order to exonerate Shivaji as an assassin who killed for the general good and not for selfish reasons (McLane 1970: 56). Tilak's advice was thus to '[g]et out of the Penal Code, enter into the extremely high atmosphere of the *Bhagavad Gita*, and then consider the actions of great men' (quoted in McLane 1970: 56). Just as Shivaji was a prototype for nationalists, in Tilak's view the *Bhagavad-Gītā* effectively became a nationalist tract, providing a Hindu rationale for violent action in the service of a higher cause. Tilak frequently protested that his championing of Shivaji encouraged neither anti-Muslim nor anti-British sentiment and also was at some pains to differentiate between Shivaji's spirit and his actions so that his spirit but not his actions were to be emulated (e.g. Tilak 1922: 50–1). Even so, it is difficult to escape the conclusion that Tilak's message to nationalists was that they should do as Shivaji had done, confident that Hinduism, on the basis of the *Bhagavad-Gītā*, would condone their actions.

In any case, the link between the *Bhagavad-Gītā*, Hinduism and nationalism was made explicit in Tilak's speech on 'The Bharata Dharma Mahamandala'. In this speech, he expressed his admiration for the *Bhagavad-Gītā* and hailed the Hindu or Vedic religion as 'Sanātana Dharma' (Tilak 1922: 35, 39). However, his concern was with the unity of the Hindu religion, identifying the *Bhagavad-Gītā* alongside the *Vedas* and the Epics as a factor making for unity (Tilak 1922: 35–6). This unity had political as well as religious importance since, by concentrating on the common adherence to the *Bhagavad-Gītā* and other texts as constituting a shared inheritance, 'we shall ere long be able to consolidate all the different sects into a mighty Hindu nation' (Tilak 1922: 36–7). The importance of the *Bhagavad-Gītā* for nationalism was thus openly acknowledged, reinforced by mention of Kṛṣṇa's promise to incarnate in order to uphold good whenever evil was on the rise (Tilak 1922: 37–8). Hinduism alone among religions, Tilak argued, offered the assurance of repeated divine interventions, defining religion as 'an element in nationality' and declaring that Hinduism supplied 'a moral as well as a social tie' (Tilak 1922: 36, 38). Consequently, he attributed the greatness of the Indian nation in ancient times to its unity, presenting religious unity as the foundation of national unity and inviting all Hindus to contribute towards the achievement of this goal (Tilak 1922: 36–7).

Tilak regarded the *Bhagavad-Gītā* as an activist work and sought to redress the imbalance in perceptions of Hinduism by reference to it. The *Bhagavad-Gītā* was significant not only because it expounded the activism that he insisted was a vital part of Hinduism but also because it was necessary to Hinduism as the grounding for nationalism.

Mohandas Karamchand Gandhi (1869–1948) similarly stressed action but, in contrast to Tilak, urged that karma-yoga entailed non-violence. Thus his interpretation of the *Bhagavad-Gītā* was very different from Tilak's despite having read his work (Gandhi 1946: 126) and referred to it in support of his own argument (Gandhi 1980: 295). Gandhi's view of Hinduism focused on both action and non-violence, the *Bhagavad-Gītā* expounding these themes so as to demonstrate their relevance to life in the world where there was no recognition of a divide between the sacred and the secular. Accordingly, the *Bhagavad-Gītā* and Hinduism underwrote his nationalist activities and justified such activities on the part of others.

Gandhi's writings on the *Bhagavad-Gītā* were published both as books and pamphlets – *The Bhagvadgita, The Gospel of Selfless Action or The Gita According to Gandhi, Discourses on the Gita* – and as excerpts in many collections of Gandhi's writings where Hinduism also featured. This prominence of the *Bhagavad-Gītā* in various publications was a reflection of the text's importance for him personally. For example, he explained that it was a source of comfort when he thought he was dying (Gandhi 1978: 14) and related that his appreciation for it increased daily (Gandhi 1980: 308). He called the *Bhagavad-Gītā* 'a spiritual reference work' (Gandhi 1946: 126), adding that '[b]efore Mother *Gita*, the earthly mother stands no comparison' (Gandhi 1980: 47). He emphasized that the *Bhagavad-Gītā* was for everyone, that in it all would find a cure for their spiritual ills (Gandhi 1980: 33, 243). As this suggests, the *Bhagavad-Gītā* was not to be studied academically without seeking to apply what it taught; he commented that reading the text had pervaded his life with prayer (Gandhi 1980: 153–4).

Yet the *Bhagavad-Gītā* was not always an important part of his life as he admitted in his autobiography. Indeed, he first read the *Bhagavad-Gītā* at the invitation and in the company of two English Theosophists and even then it was years later that he took to reading it everyday (Gandhi 1982: 76–7). It is noteworthy that Gandhi's initial encounter with the *Bhagavad-Gītā* was in Edwin Arnold's English translation, a translation of which he formed the highest opinion (Gandhi 1982: 76). Perhaps, though, of greater significance was the way in which this encounter inspired Gandhi to further investigation of the text (Gandhi 1946:126) as well as contributing towards his rediscovery of his heritage (Gandhi 1980: 9). Subsequent years of study and reflection led Gandhi to conclude that the *Bhagavad-Gītā* taught action, and since such action was to be selfless, necessarily non-violent. This involved an allegorical interpretation of the martial setting and content of the text.

Gandhi pointed to the *Bhagavad-Gītā*'s teaching on karma, its unique solution to the necessity of action when any action binds the agent being to concentrate on the motivation for its performance. His summary of the *Bhagavad-Gītā*'s teaching was as follows: 'Do your allotted work but renounce its fruit – be detached and work – have no desire for reward and work' (Gandhi 1946: 131). Accordingly, commenting on the third chapter, his interpretation of sacrifice stressed that service of others was no sacrifice at all if its motivation was selfish (Gandhi 1960: 20–1). Moreover, the practise of karma-yoga was to include both knowledge and devotion since without knowledge there was no wisdom and without devotion there was no love (Gandhi 1980: 305). His advocacy of renunciation in, not of, action was not, however, distinctive – his distinctive contribution lay in his insistence that selfless action was non-violent.

Gandhi made this connection between selflessness and non-violence in action by extolling the virtue of detachment, arguing that the issue of violence in the *Bhagavad-Gītā* was resolved because '[w]hen detachment governs our actions, even the weapon raised in order to strike an enemy down falls out of our hand' (Gandhi 1960: 21). In his view, the *Bhagavad-Gītā* associated violence with anger and hatred, and its ideal was attainment of a state in which neither anger nor hatred was possible (Gandhi 1980: 12–13). Thus he argued that the *Bhagavad-Gītā*'s portrayal of a perfected person was incompatible with actual violence (Gandhi 1946: 128). Clearly, though, in order to present the *Bhagavad-Gītā* as preaching non-violent action, he also had to provide a persuasive account of its setting in the epic when battle was about to begin and its dialogue which was directed towards convincing Arjuna to fight.

For example, Gandhi insisted that the *Mahābhārata* portrayed the pointlessness of war, asking a series of rhetorical questions regarding the outcome of the conflict and the fate of the combatants (Gandhi 1980: 12). He found evidence of the futility of physical violence in the fact that even the victors experienced defeat so that theirs was a pyrrhic victory (Gandhi 1980: 292). His approach to the *Bhagavad-Gītā* was that it was not historical and thus not to be interpreted literally; rather it was an external representation of an internal conflict (Gandhi 1946: 127–8). The battlefield of Kurukṣetra he saw as the heart and the site of constant battle though also, if God dwelt there, a field of righteousness (Gandhi 1960: 8). Duryodhana and the Kauravas, he believed, symbolized the evil, and Arjuna and the Pāṇḍavas the good, tendencies within humanity with Kṛṣṇa as the inner guide (Gandhi 1980: 13–14).[3]

In so doing, Gandhi was adopting a particular attitude towards the authority and meaning of what he called scriptures. He was dubious about claims of divine inspiration, at least insofar as such claims were exclusive to a text or extended to the entirety of its contents (Gandhi 1978: 9). Instead, he was concerned to discover the spirit and not the letter, considering that scriptures might contain elements that were not genuine and that they were not constrained by historical provenance (Gandhi 1978: 39–40). He appealed to an authority higher than the scriptures themselves – reason – and on this basis argued that any śāstric ruling that did not satisfy the criterion of truth was to be rejected (Gandhi 1978: 43). Moreover, he referred to a Hindu maxim that real knowledge of the śāstras depended on spiritual qualities, stating that the meaning of the scriptures was revealed in accordance with the exegete's realization of truth (Gandhi 1978: 10, 127). This relativization of texts was mirrored in Gandhi's treatment of traditions.

Gandhi was aware of some of the issues surrounding the word 'Hinduism' as a foreign label but nevertheless attributed to it characteristics of tolerance and inclusiveness (Gandhi 1971: 197). He did not, though, take the position that Hinduism was superior to other religions. On the contrary, he insisted that all religions combined insight with error, urging respect for other religions as for one's own (Gandhi 1971: 197). He declared his own respect for other religions was the same as for Hinduism, adding that they were appropriate for those people to whom they were given and consequently disparaging the prospect of there being only one religion (Gandhi 1958: 60–1). Yet he vested the equality of religions in the oneness of God so that all led to the same goal (Gandhi 1958: 59; 1978: 23). More than this, he subordinated Hinduism to 'the religion which transcends Hinduism, which changes one's very nature, which binds one indissolubly to the truth within and which ever purifies' (Gandhi 1971: 124). This was why Gandhi regarded the terms God and Truth as interchangeable, even if in later years he tended to favour Truth as God over God as Truth (Gandhi 1958: 69, cf. 1988: 124). Certainly he affirmed that 'the essence of Hinduism is truth' but it was to the outworking of truth in action, more particularly non-violent action, that he attached the utmost importance since the end did not justify, but instead was determined by, the means (Gandhi 1978: 42).

In answering questions about his religion and its relevance to society, Gandhi indicated his adherence to Hinduism as the 'religion of humanity' and the 'religion of Truth' (Gandhi 1988: 124). When explaining how this religious adherence was expressed in conduct, he focused on the unity of life and the principle of service as to realize truth was to identify with and care for all (Gandhi 1988: 125). In his understanding, the pursuit of truth was a quest that encompassed every aspect of life and motivated all his acts of service (Gandhi 1958: 75). On these grounds, he refused to divide religion from politics since to do so would be to place a restriction on the love that an aspirant after truth should feel for all of creation (Gandhi 1982: 453). The name he gave to his method of direct action, Satyāgraha (Truth-Force), made clear this connection between truth and action (e.g. Gandhi 1971: 65).

The connection between truth and non-violence in Gandhi's thought was even clearer.[4] He believed that truth could be realized only through non-violence (Gandhi 1982: 452–3). Indeed, though non-violence was found in every religion, it was in Hinduism that it achieved its climax (Gandhi 1978: 8). In response to the accusation that he had glossed truth and non-violence, on the one hand, with Hinduism, on the other hand, his rejoinder was to observe that Hinduism lacked a creed (Gandhi 1978: 18). This explained his decision to state 'Truth and non-violence is my creed' but he also stated, if he had to formulate a creed for Hinduism, that it would be 'search after Truth through non-violent means' (Gandhi 1978: 18). Further, the *Bhagavad-Gītā* was a point of reference for Gandhi's interpretation of Hinduism both in terms of action and non-violence.

Gandhi extolled the *Bhagavad-Gītā* 'as the very quintessence of all Shastras' so that, though many other books might be read to confirm its tenets, 'its sole authority' should suffice (Gandhi 1980: 23, 243). He even went so far as to say that the final 19 verses of the second chapter – verses that he said 'ever remained engraved in my heart' – incorporated 'the essence of dharma' (Gandhi 1980: 9). He espoused the view that the *Bhagavad-Gītā* taught what all scriptures taught, while emphasizing that the *Bhagavad-Gītā* set forth a method by which the equanimity it advised might be achieved (Gandhi 1960: 9). In similar vein, he insisted that the *Bhagavad-Gītā*, in common with all scriptures, was concerned with self-realization but reiterated that the purpose of the *Bhagavad-Gītā* was to show how that self-realization was to be accomplished (Gandhi 1946: 129). '*That matchless remedy*' was action infused by a spirit of renunciation and dedicated to the divine, dependent on both knowledge and devotion, a principle set forth in other Hindu scriptures but mostly clearly in the *Bhagavad-Gītā* (Gandhi 1946: 129). His exposition of this selfless action in the *Bhagavad-Gītā* and in Hinduism was also associated with non-violence.

On the subject of non-violence, Gandhi justified his exegetical strategy by appeal to the vocation of the poet and the nature of poetry (Gandhi 1946: 133). He explained that the *Bhagavad-Gītā* had changed the meaning of certain terms, demonstrating how sacrifice had become service of others and renunciation selfless action in the world (Gandhi 1946: 133). Taking this as his model for interpreting the *Bhagavad-Gītā*, he asserted that even if the literal meaning of the text could reconcile violence with selflessness, his own experience of living out its teaching led him to conclude 'that perfect renunciation is impossible without perfect observance of *ahimsa* in every shape and form' (Gandhi 1946: 133–4). This insistence on non-violence as a corollary of selfless action, entailing as it did a redefinition of Hindu concepts, was part of an agenda in which the religious and the political were integrated.

For Gandhi, the significance of the *Bhagavad-Gītā* lay in its holistic rejection of the notion that religion was concerned solely with other-worldly subjects. He claimed that the *Bhagavad-Gītā* showed that religion was a guide to the whole of life, declaring 'the *Gita* teaches us that what cannot be followed out in day-to-day practice cannot be called religion' (Gandhi 1946: 132). This was consistent with his description of the divine as 'ethics and morality' and, more generally, with the priority he attached to ethical or moral action (Gandhi 1958: 58). Hence he was not prepared to place the interests of India as his country or Hinduism as his religion above the demands of non-violence (Gandhi 1958: 73).

Non-violence, for Gandhi, was a moral imperative arising out of the oneness of humanity as well as an expression of the religious dimension of politics. When he described his mission, it was with reference to the *Bhagavad-Gītā* that he expressed the ambition to be at peace with everyone (Gandhi 1988: 68). What this meant in practice was evident, for example, in his opposition to Untouchability as a form of violence – an institution, antithetical to his principle of Sarvodaya (Universal Welfare), he was definite had no basis in the *Bhagavad-Gītā*'s version of Hinduism, nor that of the *Vedas* or *Upaniṣads* (Gandhi 1988: 57–8). Moreover, as he warned, '[a]nyone... who does not find the principle of non-violence in the Shastras is indeed in danger' (Gandhi 1980: 11). Gandhi himself was in no such danger as non-violence together with selfless action was the message he found in the *Bhagavad-Gītā*.

Gandhi's understanding of the *Bhagavad-Gītā* was thus a call to action though its selfless character required it also to be non-violent. This fitted with his understanding of Hinduism as a religion of action and non-violence. Indeed, both Hindu scriptures and Hinduism were relativized by his dedication to truth while truth required action and non-violence. For him, the *Bhagavad-Gītā* was perhaps the best expression of these ideals that also typified the true Hinduism.

Aurobindo Ghose (1872–1950), also known as Sri Aurobindo, however, established a marked contrast with Tilak and Gandhi. This was because the *Bhagavad-Gītā* played little part in Ghose's early career as a nationalist, only later becoming significant, and because the *Bhagavad-Gītā* was important to him in a different capacity when he had retired from nationalist politics, finally losing its special status in his universal spiritual vision. His account of Hinduism was at one stage associated with nationalism, though at another with universalism. The *Bhagavad-Gītā*, he recognized, could serve the cause of nationalism from a Hindu perspective as well as contain profound spiritual insights of relevance to all. Like Tilak, he was prepared to countenance violence; like Gandhi, he believed it possible to extend the meaning of terms.

Although Ghose's initial use of Hindu religious symbolism in the service of Indian nationalism tended to feature India as Śakti, Divine Energy or Power (e.g. Ghose 1972a: 65), the odd reference to the *Bhagavad-Gītā* did appear.[5] For example, in an article on 'The Doctrine of Passive Resistance', he appealed to the text when advocating opposition to British rule, even justifying violent opposition, finding in the battlefield and the divine admonition of the reluctant warrior a vindication of his present call to arms (Ghose 1972a: 98). Commenting on the situation of imperial India, though he recommended passive resistance, he refused to condemn other methods on the grounds that the empire rested upon violence while disallowing violent resistance on the part of its subject peoples (Ghose 1972a: 98). This meant that in certain conditions force was lawful and legitimate and in these conditions '[t]o shrink from bloodshed and violence... is a weakness deserving as severe a rebuke as Sri Krishna addressed to Arjuna when he shrank from the colossal civil slaughter on the field of Kurukshetra' (Ghose 1972a: 98). Kṛṣṇa's admonition of Arjuna was, therefore, a precedent for Indian nationalism since Ghose contended that it was morally defensible to use whatever means were necessary to overcome oppression, not excluding force.

Another example of reference to the *Bhagavad-Gītā* was in 'The Morality of Boycott' where Ghose cited the text to confound pacifist principles – disputing any demand that the oppressed adopt a higher standard of conduct than their oppressors since this favoured injustice, he stated that 'the Gita is the best answer to those who shrink from battle as a sin, and aggression as a lowering of morality' (Ghose 1972a: 124). More generally, he described politics as both 'the business of the Kshatriya' and 'the ideal of the Kshatriya' (Ghose 1972a: 122, 125). Yet the *Bhagavad-Gītā* played only a minor part in his nationalist rhetoric.

This changed as a result of a series of religious experiences when in prison that also changed Ghose's approach to nationalism. Recalling these experiences in his Uttarpara Speech in 1909, he related the divine message that his imprisonment was God's will to prepare him for his future role (Ghose 1972b: 3). Continuing, he recounted how the *Bhagavad-Gītā* had been placed in his hands and he had been enabled to follow its discipline, coming to understand Kṛṣṇa's instruction to Arjuna and through him all who wished to serve the divine purpose 'to do work for Him without the demand for fruit' (Ghose 1972b: 3). Here was the stress on action performed selflessly in obedience to God as a divine trust. The focus on action, albeit in a new context where nationalism no longer claimed ultimacy, was evident in the journals he founded in this period, *Dharma* and *Karmayogin*. *Dharma* had on its cover Kṛṣṇa's declaration of the avatāra ideal (4.7) (Minor 1991: 71). This choice of verse emphasized Kṛṣṇa's active concern with, and involvement in, the world to uphold the good and combat the evil. Similarly, *Karmayogin* had on its cover Kṛṣṇa's advice to act and dedicate all actions to him (3.30) (Minor 1991: 72). This verse underlined the significance of action performed for God in an equable spirit. Yet increasingly Ghose understood the teaching about action as a yoga, a spiritual discipline, indeed, 'the Yoga of the Gita', and as such it constituted an aspect of continuity between his earlier and later works.

After his flight from British India and effective cessation of nationalist activity, Ghose's writings still featured the *Bhagavad-Gītā*, initially in a central role and latterly in a more minor capacity. In *Essays on the Gita*, for example, he discussed Kurukṣetra in the light of his acceptance that the text had been composed when war was inevitable, though limited both by the size of the warrior class and their code of chivalry; accordingly, it offered advice to the warrior in the conduct of war (Ghose 1970: 44–7). However, war also symbolized 'the aspect of battle and struggle which belongs to all life' and, similarly, the warrior symbolized 'the fighter in man . . . striving towards mastery' (Ghose 1970: 48).[6] This emphasis on the deeper spiritual message conveyed by the *Bhagavad-Gītā* meant that Arjuna was a man of action guided by an ideal of right who was shown the way to combine action with renunciation, an approach of 'calm and self-possessed action in the world' (Ghose 1970: 48–51). Action, therefore, remained an important theme though Ghose's treatment of action reflected his changing priorities.

Certainly Ghose was critical of the recent stress on action to the detriment, if not the exclusion, of knowledge and devotion, rejecting the pervasive tendency to view the *Bhagavad-Gītā*'s activism as delivering an ethical imperative, synonymous with social duty or service, rather than a spiritual one (Ghose 1970: 27–8). Accordingly, though the *Bhagavad-Gītā* was 'a Gospel of Works', he asserted that such action led to knowledge and was informed by devotion; the *Bhagavad-Gītā*'s teaching concerned 'not a human, but a divine action' and, consequently, it was 'not a book of practical ethics, but of the spiritual life' (Ghose 1970: 27–8). This testified to the growing importance of spirituality in Ghose's life, as well as to an interpretation of action where the surrender to the divine and the divine purpose for the world was the defining characteristic.

This was consistent with his paraphrase of Kṛṣṇa's teaching in a chapter entitled 'The Message of the Gita' when he summarized '[t]he secret of action' (Ghose 1970: 553). This secret he set out in terms of both knowledge and devotion within an overarching spiritual framework where action as sacrifice culminated in self-surrender to 'the supreme and universal Spirit to do through you his own will and works in the world' (Ghose 1970: 553–4). Here too, then, action was to be performed in the service of the divine and to be directed by divine guidance. Nationalism could no longer constitute an overriding priority since it was an externally dictated duty.

This emphasis on a truth known within, probably attributable to the transformative impact of spiritual experiences on his own life, tended to relativize the authority of all scriptures yet the frequency with which he referred to the *Bhagavad-Gītā* indicated that he regarded it as having great value nevertheless. For instance, in *The Synthesis of Yoga*, he discussed revelation through the Word, stressing that the Word might be mediated by a variety of means, including scripture (Ghose 1987: 142). But he stressed that no scripture was able to encompass truth in its entirety and, accordingly, the spiritual aspirant would benefit from, but not be restricted by, scripture (Ghose 1987: 143). A scripture could exert a profound influence on an aspirant, even facilitating the experience that transcended its truths (Ghose 1987: 143). An aspirant's spiritual practice might be based on one scripture or several in succession, the *Bhagavad-Gītā*, the *Upaniṣads* or the *Vedas*, but, in the final analysis, it was what lay beyond scripture – the Infinite – that mattered most (Ghose 1987: 143). Notwithstanding this subordination of scripture to experience, the structure of *The Synthesis of Yoga*, published as volumes 20 and 21 of the Sri Aurobindo Birth Centenary Library, reflected the three paths of the *Bhagavad-Gītā*. There was the focus on action (Part One 'The Yoga of Divine Works'), knowledge (Part Two 'The Yoga of Integral Knowledge') and devotion (Part Three 'The Yoga of Divine Love') as well as Ghose's by then typical stress upon synthesis (in the introduction) and self-realization (in the fourth part) (Ghose 1987). This illustrated that for him the text retained some significance.

Subsequently, the *Bhagavad-Gītā* was largely superseded. It did not disappear entirely from Ghose's works, however. *The Life Divine* thus contained a number of references to the *Bhagavad-Gītā* in the course of considering certain themes and topics, notably in the form of short quotations in the superscriptions to the chapters (Ghose 1982: 64, 71, 136, 142, 159, 207, 228, 295, 322, 338, 352, 365, 388, 412, 439, 492, 508, 524, 577, 596, 633, 683, 742, 848, 884, 889, 987, 1019, 1050). Although in these ways the *Bhagavad-Gītā* was still present and, indeed, other scriptures (various *Upaniṣads* and the *Ṛg Veda*), it would seem that the logic of Ghose's position, privileging spiritual experience over scriptural authority, would lead him personally to the point when the text ceased to be useful and, in his later years, this was probably what occurred.

In Ghose's view, it was by advancing the interests of Hinduism that the welfare of the nation was to be secured. Furthermore, as he stated in an article on 'The Ideal of the Karmayogin', to serve India was to serve humanity at large (Ghose 1972b: 16). He believed that the preservation and dissemination of the Sanātana Dharma (translated by him as 'eternal religion', national but also universal) was India's destiny (Ghose 1972b: 17). Since foreign forces had exercised a deleterious impact on India's practise of the Sanātana Dharma, it was now necessary to rediscover her spiritual heritage (Ghose 1972b: 17). It was in this context that karma-yoga became a national duty though it was simultaneously the means whereby India could discharge her duty, to the world – not only was it through karma-yoga that India would gain 'the strength to realise her freedom, unity and greatness' but it was also to make karma-yoga 'the ideal of human life' that India was to rise (Ghose 1972b: 17). In this way, Ghose linked Hinduism as the Sanātana Dharma with nationalism through his advocacy of karma-yoga.

Speaking after his religious experiences while in prison, Ghose's account of Hinduism was thus articulated in terms of a link between the Sanātana Dharma and the nationalist cause (Ghose 1972b: 10). His understanding of the Sanātana Dharma as eternal entailed his insistence that it was the Hindu religion only in the sense that Hindus had remained faithful to it – it was not limited to one people but, on the contrary, encompassed all paths (Ghose 1972b: 9). God's message to him, as he informed his audience, was that India was being raised for the purpose of proclaiming the Sanātana Dharma (Ghose 1972b: 8). Here Ghose made two important observations: first, an identification of the Sanātana Dharma with nationalism where previously he had described nationalism as a religion; second, an assertion that the fortunes of the Hindu nation were inextricably bound up with the fortunes of the Sanātana Dharma (Ghose 1972b: 10). From these came his statements claiming 'the Sanatan Dharma . . . for us is nationalism' and '[t]he Hindu nation was born with the Sanatan Dharma' (Ghose 1972b: 10). Yet at this comparatively early period, there were already clear indications that Indian nationalism had a wider, even universal, significance as a vehicle of Hinduism, the Sanātana Dharma, with tidings for the world as a whole.

As a result of Ghose's religious experiences, as he explained in his Uttarpara speech, he came to appreciate the truth of Hinduism of which so many were ignorant (Ghose 1972b: 3). Contrasting Hinduism with other religions on the grounds that other religions were based on belief whereas Hinduism was predicated on practice, he declared the Sanātana Dharma to be 'life itself', vouchsafed to India where it was held in safekeeping for humanity as a whole (Ghose 1972b: 3–4). Hence the revival of India had a religious purpose in which '[s]he is rising to shed the eternal light entrusted to her over the world' (Ghose 1972b: 4). This vision for India's global role as a spiritual exemplar was a theme to which he returned throughout his career.

Towards the close of his life, in an address delivered on the day India achieved independence, Ghose recalled his previous comments about India's destiny in which her freedom and fortune served not just her own interests but the world's, and continued by proposing a progressive model ranging from nationalism to universalism (Ghose 1964: 40–1). Beginning with Indian independence, moving through the promotion of a post-colonial Asia and international harmony, to conclude with spiritual development and evolution to a new stage of consciousness, he lauded 'the gift by India of her spiritual knowledge and her means for the spiritualisation of life to the whole race' leading to 'a new step in... evolution which... would begin the solution of the many problems of existence which have perplexed and vexed humanity' (Ghose 1964: 40–1). On this occasion, Ghose was locating Indian nationalism in a context where it inaugurated a process with continental and global implications. Moreover, India's spirituality, for him an important aspect of her national character that would flourish with independence, was her contribution to the spiritual uplift of all humanity.

The close relationship between the *Bhagavad-Gītā* and Hinduism was evident when Ghose explained he had learnt 'what the Hindu religion meant' during his religious experiences while in prison, experiences in which the *Bhagavad-Gītā* and especially its teaching on action figured so prominently (Ghose 1972b: 3). Before that, despite his scepticism, he had been drawn 'to the truth of the Vedas, the truth of the Gita, the truth of the Hindu religion' but it was only in prison that he came to a real understanding of such truth (Ghose 1972b: 7–8). That said, in his discussion of the karma-yogin, he took the view that the '*sanātana dharma* has many scriptures' of which the *Bhagavad-Gītā* was only one example, though all these scriptures were in some sense secondary since they were subject to confirmation by experience of that which was their origin as well as the foundation of karma-yoga (Ghose 1972b: 19). But, however much this might imply that the text was not of any particular note, this was far from the case. Still a nationalist, albeit an advocate of a spiritualized nationalism, commenting on 'The Gita and Terrorism', he hailed 'the yoga of the *Gītā*' as 'our chief national heritage' (Ghose 1972b: 401).

This was significant because Ghose was addressing the issue of the *Bhagavad-Gītā*'s involvement in political violence 'as a gospel of Terrorism' (Ghose 1972b: 400). Refuting the allegation that the text was a terrorist tract, he suggested that the only tenet that could be corrupted by a terrorist was the teaching that a warrior's duty was to kill and that to do so incurred no sin if the action was selfless and dedicated to the divine (Ghose 1972b: 400). If on such grounds this teaching was to be rejected, he believed there would be 'no moral basis for the hero, the soldier, the judge, the king' (Ghose 1972b: 400). Acknowledging that in contemporary conditions the *Bhagavad-Gītā* was not so much 'a transcendental philosophy' but rather 'a rule of life', he characterized the morality of the text in terms of 'selflessness, courage, a free and noble activity' (Ghose 1972b: 400). Such a message, he insisted, had been denounced by no other nation and for this reason he rejected criticism of the *Bhagavad-Gītā* (Ghose 1972b: 400–1).

After he had abandoned political campaigning in pursuit of spiritual goals, he proclaimed the *Bhagavad-Gītā*'s importance, its religious authority and practical influence, especially its role as 'a powerful shaping factor in the revival and renewal of a nation and a culture', in *Essays on the Gita* (Ghose 1970: 543). Again, though hedged about with warnings about falsely elevating scripture over experience, he stated in no uncertain terms that even after religious experience the *Bhagavad-Gītā*, widely recognized to be 'one of the world's great scriptures', offered 'a large inspiration and guidance' (Ghose 1970: 543–4). More than this, there were hints of the *Bhagavad-Gītā*'s wider significance. Perhaps this lay behind his declaration that 'the *Gītā* will become the universally acknowledged Scripture of the future religion' (Minor 1991: 71; cf. Ghose 1972c: 57) where earlier he had argued that Hinduism, understood in the broadest manner possible, was 'the basis of the future world religion' (Ghose 1972b: 19). In any case, for a major part of Ghose's career, the *Bhagavad-Gītā* was fundamental to his understanding of Hinduism, cited in support of both nationalist and universalist ideas.

In the *Bhagavad-Gītā*, Ghose had a Hindu frame of reference for his nationalist critique of imperial India. As he explained in 'The Awakening Soul of India', contrary to Kṛṣṇa's injunction to perform one's own duty, imperial India had been content to ape Western norms and values (Ghose 1972b: 36). He lamented this alienation from India's own duty, involving as it did 'forgetting the deep saying of the Gita' concerning the connection between one's being and one's duty (Ghose 1972b: 36). Yet, where nationalism had been defined against European norms, he warned that it should not amount to an uncritical acceptance of all things Indian because that would be at odds with 'the spirit of Hinduism' where what was required was to be true to the national soul (Ghose 1972b: 40–1). In like manner, as evident in 'God and Man', the *Bhagavad-Gītā* provided Ghose with a Hindu basis for an activism that was simultaneously a spiritual discipline (Ghose 1972b: 105). Urging that setbacks should not lead to an abandonment of action, he reposed confidence in the working of God's will, referring to the teaching of the *Bhagavad-Gītā* '[r]emember me and fight' as well as the divine assurance that 'thou shalt pass safe through all difficulties and dangers' (Ghose 1972b: 105). He also insisted that 'the Yoga of the Gita' would make a major contribution to the welfare of the Indian nation (Ghose 1972b: 105). Still, in addition to these overtly nationalist appeals to the *Bhagavad-Gītā*, whereby Hindu precepts were associated with India's political future, the text was also cited in a universal context.

Accordingly, in *Essays on the Gita*, Ghose suggested that Hinduism acquired a much wider relevance through the *Bhagavad-Gītā*. He made clear that the text's insights were not limited to a specific time or place, identifying general spiritual truths informing particular Hindu ideas and institutions (Ghose 1970: 3–4). His interpretation of the *Bhagavad-Gītā* was based upon what he regarded as the text's own tendency to draw out the general from the particular, cautioning against a narrow and literal interpretation of the text since this would 'deprive it of its universality and spiritual depth and limit its validity for mankind at large' (Ghose 1970: 4–5). Discussing the variety of Hindu philosophical and theological views informing the *Bhagavad-Gītā*, he emphasized the text's openness and inclusivity as a work of synthesis, harmonizing action, knowledge and devotion as ways to reach the divine (Ghose 1970: 5–7). Although he did not think it necessary or desirable to be restricted by adherence to its teaching, when he looked forward to 'a new, a very rich, a very vast synthesis' beyond Hinduism, encompassing other religions and modern discoveries, he affirmed the value of the *Bhagavad-Gītā* as a foundation for this future development (Ghose 1970: 8). Thus the *Bhagavad-Gītā* could represent yet also transcend Hinduism, contain a nationalist message for India yet also offer a spiritual truth to the world.

Over time Ghose's account of the *Bhagavad-Gītā* changed though action remained a major theme of his exposition. He interpreted the *Bhagavad-Gītā*, as he did Hinduism, in the light of his earlier nationalist and later universalist convictions. In spite of some statements that suggest a subordination of scripture, he accorded the *Bhagavad-Gītā* a privileged position in his account of Hinduism and, by means of his interpretation of the text, gave the tradition a national and also a universal significance.

With Tilak, Gandhi and Ghose, the *Bhagavad-Gītā* became an activist work underwriting Indian nationalism by providing it with a Hindu rationale. Together, albeit differently, they gave an activist flavour to the *Bhagavad-Gītā* and hence to Hinduism. The relevance of this to the India of their time was obvious, as nationalists sought an indigenous basis for social and political action.

For Tilak, the *Bhagavad-Gītā* advocated action, if need be violent action, performed selflessly for the greater good, an aspect of Hinduism that he was insistent had been ignored with damaging consequences for India. For Gandhi, the *Bhagavad-Gītā* also advocated action but he excluded violence on the grounds that violence was incompatible with selflessness, consistent with his understanding of Hinduism in terms of both action and non-violence. Tilak and Gandhi were lifelong nationalists, whereas Ghose withdrew from nationalism to concentrate on the religious life. For Ghose, the *Bhagavad-Gītā* did advocate action but, as he gained in spiritual understanding, his view became more sophisticated, going beyond the straightforward nationalist interpretation and eventually beyond nationalism altogether. In like manner, notably through the *Bhagavad-Gītā*, he appealed to Hinduism in the cause of Indian nationalism and then in expounding a universalism that transcended even Hinduism.

3

CHRISTIAN THEOLOGICAL AND MISSIONARY CRITIQUES

Christian theologians and missionaries were among the most prolific writers on the *Bhagavad-Gītā*, a text to which they referred often in the course of arguments about the relationship between Hinduism and Christianity. This relationship has been seen as: oppositional, Hinduism and Christianity as advancing antagonistic claims; progressive, Hinduism as preparing for and pointing to Christianity; and complementary, Hinduism and Christianity as mutually supportive insights into reality. Consequently, the *Bhagavad-Gītā* has been cited as proof of both the failings and the achievements of Hinduism, notably as evidence of the relative truth of Hinduism contrasted with the absolute truth of Christianity and as the basis of dialogue between Hinduism and Christianity predicated on the equality of these religions.

Although the history of Christianity in India has been traced to St Thomas, it owed much to European imperial expansion in the subcontinent from the sixteenth century onwards. Consequently, reflection on the relationship between Hinduism and Christianity was a feature of the modern period. Indeed, the association with imperialism posed some problems for proselytization as conversion to Christianity could be regarded as tantamount to 'denationalization' such that the enculturation of Christianity seemed to many to be a contradiction in terms. However, the study of Indian beliefs and practices, the need to understand indigenous society, was motivated not only by the imperative to make converts but also inspired by a spirit of openness eschewing any sense of Christian superiority. In this connection, the *Bhagavad-Gītā* presented Christian theologians and missionaries with some strikingly familiar ideas in sometimes unfamiliar guise – faith in God and reliance on divine grace, albeit focused on Kṛṣṇa as incarnate deity in a context where living beings had many lives and Viṣṇu, a member of a polytheistic pantheon, had many incarnations.

Overall, the question that Christian theologians and missionaries were seeking to answer from the standpoint of Christian faith was how the *Bhagavad-Gītā* compared with the Gospel, and Hinduism with Christianity. For some, the answer has not been simply appreciation of the qualities of the *Bhagavad-Gītā* and respect for Hinduism, attributing to the Bible alone the fullness of divine revelation and to Christianity a unique message of universal salvation; on the contrary, it has been to value the *Bhagavad-Gītā* as highly as the Bible and to accord the same status to Hinduism as to Christianity.

R.D. Griffith, a member of the Wesleyan Missionary Society, was one of the contributors to a volume on the *Bhagavad-Gītā* edited by John Garrett, the Director of Public Instruction in Mysore, and published by the Wesleyan Missionary Press in 1849. This volume contained Sanskrit, Canarese and English versions of the text along with a critical apparatus in the form of scholarly essays, notes and appendices. Additionally, the advertisement prefacing the volume contained quotations from Western writers praising the *Bhagavad-Gītā* (Garrett 1849: iii–iv). Yet, despite the esteem apparently enjoyed by the text, Garrett emphasized the extremely limited availability of both its English translation and the Sanskrit original (Garrett 1849: iv). It was this want that the volume was intended to supply and at a relatively early date (Garrett 1849: iv). Thus the editor of the volume expressed the hope that it would prove especially useful to missionaries (Garrett 1849: iv). Moreover, he allowed himself to hope that it would also inspire Hindus to compare the basis of their faith with that of Christianity and 'to contrast the glimmerings of truth which the work is admitted to disclose, with the perfect brightness of that "life and immortality" which the "glorious Gospel of the blessed God," reveals to us' (Garrett 1849: iv). Accordingly, Griffith's essay approached the *Bhagavad-Gītā* from a confessional stance, thereby establishing some significant themes and trends in Christian interpretation of the text.[1]

Griffith was ambivalent about the *Bhagavad-Gītā* on the grounds 'that its reputation is fabulous, though its purport happens to be so notably excellent: that there are flaws in its title, though its contents are mixed up with doctrines of the highest speculative value' (Griffith 1849: xxxviii). Defending this judgement, he insisted that the methodology employed was the same that others could employ to examine the Christian scriptures (Griffith 1849: xxxviii). Certainly, in presenting his argument about the *Bhagavad-Gītā*, he often couched his criticism of the text in terms of the superiority of the Bible. For instance, Griffith's criticism of the setting of the *Bhagavad-Gītā* on the grounds of the improbability of such a dialogue occurring as great armies were about to engage in battle was contrasted with his praise of the Bible for its congruity between the content and context of revelation – the thunder and lightning that marked the giving of the law on Mount Sinai testifying to the glory of God while the ordinary surroundings in which Jesus taught his followers stressed his humanity and the accessibility of his message (Griffith 1849: xxxviii). Or again, Griffith's criticism of the consistency of the *Bhagavad-Gītā* on the grounds of its internal contradictions was contrasted with his praise of the Bible for its freedom from such faults as authenticated by miracle and prophecy, on the one hand, and reason, on the other – the progressive nature of the unfolding of the divine purpose in history meaning that the Gospel built upon and brought to completion earlier communication between God and his people while simultaneously satisfying the requirements of rationality (Griffith 1849: xxxviii–xxxix). Griffith went further, however, querying the age and authority of the *Bhagavad-Gītā* on the basis that the *Laws of Manu* made no mention of the events and figures portrayed in the *Mahābhārata* (Griffith 1849: xl). He was similarly disparaging about the fragmentary character of the truth the *Bhagavad-Gītā* disclosed and that only after considerable effort (Griffith 1849: xl).

Turning to a more detailed analysis of the *Bhagavad-Gītā*, Griffith was indebted to the work of Baron William de Humboldt (cf. de Humboldt 1849) to identify specific subjects (Griffith 1849: xl). The first of these concerned psychology and ethics (Griffith 1849: xl–xliii). Here he drew a clear distinction between Kṛṣṇa's teaching on the soul, which he admired, and his instruction on right living, which he denigrated, suggesting a general principle of the priority of metaphysical over moral truth (Griffith 1849: xli–xlii). As for ethics, in his judgement, it was unacceptable to separate the morality of actions from their consequences or to ground the morality of actions in the concept of duty, also objecting to what he thought of as a determinism that tended to fatalism and a reliance on the divine that detracted from moral responsibility (Griffith 1849: xlii–xliii). He then examined various theological ideas. First, he concluded that image-worship was a latter-day popular degeneration from a pure philosophic faith, though he was at pains to point out the existence of anthropomorphic and other material imagery for the divine in the Christian scriptures (Griffith 1849: xliii–xlv). Second, he likened the pantheism of the *Bhagavad-Gītā* to that of the writings of St John and the incarnation of Kṛṣṇa to that of Christ, albeit representing the *Bhagavad-Gītā* and Kṛṣṇa as partial, inadequate and ineffective versions of their Christian counterparts (Griffith 1849: xlv–xlviii). Third, he made comparisons in terms of the reconciliation of divine unity and plurality between the trimūrti (the Hindu 'trinity' of Brahmā, Viṣṇu and Śiva), expressed in the mystic syllable aum, and the trinity, itself linked with the tetragrammaton (the Hebrew letters of the name YaHWeH or JeHoVaH), before asserting the superiority of the Christian formulation (Griffith 1849: xlviii–l).

The ambivalence that ran through so much of Griffith's account of the *Bhagavad-Gītā* remained in evidence in his treatment of the remaining two subjects, namely reincarnation and Yoga. In his understanding, reincarnation was contrary to the general principle of progress and its particular application to human destiny, confusing the characters of higher and lower forms of life and conflicting with its desired object of divine union; here he contrasted reincarnation with the Christian belief in one life, an intermediate state between death and resurrection, final judgement and the prospect of paradise (Griffith 1849: l–liii). If his view of reincarnation was negative, his assessment of Yoga was positive. He expressed appreciation of it as a means of attaining the divine through improving the mind and restraining the flesh hence, without endorsing the discipline of asceticism, he stated that it was predicated upon an understanding of human nature; here he cited verses from the New Testament about the mortification of the body to establish a comparison with Yoga (Griffith 1849: liii–lv). Overall, he detected some significant similarities between the *Bhagavad-Gītā* and the Bible but he insisted on the unique qualities of the latter. He adopted much the same position in defining the relationship between Hinduism and Christianity, identifying areas of agreement while upholding the primacy of Christianity.

Certainly it was clear that, for Griffith, Hinduism could not meet the challenge posed by Christianity though he did not regard it as worthless. Despite acknowledging that many would reject any idea of Hinduism having value considering the debased and dissolute nature of popular religiosity, he asserted that the failings of some were not the failings of all and, in any case, that few would be prepared to judge Christianity by the conduct of Christians (Griffith 1849: lv–lvi). That said, in the final analysis, 'Hindooism cannot conceal its great cardinal, crying defect' (Griffith 1849: lvi). It was his contention that Hinduism could not bring about the reconciliation of humanity to God; hence his observation that '[t]here are wounds within, which Hindooism cannot heal' (Griffith 1849: lvi). On this line of argument, Hinduism could go so far but could not achieve the atonement because that was achieved by Jesus Christ alone (Griffith 1849: lvi). In this respect, he proposed that Hinduism had much the same strengths and weaknesses as Natural Theology: it could come to an understanding of the divine nature but could not offer a satisfactory account of the place and purpose of humanity; it could describe the spiritual predicament of humanity but could not prescribe a remedy by which to answer the question of salvation (Griffith 1849: lvi–lvii). Still, not only in fairness to Hinduism but also as a strategy for successful evangelism, he deemed it better 'to direct the minds of the Hindoo to the fragments of truth which their superstitions overlay; than to exasperate their temper and outrage their prejudices' (Griffith 1849: xlv). Rather than an arrogant assertion of Christian truth that would provoke resentment on the part of potential converts, he argued that proselytization would be expedited by appealing to features common to Hinduism and Christianity (Griffith 1849: xlv). For all the differences he detected, his recommendation was thus that the missionary enterprise be conducted in a manner that exploited equivalences between Hinduism and Christianity as, in his opinion, this would advance the cause of conversion (Griffith 1849: xlv).

Interestingly, notwithstanding the way Griffith's treatment of the *Bhagavad-Gītā* gave him a platform from which to make more general statements about Hinduism, he commented that '[t]he orthodoxy of the Geeta in many of its fundamental tenets, much less as a whole, no intelligent Hindu would allow' (Griffith 1849: xxxix).[2] Certainly he did emphasize the text's specific sectarian nature, adopting the position that the philosophical basis of the *Bhagavad-Gītā* was Patañjali's Yoga system (Griffith 1849: xxxix). However, he cited evidence of the partiality of Patañjali's system, referring to the divergent views espoused by other philosophers associated with the Vedānta, Nyāya and Sāṃkhya schools (Griffith 1849: xxxix). These differences led him to conclude that the teachings of the *Bhagavad-Gītā* could not command universal acceptance and, consequently, that they had to be treated with some caution in terms of their authority (Griffith 1849: xxxix). Such a view obviously entailed denying the *Bhagavad-Gītā* the same foundational role and prime status for Hindus that the Bible had for Christians.

Indeed, the ambivalence that characterized Griffith's account of the *Bhagavad-Gītā*, especially in relation to the Bible, typified his response to Hinduism as a whole, conceding its insights yet also being convinced that Christianity succeeded where it failed.

Notably, Griffith represented the *Bhagavad-Gītā*'s publication as serving the cause of truth (Griffith 1849: xxxvii). Not only did he believe that Hindu philosophy merited serious study for its innate properties, great age and wide influence, but he declared that hitherto it had hardly received an unprejudiced assessment (Griffith 1849: xxxvii). Furthermore, such a study was located in a context that had it promote the Christian faith since '[t]ruth wherever it lie, and in whatever form it be developed, must sooner or later become the handmaid of Christianity' (Griffith 1849: xxxvii). Insofar as the *Bhagavad-Gītā* was concerned, he regarded it as part of Hindu philosophy and hence worthy of reflection (Griffith 1849: lv). Yet none of this meant that he felt unalloyed admiration for the *Bhagavad-Gītā*. On the contrary, for all its virtues, 'we look upon the system propounded by Krishna, with painful feelings' (Griffith 1849: xxxvii). The working of human reason without the benefit of divine revelation, the reaching out on the part of others for what was only fully present in the Bible, might inspire sympathy (Griffith 1849: xxxvii). Yet, in the end, by incorporating some insight into truth, he implied that the *Bhagavad-Gītā* pointed to truth itself (Griffith 1849: xxxvii). This would be in accord with his declaration that '[e]very error presupposes some truth' whereby all mythology rested upon principles that were the common property of humanity and the product of divine providence (Griffith 1849: xxxvii). Whatever the attributes of the *Bhagavad-Gītā*, it was found wanting when measured against criteria set by the Bible. As a result, it demonstrated that Hinduism was inferior to Christianity, though it might act as a preparation for the preaching of the Gospel if appropriated in the right way.

Griffith recognized good qualities in the *Bhagavad-Gītā* though, for various reasons, he subordinated it to the Bible. Consistent with this, Hinduism was not regarded as sufficient for salvation while there were correspondences between the two religions upon which Christian missionaries could draw. If the *Bhagavad-Gītā* did not seem to him to have general validity for Hindus, nevertheless he used the text as a springboard for a survey of Hinduism. In the *Bhagavad-Gītā* and in Hinduism, he saw some glimpses of truth; in the Bible and in Christianity, he saw saving truth in its entirety.

J.N. Farquhar (1861–1929) was one of Griffith's successors who, writing half a century later, devoted much attention to the *Bhagavad-Gītā*.[3] Although Farquhar differed markedly from Griffith in his estimation of the text's importance, his argument was reminiscent of his predecessor's in his insistence on the necessity for revelation to supplement the exercise of human reason and thus the superiority of Christianity over Hinduism. Farquhar saw the *Bhagavad-Gītā* as significant for its proclamation of a personal deity and a practical morality in a religious message for ordinary people. He was knowledgeable about both the historical development of Hinduism and its contemporary movements but convinced that

Hinduism was fulfilled in Christ. His treatment of the *Bhagavad-Gītā* was one that acknowledged its past and present prominence within Hinduism, explaining how and why this came to be the case, and thus through his discussion of the text he was able to draw conclusions about Hinduism as a whole. By reference to what were the special qualities of the *Bhagavad-Gītā*, he argued that, even at its best, Hinduism was in need of the fulfilment provided by Christ.[4]

Farquhar treated the *Bhagavad-Gītā* in *An Outline of the Religious Literature of India* when discussing theistic trends in Hinduism and the rise of Vaiṣṇavite devotion in relation to epic literature and the doctrine of incarnation (Farquhar 1920: 78, 81–5). Acknowledging that '[t]he poem is a very remarkable one, and has had an immeasurable influence on religion in India', he regarded the *Bhagavad-Gītā* as the product of the earliest Indian effort at theism (Farquhar 1920: 86). What this involved was an identification of Kṛṣṇa with Viṣṇu as Brahman, devotion to whom would bring salvation, thereby creating a spiritual discipline for lay people that began as heterodox but became orthodox (Farquhar 1920: 87–9, 91). Although he regarded the *Bhagavad-Gītā's* theology as flawed because it combined theism with other influences, he acclaimed the greatness of the text (Farquhar 1920: 89–90). Its greatness lay in the portrayal of the divine as the incarnate teacher of Arjuna, the skilful characterization of Kṛṣṇa, the vivid setting for Kṛṣṇa's teaching and the literary excellence of the composition as a vehicle for this teaching (Farquhar 1920: 90–1).

Farquhar gave lengthy consideration to the *Bhagavad-Gītā* in works such as *The Age and Origin of the Gita* and *Permanent Lessons of the Gita*. In *The Age and Origin of the Gita*, for example, he stated that the author of the *Bhagavad-Gītā* established the ultimacy of Kṛṣṇa and the principle of action (Farquhar 1904: 22). What was important about Kṛṣṇa was his being Brahman, 'the object of all the meditation of the sages of the Upanishads', and also a personal deity 'approachable with sacrifices and prayer' (Farquhar 1904: 22). What was important about karma-yoga was similarly 'its combination of philosophy with the popular life' whereby it combined 'philosophic renunciation of the world with practical everyday life' (Farquhar 1904: 22–3). These points were examined in more detail in *Permanent Lessons of the Gita*. Explaining Kṛṣṇa's significance, Farquhar declared that people 'longed for a personal God, who could be the object of their devotion and their adoration' (Farquhar 1912: 8). This was Kṛṣṇa whose relationships with those who worshipped him were characterized by divine love and grace (Farquhar 1912: 9). Defining karma-yoga, he indicated that it meant to discharge those duties prescribed by Hindu legal literature but to do so selflessly (Farquhar 1912: 13). This command to do one's duty without desire for reward thus 'seeks to retain moral activity, while destroying utterly the selfish principle' (Farquhar 1912: 14). In such ways as these, Kṛṣṇa as both personal and ultimate, karma-yoga as both renunciatory and active, Farquhar believed that the *Bhagavad-Gītā* was of particular importance.

Farquhar's understanding of Hinduism was set out in relation to Sanskrit literature, whether a survey of trends associated with its different types or a chronicle of the development of ideas found within it. His view as expressed in *The Age and Origin of the Gita* was that there were two strands of Hinduism: the one labelled '*philosophical*', portrayed in the *Āraṇyakas* (forest treatises), *Upaniṣads* and various other works; the other labelled '*ceremonial*' and connected with the *Brāhmaṇas* (priestly treatises), *Kalpa Sūtras* (ritual compendia) and *Dharmaśāstras* (Farquhar 1904: 23). Further, writing in *Permanent Lessons of the Gita*, he analysed the key concepts contained in certain works: he attributed to the *Ṛg Veda* the belief in sacrifice and the hope for a heavenly existence after death; to the *Brāhmaṇas* the belief in transmigration and the law of action; to the *Upaniṣads* the belief in liberating knowledge of Brahman, the identity of the self with Brahman and the irrelevance of the *Vedas* and their teaching; and to philosophical theories diverse tenets including the Sāṃkhyan doctrine of the eternal actionless nature of the self and the Vedāntic doctrine of the illusory nature of the world (Farquhar 1912: 2–5). Yet his knowledge of Hinduism also took account of contemporary changes such as the rise of the 'Neo-Kṛishṇa movement', noting the emphasis on the Vaiṣṇavite doctrine of incarnation in human form where Rāma and especially Kṛṣṇa were dominant (Farquhar 1977: 294, 440). Throughout he was concerned with the relationship between Hinduism and Christianity.

This subject was addressed at length in Farquhar's *The Crown of Hinduism*. Christ, of course, was the crown of Hinduism to which the title referred and thus Farquhar looked forward to the time when 'the wonderful religious genius of India will reveal its power anew in its interpretation of Christ' (Farquhar 1913: 64). His comparative study of Hinduism and Christianity was located in the context of his rejection of Christian accounts of Hinduism that were unduly and unfairly condemnatory (Farquhar 1913: 35). His own approach, in contrast, was one predicated upon the notion that it was necessary to judge Hinduism by its own standards and not by the failure of Hindus to live up to these standards (Farquhar 1913: 53). Moreover, he was insistent that Christianity was not to be confused with Christianity as practised by any nation or church since its source was Christ alone who was not the property of a specific civilization or denomination (Farquhar 1913: 58). Nevertheless, his treatment of Hinduism was ambivalent, combining criticism of its failings with the claim that there was some value and validity even to what he regarded as its worst features (Farquhar 1913: 446–7). Summing up his thesis, he declared that 'Christ provides the fulfilment of each of the highest aspirations and aims of Hinduism' (Farquhar 1913: 457–8). Moreover, the *Bhagavad-Gītā* served as evidence in his argument that Hinduism was fulfilled in Christ since it embodied Hinduism as a historical tradition and a contemporary presence.

Acknowledging the vital role and status of the *Bhagavad-Gītā*, Farquhar analysed the reasons for this. In *The Age and Origin of the Gita*, he suggested that its popularity was due to its literary qualities, philosophic basis, religious sentiment, moral ambition and especially the characterization of Kṛṣṇa (Farquhar 1904: 3–4). Further, he explained that '[i]t is because the *Gita* is to Hindus a divine revelation, a book in which God Himself speaks to the individual soul, that this poem has won the supreme place it holds to-day' (Farquhar 1904: 4). Similarly, in *Permanent Lessons of the Gita*, he stressed the special part played by the text in Hindu belief and practice as a rationale for his examination of its message, impact and implications (Farquhar 1912: 1). Thus he observed, unlike the *Vedas* and the *Upaniṣads* that were venerated and the Epics that were loved, 'the *Gītā* is the object of at once unbounded reverence and affectionate study' (Farquhar 1912: 1). In such ways, his investigation of the *Bhagavad-Gītā* was intended to demonstrate that it represented and reproduced Hinduism as a whole as well as containing some distinctive elements.

To return to the two strands of Hinduism, the 'philosophical' and 'ceremonial', Farquhar indicated that 'in the *Gita* these two streams unite and flow together' whereby 'it sums up Hinduism on both sides' (Farquhar 1904: 23). Indeed, he argued that the *Bhagavad-Gītā* was not so much innovative in tendency but developmental so that the supremacy of Kṛṣṇa was a development of Kṛṣṇa as a demi-god and the advocacy of karma-yoga was a development of ideas found in the *Upaniṣads* (Farquhar 1904: 23). Or again, with reference to the key concepts contained in certain works, he insisted that 'the whole of this long evolution of religious and philosophic thought reappears in one way or another in the Song' (Farquhar 1912: 7). Here though, when identifying the supremacy of Kṛṣṇa and the advocacy of karma-yoga, he did seem to suggest that this teaching was innovative in some respects: where the *Upaniṣads* had taught that Brahman was impersonal and unmanifest, the *Bhagavad-Gītā* taught that Kṛṣṇa was a personal manifestation of Brahman in human form (Farquhar 1912: 8); and where the *Upaniṣads* had taught that renunciation was conducive to liberation, the *Bhagavad-Gītā* taught that karma-yoga was a form of renunciation in action that was spiritually and socially beneficial (Farquhar 1912: 11).

When Farquhar directed attention towards recent trends as he did in *Modern Religious Movements in India*, the *Bhagavad-Gītā* was also central to his account. Noting the Hindu tendency to 'lay all the stress nowadays on the best parts of Hinduism', downplaying its legal, customary and ritual aspects, he added that in contemporary movements the *Bhagavad-Gītā*, along with the *Upaniṣads*, had pride of place (Farquhar 1977: 438). The 'Neo-Kṛishṇa movement', literary and apologetic in character, was of particular importance in this analysis of recent developments (Farquhar 1977: 295). In his view, the very prominence of Kṛṣṇa was attributable to Kṛṣṇa's portrayal in the *Bhagavad-Gītā*, enabling the text's depiction of the divine to be promoted 'as a satisfactory Hindu substitute for Christ and the Gospels' (Farquhar 1977: 440). Yet, in order to serve in this capacity, Hindus had to defend Kṛṣṇa and the *Bhagavad-Gītā* from criticisms 'that the incarnation-stories of… Kṛishṇa were myths, and that the *Gītā* did not come from Kṛishṇa' (Farquhar 1977: 295). Despite his admiration for the *Bhagavad-Gītā*'s depiction of Kṛṣṇa, Farquhar himself was the author of such criticism and thus the issue of historicity was one he addressed in some detail.

Certainly Farquhar regarded the *Bhagavad-Gītā* as epitomizing Hinduism and embodying its most estimable and excellent aspects. Yet he also saw it as a testament to the ultimate inadequacy of Hinduism. Calling the *Bhagavad-Gītā* 'the spiritual autobiography of Hinduism', he praised it in extravagant language as 'the concentrated essence of Hinduism' and added that '[i]f anyone wants to understand the Hindu people, let him steep himself in the thought of the *Gita*' (Farquhar 1904: 23–4). The importance he vested in the text rested on its theistic nature and its appeal to the religious instinct. However, he contrasted the power of the teaching with its lack of historical foundation, considering how this could have come about (Farquhar 1904: 24). He suggested two possibilities – an irrational act of imagination and an important response to need – where to adopt the stance that the *Bhagavad-Gītā* was a fond but futile wish for a fictive object was to give way to despair and doubt whereas to adopt the stance that it was a sign of spiritual hunger to be satisfied by God meant that it bore some relationship to reality (Farquhar 1904: 24). Finally he asked '[w]hat is the reality which is adumbrated by the Kṛishṇa of the *Gita*?' (Farquhar 1904: 24). Although *The Age and Origin of the Gita* ended with this question, he gave an answer to it in *Permanent Lessons of the Gita*.

The lessons taught by the *Bhagavad-Gītā*, from which Farquhar drew the most profound and sweeping conclusions about religion in general and Hinduism in particular, were fourfold. His 'First Lesson' was that '[p]hilosophy cannot take the place of religion' on the grounds that religion was fundamental to society as a unifying factor (Farquhar 1912: 25). His 'Second Lesson' was that '[r]eligion demands a Personal God' on the grounds that such a conception of deity was the focus of the devotee's prayer and worship as well as the source of grace and love (Farquhar 1912: 25–6). His 'Third Lesson' was that '[m]orality consists, not in abandoning life, but in living rightly' on the grounds that morality involved an attitude of detachment combined with the discharge of one's duty (Farquhar 1912: 26–7). Yet 'The Supreme Lesson' of the *Bhagavad-Gītā* was the appeal of Kṛṣṇa and hence the attraction of its teaching (Farquhar 1912: 27). In discussing this further, Farquhar rejected the historicity of the text as an imaginative work and also the historicity of Kṛṣṇa as the divine incarnate in human form (Farquhar 1912: 27–8). Such a rejection of the historicity of both dialogue and deity posed other problems from the perspective of one to whom the historicity of the Gospels and Jesus Christ was of foundational significance: one problem was the origin of the belief that Brahman assumed human form, 'taking his seat in a chariot, and giving teaching on a battle-field'; another was the source of the fascination for Kṛṣṇa and his discourse, 'the imaginary commands of this mythical god' (Farquhar 1912: 29). It was in reflecting on the nature and influence of Kṛṣṇa that Farquhar advanced a view of human nature according to which 'man needs an incarnate Saviour' – where there was no such saviour, he insisted, this saviour would be imagined and even a mythological substitute was capable of inspiring faith and devotion (Farquhar 1912: 29–30). This explained how the author of the *Bhagavad-Gītā* had come to conceive of Kṛṣṇa and how Kṛṣṇa had come to exert so strong a hold. Moreover, on this line of argument, the need for an incarnate saviour had been created in humanity by God whose faithfulness was an assurance of the saviour's advent (Farquhar 1912: 30–1).

It was at this juncture that Farquhar gave his definitive answer to the question asked in *The Age and Origin of the Gita* concerning the reality to which the Kṛṣṇa of the *Bhagavad-Gītā* pointed. This answer was Jesus Christ, the incarnate saviour of history, both 'Son of Man' and 'Son of God' (Farquhar 1912: 31). The Kṛṣṇa of the *Bhagavad-Gītā* was myth, the Christ of the Gospels was history, but Farquhar established a continuity between them when claiming that 'Jesus is the reality of which the Gita gives an imaginative picture' (Farquhar 1912: 31). On the basis of this continuity, he declared that the author of the *Bhagavad-Gītā* would have become a Christian if afforded the opportunity and likewise that the Hindu would become a Christian having accepted the teachings of the *Bhagavad-Gītā* (Farquhar 1912: 31). In this way, Farquhar presented the *Bhagavad-Gītā* as prefiguring the Gospel, 'a marvellous prophecy', and so presented Hinduism as preparing for Christianity (Farquhar 1912: 31).

Farquhar praised the *Bhagavad-Gītā*, notably for its characterization of Kṛṣṇa and its championing of karma-yoga. He recognized the historic diversity of Hinduism as well as contemporary developments, without conceding his conviction of the need for Christ to fulfil Hinduism. The *Bhagavad-Gītā*, he realized, was important to Hindus; moreover, the *Bhagavad-Gītā* replicated Hinduism's historical diversity and was of great significance to contemporary developments in Hinduism. However remarkable the *Bhagavad-Gītā*, nevertheless it demonstrated the superiority of Christianity since, where Kṛṣṇa and his teaching were myth, Christ and his teaching were history. Even so, any superiority arose out of Christianity's fulfilment of Hinduism's hopes and dreams as Hindus would come to see in Christianity the best of Hinduism brought to completion.

Bede Griffiths' (1906–93) career in India saw his view of the nature and relationship of religions change from that espoused by Farquhar, where Christianity constituted the fulfilment of religions, to a position that no longer privileged Christianity but regarded religions as complementary. This had obvious implications for his understanding of the *Bhagavad-Gītā* as well as Hinduism. His commentary on the *Bhagavad-Gītā* was based on a symbolic interpretation of the text, emphasizing the rise of devotion to a personal deity as the true meaning and purpose of both knowledge and action. He surveyed Hinduism generally, though his assessment of the comparative merits of Hinduism and Christianity changed markedly over the years until finally he equated the two religions. Certainly he accorded the *Bhagavad-Gītā* a pivotal role in Hinduism but its importance as a declaration of Kṛṣṇa bhakti was not the limit of its significance since he deemed it to be significant for the whole of humanity. Moreover, he saw the *Bhagavad-Gītā* as of great value for Christians as well as the springboard for a comparison of Hinduism and Christianity, identifying areas of agreement between them consistent with the fundamental unity of religions.

Griffiths' knowledge of the *Bhagavad-Gītā* predated his arrival in India. He recollected how he had first read the *Bhagavad-Gītā* and the impact the text had made upon him when explaining how his scholarly and personal interest in Indian spirituality had developed over many years (Griffiths 1966: 10, 17).[5] Accordingly, the *Bhagavad-Gītā* featured in his general works: in *Christian Ashram: Essays Towards a Hindu–Christian Dialogue*, he stated that the text set forth an asceticism combined with a commitment to social service, that it constituted one of the sources of Indian monasticism and that it contained vital truths of Hinduism (Griffiths 1966: 10, 19, 22); in *Vedanta & Christian Faith*, he aligned the text with the movement of devotion to a personal deity and attributed to it worship of Kṛṣṇa as the supreme Lord (Griffiths 1973: 2, 35). However, his most detailed account of the *Bhagavad-Gītā* was in his commentary on the text, *River of Compassion*. This commentary, a revised form of talks he gave to members of Shantivanam Ashram, drew upon Mascaró's translation and other works on the *Bhagavad-Gītā* by Annie Besant and Bhagavan Das, Sri Krishna Prem and R.C. Zaehner, thereby acknowledging that a range of reading informed his avowedly non-academic treatment with its experiential emphasis (Griffiths 1987: 6).

For Griffiths, the *Bhagavad Gītā* was best approached as poetry, likening its structure to a musical composition in the variety of its themes and their complex interrelation (Griffiths 1987: 6). The account he gave of the text was allegorical, an interpretation he justified on the grounds that from antiquity the battle had been understood symbolically with the Pāṇḍavas as the righteous, the Kauravas as the unrighteous, Arjuna as the human soul, the chariot as the human body and Kṛṣṇa as the spirit within (1) (Griffiths 1987: 8). Hence, identifying the main themes of the *Bhagavad-Gītā* as being 'how to face the battle of life, how the spirit will counsel us, and how each of us will undertake the battle', the text represented human nature in symbolic terms; spirituality had been exiled and the self was dominated by the ego (1) (Griffiths 1987: 8–9).

Yet Griffiths also analysed the historical development of the Kṛṣṇa cult, outlining different ideas about Kṛṣṇa's origins, as god and hero, and different dimensions of his character, as cowherd, warrior and sage (Griffiths 1987: 3–4). Further, he suggested that Kṛṣṇa had been a non-Aryan deity absorbed into the Hindu pantheon through his identification with Viṣṇu (Griffiths 1987: 4). Griffiths' argument was that the message of the *Bhagavad-Gītā* set forth devotion to Kṛṣṇa, where action was inspired by love for the divine and knowledge was defined as knowledge of the divine (Griffiths 1987: 5–6). Thus he insisted that 'in the *Gita* the personal God becomes an object of love', that '[t]he climax of the *Gita*'s teaching on the love of God is the recognition that God loves us' and that 'the highest yoga is described as the yoga of faith and love' (6.19, 47; 18.64) (Griffiths 1987: 117, 130, 321).

Griffiths' exposition of the *Bhagavad-Gītā* reflected his emphasis on devotion to Kṛṣṇa. Nevertheless, he did not rank the personal deity and the impersonal absolute since his reading of the text suggested to him that these were two dimensions of one divine reality and, consequently, that the divine could be known in both capacities (12) (Griffiths 1987: 220). Indeed, he stated that the *Bhagavad-Gītā* was written to redress an imbalance favouring knowledge of the impersonal absolute by demonstrating that the 'personal aspect of Brahman is supremely important and that it is known by faith and love' (12.1–2) (Griffiths 1987: 221). Accordingly, it was Kṛṣṇa who received the worship offered to all deities, devotion was a means to liberation from the cycle of existence and, in contrast to other spiritual disciplines, devotion promised salvation to all irrespective of sex or social status (8.15; 9.23, 32) (Griffiths 1987: 155, 177, 180). Similarly, the revelation of Kṛṣṇa to Arjuna was explained in terms of Arjuna's love for Kṛṣṇa and Kṛṣṇa's friendship for Arjuna, a relationship of devotion (4.1–3) (Griffiths 1987: 63–4). Defining devotion, Griffiths declared that '[i]t is a total self-surrender'; it was also essential to knowledge, culminating in 'the knowledge of the personal being of God', and to action, where finally 'we relate it to the Supreme, we surrender to God' (3.29; 18.55, 57) (Griffiths 1987: 57, 318–19). In any case, it must be borne in mind that *River of Compassion* belonged to a specific period of Griffiths' evolving outlook on Hinduism in particular and religions in general in relation to his own Christian faith.

In Griffiths' earlier work, he espoused a theology of fulfilment that viewed Hinduism as preparation for Christianity whereas, in his later work, he espoused a theology of complementarity that viewed Hinduism and Christianity as founded on the same truth and subject to the same imperfections.[6] An example of his earlier work was *Christian Ashram: Essays Towards a Hindu–Christian Dialogue*, addressing the issue of inter-religious dialogue and the prospect for Christian monasticism in India (Griffiths 1966: 16–17). As impressed as he then was by Hinduism, he was insistent that its completion lay in Christ, asserting that '[t]he more one knows Hinduism, the more one realizes what wonderful resources … of true religion are present there' but also that 'I do not think it is too much to say that they [Hindus] can only find the fullness of that religion in Christ' (Griffiths 1966: 190). In comparing Hinduism with Christianity, despite acknowledging Hinduism's depth of religious feeling and philosophical insight, he contrasted its mythological basis with the historical foundation of Christianity where, in the person of Christ, God acted in and changed history (Griffiths 1966: 109–11). Rejecting any notion that other religions were false, instead he regarded them as true, deformed in part but still genuine in essence; thus Christ would not bring about their destruction but their correction and completion (Griffiths 1966: 91–2). So it was that he saw other religions as 'providential preparation for Christianity, by which the people of the East have been led through the course of their history towards their fulfilment in Christ' (Griffiths 1966: 92). This approach was rather different from the one he later took in *Vedanta & Christian Faith* where a belief in the complementarity of religions superseded a belief in their fulfilment in Christianity.

Vedanta & Christian Faith was Griffiths' attempt to compare the orthodox traditions of Christianity and Hinduism with a view to facilitating mutual benefit and achieving ultimate unity through concentration on the common experience of the divine (Griffiths 1973: vii). This position was thus one in which Christianity was no longer superior to other religions. It was now his contention, not only that 'the divine Mystery, the eternal Truth, has been revealing itself to all men from the beginning of history', but also that 'every religion, from the most primitive to the most advanced, has its own unique insight into the one Truth' (Griffiths 1973: vii–viii). His advocacy of a complementarity of religions, each with faults and scope for development, meant that he was seeking to promote inter-religious harmony (Griffiths 1973: viii). Turning to Hinduism and Christianity, he recognized their historical independent existence and their contemporary mutual influence while hailing them for the profundity of their thought regarding ultimate reality (Griffiths 1973: 1). His conclusion, having examined the themes of the divine or the real, humanity and creation and the supreme goal of life in comparative perspective, was that the Hindu and Christian as well as the adherents of other religions were united when it came to 'the ultimate mystery of being, which is the beginning and the end of all our human aspirations' (Griffiths 1973: 84). *River of Compassion* belonged to this later stage of Griffiths' career where he evaluated Hinduism and Christianity equally as expressions of one truth. Referring to a range of religions including Hinduism and Christianity in this commentary on the *Bhagavad-Gītā*, he declared that '[t]he same one light is shining in each and each one is receiving the truth in its own way', which was consistent with his belief that divine providence encompassed the whole of humanity communicated in culturally appropriate forms and styles (17.1) (Griffiths 1987: 290).

In *River of Compassion*, Griffiths explained that Hindus called their religion Sanātana Dharma, adding that '*Dharma* is the law, the cosmic order, and their religion is the expression of this eternal law' (7.10) (Griffiths 1987: 138–9). His treatment of Hinduism featured the rise of the bhakti movement inculcating devotion to a personal deity, distinguishing between an emotional love of God as the preliminary sentimental stage and a profound love as the final transformatory stage (5.29) (Griffiths 1987: 102–3). He saw Hinduism as developing in certain directions over time. Taking as his model the progress from law to spirit, from external authority to internal prompting, he traced changes in the Hindu pantheon in which Indra, god of war, ceased to feature and Śiva, initially an awesome and terrible figure, became a god of love (16) (Griffiths 1987: 277–8). He also surveyed a range of Hindu sacred literature, the *Vedas*, *Brāhmaṇas*, *Āraṇyakas* and *Upaniṣads* with their respective emphases on the priestly function in sacrifice, the importance of ritual, the practice of meditation and the cultivation of insight (Griffiths 1987: 3). In his view, Hinduism was the product of Aryan Sanskrit and indigenous Dravidian religions, dating from the period of the Epics and witnessing the rise of devotion to the personal divine (Griffiths 1987: 2). The *Bhagavad-Gītā* was central to this account of Hinduism as, in his opinion, it was to the wider context of religion in general.

In the opening words of his introduction, Griffiths declared that the text's significance as 'a spiritual classic' transcended even Hinduism to become the common property of humanity (Griffiths 1987: 1). Still, the importance of the *Bhagavad-Gītā* for Hinduism was a point he made throughout the commentary. He aligned the *Bhagavad-Gītā* with the rise of the bhakti movement and the tendency towards higher bhakti where divine love takes possession of the soul, concluding that it was in the *Bhagavad-Gītā* that a personal deity became the focus of love (6.19) (Griffiths 1987: 117). When it came to morality, he stated that the *Bhagavad-Gītā* was transitional on the grounds that in it the notion of external battle was giving way to internal conflict in which warfare was increasingly understood to be waged against the passions to achieve surrender to the divine (8.7; 16) (Griffiths 1987:152, 278). Relating the *Bhagavad-Gītā* to Hindu sacred literature, he insisted that the text was a synthetic and inclusive work that reflected the range of religious movements contemporaneous with its composition, also that it summarized Hindu teaching and epitomized Hindu religiosity (Griffiths 1987: 2–3). He linked the *Bhagavad-Gītā* with the Epic period, observing that in the *Bhagavad-Gītā* devotion to the personal deity took the form of Kṛṣṇa worship influenced by the Bhāgavata movement (Griffiths 1987: 2–3). Reiterating the emphasis on devotion to Kṛṣṇa as the personal divine, he indicated that it was the accessibility of the *Bhagavad-Gītā's* message to the ordinary householder in the midst of worldly life that explained its role as 'a handbook for the Hindu, a kind of New Testament' (Griffiths 1987: 5). So it was that Griffiths accorded the *Bhagavad-Gītā* a crucial role in the development of Hinduism.

Yet Griffiths' exposition of the *Bhagavad-Gītā* did not only relate it to Hinduism but also mentioned Buddhist, Jain, Taoist and Sikh material as well as making numerous references to the literature, philosophers, theologians, saints and mystics of Christianity alongside those of Hinduism (Griffiths 1987). Convinced that no religion could exist in isolation, he emphasized the commonality of all people and hence the necessity to hold in common the wisdom of all religions (Griffiths 1987: 1). Notwithstanding this, considering his own Christian faith and the *Bhagavad-Gītā*'s Hindu identity, Christian–Hindu parallels dominated the commentary. Griffiths called *River of Compassion* 'a "Christian reading"', principally concerned with the way in which the *Bhagavad-Gītā* could serve as 'a practical spiritual guide to a Christian' (Griffiths 1987: 1). Although he excluded any notion of Christian impact on the text and refrained from appropriating it as somehow Christian, it was his claim that a Christian could gain from it a deeper appreciation of the Gospel (Griffiths 1987: 1). Accordingly, while he indicated that his commentary could be useful to all people drawn to the *Bhagavad-Gītā* and moved to apply its teachings in their lives, he concentrated on the text's significance for Christians (Griffiths 1987: 1).

When it came to comparisons between Christianity and Hinduism, Griffiths' commentary on the *Bhagavad-Gītā* made clear that there were some major differences. On the subject of incarnation, for instance, he argued that the Hindu idea was different because it was mythological in character and related to a cyclical concept of time whereas Christ was a historical figure who made a decisive intervention in history (4.7–8) (Griffiths 1987: 66–9). However, there were similarities too as he acknowledged when making the point that Christianity as well as Hinduism distinguished between the divine as immanent and transcendent (12.8) (Griffiths 1987: 222–3). Moreover, he declared that the *Bhagavad-Gītā* in its stress on the ultimacy of love was making the same point as the Gospel in its proclamation of Christ (6.30) (Griffiths 1987: 125). Indeed, in his view, the teaching that God was love was the *Bhagavad-Gītā's* chief accomplishment in Hinduism as it was the crux of the Gospel in Christianity (5.17) (Griffiths 1987: 94). He even advanced a Christian inclusivism based on Kṛṣṇa's statement that all paths led to him whereby, through Christ, divine grace drew people towards God in their various ways (4.11) (Griffiths 1987: 71).

Overall, Griffiths' approach to the *Bhagavad-Gītā* was predicated upon the belief that reflection on the text would benefit Christians. Closing his commentary, he eulogized the *Bhagavad-Gītā* as 'a work to fill the soul with awe and wonder'; a work that, when read by a Christian, was also 'a wonderful confirmation of the revelation of God's love contained in the Gospel' (18.74–8) (Griffiths 1987: 325). Thus the significance of the *Bhagavad-Gītā* for Hinduism was at least in part the common ground it established with the Gospel and Christianity, an exercise in inter-religious dialogue in which Hindus and Christians engaged on a basis of equality.

Griffiths' commentary on the *Bhagavad-Gītā* was a detailed exposition of the text, making use of allegory in interpreting its message of the personal nature of the divine and the path of devotion. As a later work, it embodied a theology of complementarity where Christianity and Hinduism were two expressions of the same truth. Thus, though he accorded the text a special status in Hinduism, he also insisted on its importance in a global context. Paying particular attention to Christian–Hindu parallels, his account of the *Bhagavad-Gītā* addressed primarily to a Christian audience demonstrated that there were significant points of contact between the religions.

This variety of Christian theological and missionary critiques of the *Bhagavad-Gītā* offered different perspectives on the relationship between Christianity and 'other religions' such as Hinduism. The *Bhagavad-Gītā* evoked responses ranging from qualified admiration to unreserved acclamation. Similarly, Hinduism was judged to be: inferior; preparatory; and equal to Christianity.

R.D. Griffith was ambivalent towards the *Bhagavad-Gītā*, alive to its power and profundity yet regarding it as seriously flawed; consistent with this, he believed that Hinduism could not in the end compete with Christianity, which alone was revealed. Farquhar was full of praise for the *Bhagavad-Gītā*, focusing on personal deity and practical morality; while acknowledging its importance for Hinduism, he interpreted it as a prophecy of the Gospel and Christianity. Griffiths, in contrast, produced a commentary on the *Bhagavad-Gītā* that did not subordinate it to the Gospel; instead, his comparative observations rested on the parity of Hinduism and Christianity, where both were true yet subject to error.

4

UNIVERSALIST VISIONS

Various Hindu writers presented universalist visions of the *Bhagavad-Gītā*. These involved a stress on the inclusivity and openness of the text, setting out different disciplines to reach the divine and harmonizing different forms of religious belief and practice. In this way, it proved possible to attribute to Hinduism the qualities of tolerance and liberality that were so highly prized and so widely believed to typify Hinduism in contrast to Christianity. Moreover, on this basis, the *Bhagavad-Gītā* could be represented as a universal work and/or Hinduism as the universal religion. At the same time, it was deemed necessary to provide a rationale for action in the service of others and here the *Bhagavad-Gītā* was evidence by which to reject the charges levelled against Hinduism by critics, including Christians, who often alleged that it lacked ethics.

Though continuous with earlier ideas, especially those associated with Śaṅkara's Advaita Vedānta, such universalism, especially with an activist emphasis, was well suited to a defence of Hinduism. As a philosophy of Hinduism, it lent itself to an assertion of Hindu spirituality and morality that upheld India's national pride and international prestige. The *Bhagavad-Gītā*, already one of the traditional sources of Vedāntic thought, thus became a pervasive point of reference for universalist theories.

Swami Vivekananda (1863–1902), previously known as Narendranath Dutt, focused upon the *Bhagavad-Gītā* as preaching the unification of different disciplines and the importance of acting without attachment. His account of Hinduism, often identified with Vedānta, emphasized its tolerance whereby it recognized the truth of all religions and its diversity which was reconciled in an ethic of action. Recognizing the qualities of the *Bhagavad-Gītā*, its popularity and authority for Hindus, he attached great significance to its message for his characterization of Hinduism, notably the existence of one goal though many paths and the importance of work within the world.

Vivekananda offered an exposition of the *Bhagavad-Gītā* in three discourses delivered in San Francisco in 1895 ('The Gita I–III') and one discourse delivered in Calcutta in 1897 ('Thoughts on the Gita') but cited the *Bhagavad-Gītā* far more frequently in making statements about a wide variety of subjects.[1] His lecture to young monks demonstrated his awareness of literary and critical questions surrounding the *Bhagavad-Gītā* but even here, without excluding issues of historicity, he subordinated these to the spiritual quest (Vivekananda 1985: 102–6). On this occasion, he referred to the allegorical interpretation of the setting that he allowed might have some value (Vivekananda 1985: 105). Certainly elsewhere, as in his second address on the *Bhagavad-Gītā*, though he might present the setting in historical terms, he was concerned to establish its relevance to the whole of humanity for whom life is a battle too (Vivekananda 1994a: 459). Moreover, in a conversation with a disciple, he described Arjuna as a representative of the soul, within which Kṛṣṇa dwelt and with which Kṛṣṇa communicated (Vivekananda 1992b: 200). Or again, citing the *Bhagavad-Gītā* in a lecture on knowledge and action, he stated that the soul sat in the chariot of the body, where the horses were the senses, the reins were the mind and the charioteer was the intellect (Vivekananda 1994b: 227). In 'Discourses on Jnana Yoga', he stressed that spirituality had to be developed in the midst of life and that, as the *Bhagavad-Gītā* dealt with such struggle, it was appropriate to set it on a battlefield (Vivekananda 1994b: 8). On such a basis, he could present the *Bhagavad-Gītā* as relevant to Hindus and non-Hindus alike.

When addressing an audience about Kṛṣṇa, Vivekananda identified two themes in his teaching – '[t]he first is the harmony of different ideas; the second is non-attachment' – in the context of an affirmation that spiritual fulfilment could be achieved even as a political or military leader, hence the setting for Kṛṣṇa's sermon (Vivekananda 1994a: 439). Vivekananda's investigation of these issues ran through his lecture on Kṛṣṇa and those on the *Bhagavad-Gītā* as well as lectures on 'Practical Vedanta' and 'The Mission of the Vedanta' among many others. His argument that there were different paths but that the goal was the same was advanced by quoting Kṛṣṇa's statement that the worship offered to other deities was in reality worship offered to him (9.23) and also by asking whether God would be offended to be called by another name or insulted to be revered in another form (Vivekananda 1994a: 468). Similarly, he quoted Kṛṣṇa's statement that he was the source and object of all faith (4.12) as well as appealing to Kṛṣṇa's tolerance for different modes of worship (Vivekananda 1994a: 440). This stance was associated with the insistence that one should follow one's own path, predicated upon the view that action was determined by one's nature (3.33) and that it was better to die doing one's own duty than to attempt to do another's (3.35) (Vivekananda 1994a: 472–3). Accordingly, Vivekananda concluded that it was better to die following one's own religion than to follow another's irrespective of its apparent virtues (Vivekananda 1994a: 474).

Vivekananda's understanding of selflessness took as its exemplar Kṛṣṇa who worked for work's sake (3.22–3) (Vivekananda 1994a: 441). Further, citing various verses from the fourth chapter of the *Bhagavad-Gītā* where Kṛṣṇa declared that he acted without desire for result and set the standard for detached action, Vivekananda asserted that it was impossible to refrain from action (Vivekananda 1994a: 476–7). Yet the imperative to act derived at least in part from the plight of the people since the divine was to be served in serving others; in all this,

Vivekananda's ideal was the sage, calm in the midst of activity (4.18) (Vivekananda 1994a: 441–3). This perspective was premised on an identification of the all with the one, regarding as the essence of the *Bhagavad-Gītā* Kṛṣṇa's declaration that true insight saw the Supreme Lord in all beings and equating this insight with the achievement of the greatest good (13.27–8) (Vivekananda 1995b: 193–4). Calling this philosophy Vedānta, Vivekananda commented that its dissemination was necessary 'for the amelioration and elevation of the human race' (Vivekananda 1995b: 194). Hence his treatment of Hinduism expounded its tolerance of different religious disciplines as a unity in diversity and its synthesis of different religious tendencies as a renunciation in action.

Vivekananda's view of Hinduism was complicated by its equation with Vedānta. In an address on Vedānta, he justified this equation by arguing that Vedānta pervaded Hinduism and thus that 'we live in the Vedanta... and we die in the Vedanta, and every Hindu does that' (Vivekananda 1995b: 323). This meant that he could advance arguments about Hinduism by reference to Vedānta and also assert that Vedānta epitomized the best features of Hinduism, perhaps all religions. Indeed, the interchangeability of Hinduism and Vedānta pervaded Vivekananda's treatment of both tolerance and action as major themes.

Vivekananda's picture of Hinduism/Vedānta, especially when abroad, stressed its tolerance.[2] This was not only expressed in relation to various Hindu perspectives but also in relation to various religions. Speaking at the Parliament of Religions, he declared his pride at belonging 'to a religion which has taught the world both tolerance and universal acceptance' (Vivekananda 1994a: 3). This was why his discussion of the features of 'a universal religion', typified by inclusivity and openness, bore a striking resemblance to his portrait of Hinduism (Vivekananda 1994a: 19). Not surprisingly, in some instances, he stated unequivocally that Vedānta was this universal religion (e.g. Vivekananda 1995b: 250–2). Hence his definition of Hinduism in 'The Hindu Religion' was one that proclaimed the truth of all religions (Vivekananda 1994a: 329). From this it followed that the range of religions were so many ways to reach the same goal (e.g. Vivekananda 1994a: 4).

A point Vivekananda made frequently, perhaps most prominently in his 'Paper on Hinduism', was that a Hindu accepted the truth of all religions though here he presented a hierarchy of the progress from lower to higher truth with the obvious implication that Hinduism, and especially Vedānta, was the pinnacle of achievement (Vivekananda 1994a: 17). Another point he made frequently was that there was nothing to be gained by conversion from one religion to another. In his remarks at the closing session of the Parliament, he rejected any suggestion of change yet expressed the hope that individual identity could be maintained while mutual learning took place (Vivekananda 1994a: 24).

Another topic running through Vivekananda's comments on Hinduism/Vedānta was the nature and role of action. For example, considering 'Work Without Motive', he outlined two different stances on action: the one endorsing action in the form of sacrifice as constituting religion; the other advocating inaction in order to gain the knowledge essential to liberation (Vivekananda 1992a: 246). In like manner, surveying India's historical development, he contrasted the priestly tradition of ceremony and ritual with the philosophical tradition of speculation and meditation (Vivekananda 1995c: 159–60). With reference to such different views, he did not accept either that action could or should be abandoned but instead stressed that the spirit in which action was performed determined whether it led to continued transmigration or release from the wheel of existence. At the same time, he defined action more as work for the world, emphasizing its ethical over its ritual character. Thus, in instructing a disciple about action, he opposed the Pūrva Mīmāṃsā view that motivated action achieved the intended end, instead proposing karma-yoga as a way of acting conducive to spiritual realization (Vivekananda 1992b: 179). This teaching was simultaneously opposed to the renunciatory trend that sought to avoid action altogether since, with his commitment to 'Practical Vedanta', he was not prepared to counsel passivity (Vivekananda 1995a: 292). What he recommended was not Śaṅkara's insistence upon the renunciation of all actions by the wise but action performed with an equability of mind unmoved by triumph or disaster (Vivekananda 1995a: 292–3).

Certainly Vivekananda held the *Bhagavad-Gītā* in high esteem. In a letter to an American correspondent, he referred to setting off alone to read the text, indicating his personal engagement with its tenets (Vivekananda 1995c: 309). He also recommended study of the *Bhagavad-Gītā* to others on a number of occasions (Vivekananda 1992b: 137; 1994b: 280; 1995c: 333). More generally, he praised the text (Vivekananda 1994a: 456; 1994b: 8; 1995b: 50). Indeed, in one letter, he went so far as to write that it was 'the Bible of Hinduism', suggesting that it had a special status (Vivekananda 1992a: 130). This special status was a subject that he dealt with in an address on 'The Mahabharata' where he explained that the *Bhagavad-Gītā* was 'the popular scripture of India and the loftiest of all teachings' and that it had influenced American thinkers in the Transcendentalist movement (Vivekananda 1985: 95).

One way in which Vivekananda often established the importance of the *Bhagavad-Gītā* was by referring to it as a commentary on the *Vedas* (Vivekananda 1994b: 8; 1995b: 244–5, 261), the *Upaniṣads* (Vivekananda 1994a: 446) and the Vedānta (Vivekananda 1995a: 292). Other ways in which he tended to establish the importance of the *Bhagavad-Gītā* were by comparing it with other Hindu texts and considering its role in the Vedāntic tradition. For example, in 'The Freedom of the Soul', he likened the *Bhagavad-Gītā* to a bouquet of flowers though in this case what was gathered together was Upaniṣadic wisdom (Vivekananda 1995a: 189, cf. 1985: 106). Discussing 'The Vedanta in all its Phases', he hailed the *Bhagavad-Gītā* as one of 'the true Shastras' (Vivekananda 1995b: 341); discussing 'Modern India', he identified the text as evincing 'an extreme devotion to the highest spiritual truths' (Vivekananda 1985: 460); and, in a letter, he nominated the *Upaniṣads* and the *Bhagavad-Gītā* alone as 'the true scriptures' (Vivekananda 1995c: 394).

When giving an account of Vedānta, Vivekananda accorded the text high authority, expressing admiration for Śaṅkara's commentary and referring to Śaṅkara's work as establishing the precedent for the production of other commentaries (Vivekananda 1995b: 328). In similar manner, also expounding the Vedānta, he insisted that the *Bhagavad-Gītā* with the *Upaniṣads* and *Vyāsa Sūtra* (otherwise known as the *Brahma* or *Vedānta Sūtra*) had 'been taken up by every sect in India that wants to claim authority for orthodoxy' (Vivekananda 1995b: 396). Clearly, his references to the *Bhagavad-Gītā* would also feature prominently in his proclamation of the message that Hinduism was tolerant, both in respect of the variety of Hindu teachers and movements and the variety of religions, and that it was activist, commending especially activity that integrated elements of renunciation. Thus the *Bhagavad-Gītā* enabled Vivekananda to present the Parliament of Religions as fulfilling Kṛṣṇa's words and so provide divine sanction for opposition to religious exclusivism (Vivekananda 1994a: 4). In portraying the Parliament as 'a declaration to the world of the wonderful doctrine preached in the Gita', Vivekananda quoted Kṛṣṇa's assurance that he would receive all who came to him by whatever means (4.11) (Vivekananda 1994a: 4). Consistent with this sense of many paths to one goal, Vivekananda appealed to the avatāra ideal as set out in the *Bhagavad-Gītā* to support his contention that divine providence ensured appropriate guidance would be available to all people (Vivekananda 1995b: 250). Of 'The Sages of India', Vivekananda commented that the role of teachers in providing guidance corroborated 'the celebrated saying of Shri Krishna in the Gitâ' that he would incarnate whenever necessary to uphold the cause of morality and religion (4.7–8) (Vivekananda 1995b: 250). This meant that a Hindu could worship any incarnation of the divine and, on this basis, Vivekananda acknowledged the need for a personal deity especially in the form of a deity who lives in the world (Vivekananda 1995b: 250–1). Another aspect of the inclusivism he attributed to the *Bhagavad-Gītā* was the way in which it sought to bring together different approaches. In his 'Thoughts on the Gita', he explained that, where previously each yoga had advocates asserting its ascendancy, '[i]t was the author of the Gita who for the first time tried to harmonise these' (Vivekananda 1985: 106–7). This attempted reconciliation of alternative Hindu spiritual methods could serve, in turn, as a prototype for Hinduism's reconciliation of all religions.

Replying to the address of the Maharaja of Khetri, Vivekananda called 'the teachings of the Gita...the essence of philosophy, of liberality, of religion' (Vivekananda 1985: 325). A characteristic of these teachings outlined in a discourse on the *Bhagavad-Gītā* was that Kṛṣṇa was unifying different types of religiosity through his championing of the attitude of non-attachment (Vivekananda 1994a: 456). In respect of opposing views on sacrificial action and renunciant inaction, Vivekananda affirmed that these were reconciled in the *Bhagavad-Gītā*'s doctrine of selfless action (Vivekananda 1992a: 246). Thus was created a spirituality accessible to all, a change chronicled in Vivekananda's version of the 'Historical Evolution of India' (Vivekananda 1995c: 160).

Against the Pūrva Mīmāṃsā view, he thought that the *Bhagavad-Gītā* proposed that work be performed disinterestedly (Vivekananda 1992b: 179) and, against the renunciatory trend, that it be performed calmly (Vivekananda 1995a: 292). This focus upon selfless action was crucial because, as he suggested in a discourse on the *Bhagavad-Gītā*, it allowed ordinary people to discharge their worldly duties and pursue the spiritual life (Vivekananda 1994a: 457).

Vivekananda saw the *Bhagavad-Gītā* as teaching that there were different paths and that action should be performed. Related themes in his representation of Hinduism were tolerance of different paths to the same goal and advocacy of action performed in the proper spirit. In general, he articulated a strong sense of the *Bhagavad-Gītā*'s importance but, in particular, referred to it to substantiate his claims concerning the tolerance of Hinduism and the prominence of action as a spiritual discipline.

Sarvepalli Radhakrishnan (1888–1975) was influenced by Vivekananda as he himself acknowledged. Like Vivekananda, he interpreted the *Bhagavad-Gītā* as a text that described different paths and did not separate the spiritual life from an ethic of service. Also like Vivekananda, his admiration for the *Bhagavad-Gītā* led him to stress its significance for Hinduism and beyond, using the text to prove that Hinduism attached a positive value to a diversity of perspectives and maintained a commitment to the welfare of the world. Unlike Vivekananda, he wrote a full-length commentary on the *Bhagavad-Gītā* as well as various academic books and articles on Hinduism, Indian philosophy and Eastern religions that included lengthy discussions of the text or contained frequent references to it.[3]

Radhakrishnan devoted a chapter to 'The Theism of the Bhagavadgītā' in the first volume of his work on *Indian Philosophy*. Here he described the *Bhagavad-Gītā* as being 'midway between a philosophical system and a poetic inspiration' (Radhakrishnan 1929: 522). Although he gave some consideration to the date of the text, an issue he admitted incapable of easy resolution, he stressed the text's symbolic aspect and hence its significance for humanity as a whole (Radhakrishnan 1929: 522–4). On this line of reasoning, Arjuna represented the soul, Kurukṣetra the field of life, the Kauravas negative influences and Kṛṣṇa the divine voice (Radhakrishnan 1929: 520–1). Accordingly, the war chariot became a place of meditation and the battlefield an occasion for spirituality (Radhakrishnan 1929: 521). Radhakrishnan took much the same approach in introducing his commentary on the *Bhagavad-Gītā* in which context he called the text 'more a religious classic than a philosophical treatise' (Radhakrishnan 1989a: 11). Again, he discussed the date of the text, though quite briefly, but did not attach priority to historical questions such as the existence of Kṛṣṇa (Radhakrishnan 1989a: 14–15, 28). As in his earlier work, he regarded Arjuna as representing the soul and thus showed how the dialogue spoke to everyone since in everyone's life there was a time of complete despair and desperate need (Radhakrishnan 1989a: 51). So, in his commentary, he referred to the world as the arena of conflict where battles are constantly being fought (1.1)

(Radhakrishnan 1989a: 79). This emphasis upon the ethical dimension of the *Bhagavad-Gītā* was a defining characteristic of his treatment of the text.

As Radhakrishnan explained in *Indian Philosophy*, the setting of the *Bhagavad-Gītā* demonstrated that it was 'an ethical treatise, a yoga śāstra' (Radhakrishnan 1929: 532). As was the case with Vivekananda, this focus on ethics was associated with an insistence upon the plurality of paths; in Radhakrishnan's view, reflecting the nature of the divine and the differences between people. However, if not in the paths, then in the description of godhead, his preference for an Advaitin stance found expression. Thus he referred to the divine in absolutist terms as 'sat, cit and ānanda, reality, truth and bliss', while also suggesting that 'as God combines in Himself wisdom, goodness and holiness, so should men aim at the integral life of spirit' (Radhakrishnan 1929: 553). In this process, he was at pains to establish that all paths led to the same goal and that the progress of the soul encompassed knowledge, action and devotion (Radhakrishnan 1929: 554). Challenging the objection that there seemed to be some antagonism between the paths, he rejected this as indicative of faulty judgement since Kṛṣṇa taught that the particular path did not matter so that '[k]nowledge, feeling and will are different aspects of the one movement of the soul' (Radhakrishnan 1929: 554–5). This universalist neo-Vedāntic reading that unified the paths continued to characterize his account of the text throughout his career.

In the introduction to his commentary on the *Bhagavad-Gītā*, Radhakrishnan reiterated these points, sometimes in very similar terms. There, for example, he observed that the *Bhagavad-Gītā* was 'a comprehensive yoga-śāstra' (Radhakrishnan 1989a: 50). Not only did he stress the ethical message of the text but he also stressed that the paths were suited to specific types of people with specific temperaments. So it was that he declared it possible to 'attain the saving truth in three different ways', these being knowledge, devotion and action, appropriate to people 'reflective, emotional or active' in character (Radhakrishnan 1989a: 53). There again, asserting the unity of the paths and their complementarity, he accepted that they were equally effective in achieving the greatest good. In what has become a much quoted (and misquoted) statement, he asserted that '[w]e may climb the mountain by different paths but the view from the summit is identical for all' (Radhakrishnan 1989a: 75). Nevertheless, though he gave a full account of all three paths in both his books on Indian philosophy and the *Bhagavad-Gītā*, his account of karma-yoga or the way of action addressed most acutely one of his primary apologetic concerns.

This was the imperative to conduct the spiritual life while serving others, a theme Radhakrishnan treated in *Indian Philosophy* where he appealed to Kṛṣṇa as the model for selfless action and affirmed such action's liberating potential (Radhakrishnan 1929: 568–9). Just as God acted for the good of the world, so should Arjuna fight, and to act in such a way for the welfare of others did not bind the agent to the wheel of existence (Radhakrishnan 1929: 568–9). Indeed, Radhakrishnan made the point that those who were liberated had a duty to assist others where '[s]ervice of humanity is worship of God', throughout insisting on the compatibility of spiritual progress and worldly activity when action was performed selflessly (Radhakrishnan 1929: 568–9). The introduction to Radhakrishnan's commentary on the *Bhagavad-Gītā* took the same line, stressing that the text opened with Arjuna's refusal to fight and closed with Arjuna's acceptance of the need to do so (Radhakrishnan 1989a: 66). What changed Arjuna's mind and convinced him of the value of action was Kṛṣṇa's instruction; refusing to regard the world as unreal and action as binding, Kṛṣṇa 'recommends the full active life of man in the world with the inner life anchored in the Eternal Spirit' (Radhakrishnan 1989a: 66–7). What Radhakrishnan had to say about the *Bhagavad-Gītā*, its many paths and its social conscience, was consistent with his more general discussion of Hinduism, in particular its tolerance resting on its inclusivity and its moral sense founded upon the oneness of humanity.

A potential area of confusion in Radhakrishnan's argument, as in Vivekananda's, was the relationship between Hinduism and Vedānta. As Vivekananda had before him, Radhakrishnan equated Vedānta with Hinduism whereby it became the core of Hinduism and, indeed, the essence of religion. This was evident in *The Hindu View of Life* where Radhakrishnan explained the importance of Vedānta to Hinduism but also emphasized that it transcended Hinduism, observing that '[a]ll sects of Hinduism attempt to interpret the Vedānta texts in accordance with their own religious views' and that '[t]he Vedānta is not a religion, but religion itself in its most universal and deepest significance' (Radhakrishnan 1927: 23). Here Radhakrishnan took as his basis the priority of religious experience and on such grounds claimed that Hindus accepted and valued other beliefs (Radhakrishnan 1927: 19). His reasoning was that divine providence must encompass all of humanity as God's children and hence that '[w]hen the Hindu found that different people aimed at and achieved God-realisation in different ways, he generously recognised them all and justified their place in the course of history' (Radhakrishnan 1927: 19–20). Certainly Radhakrishnan's account of Hinduism emphasized its internal diversity, the multiplicity of texts and traditions held together not by dogma or creed (Radhakrishnan 1927: 20–1). At the same time, he stressed the dynamism of Hinduism as it developed over the ages, a process of development that constituted an ever greater insight into reality and centred on the Vedānta as its common factor (Radhakrishnan 1927: 21–2).

Consequently, Radhakrishnan's picture of Hinduism was of the coexistence of many different beliefs and practices – its capacity to contain a variety of views meant that it adopted an inclusive attitude (Radhakrishnan 1927: 37). This attitude, contrasted by him with the Semitic religions and what he regarded as their exclusive truth claims as well as the threat of eternal damnation for unbelievers, went beyond Hinduism (Radhakrishnan 1927: 37). Although he did not argue for relativism because tolerance rested on a hierarchical model of spiritual growth with Vedānta at its apex, Hinduism offered a means of coping with inter-religious conflict that involved seeking 'the unity of religion not in a common creed but in a common quest' (Radhakrishnan 1927: 58–9). Further, he was confident that the approach taken by Hinduism would be more widely adopted, appealing to inter-religious dialogue and comparative religions as evidence of a growing recognition of the unity of religions (Radhakrishnan 1927: 59–60). Summing up his understanding of Hinduism, he contended that Hinduism accepted 'that the theological expressions of religious experience are bound to be varied' and, at the same time, accepted 'all forms of belief and lift[ed] them to a higher level' (Radhakrishnan 1927: 125). This focus upon religious experience and, therefore, the preparedness to endorse diverse forms of religiosity, even if ranking them, enabled Radhakrishnan to insist that Hinduism was tolerant because it was inclusive.

The need to defend Hinduism's ethical credentials was another major aspect of Radhakrishnan's presentation of Hinduism. In *Eastern Religions and Western Thought*, he rebutted the allegation that the Hindu spiritual ideal lacked a moral dimension by showing how the liberated person acted for the well-being of others inspired by the recognition of the identification with everyone else, 'I, yet not I' (Radhakrishnan 1989b: 54). If, as he acknowledged, India had failed to flourish, the problem was not over-concentration on spiritual goals but not living up to its own spiritual standards (Radhakrishnan 1989b: 56). Thus his definition of spiritually realized persons combined various qualities, including social concern (Radhakrishnan 1989b: 57). Radhakrishnan also rejected the suggestion that Hinduism tended towards world-denial with the result that it was unable to effect change in the world (Radhakrishnan 1989b: 64). Against this allegation, he cited Hindu examples of spiritual perfection with a strong activist element (Radhakrishnan 1989b: 68). Similarly, with reference to the distinction he drew between religion and humanism, Radhakrishnan resisted any separation of spirituality from ethics (Radhakrishnan 1989b: 75–6). Dealing with criticisms of Hinduism's moral shortcomings (e.g. Radhakrishnan 1989a: 76), he made a number of observations supporting his contention that '[v]ision and action go together' (Radhakrishnan 1989b: 80). In his view, spirituality involved action and a concern for the world, hence the truly liberated person was committed to the welfare of others and the religious life necessarily included moral endeavour (Radhakrishnan 1989b: 97–8, 100, 108). One reason for this was that he linked spiritual truth with ethical conduct, the Advaitic insight that the self is identified with the all delivering the neo-Vedāntic imperative to serve others (Radhakrishnan 1989b: 100–2). Certainly the *Bhagavad-Gītā* offered him the opportunity to demonstrate that Hinduism was both tolerant and moral. More than this, Radhakrishnan praised the *Bhagavad-Gītā* in its own right.

In various speeches delivered in his diplomatic and political capacity, Radhakrishnan represented the *Bhagavad-Gītā* as a treasured part of India's heritage that gave a clear impression of the basis of Indian glory (Minor 1991: 168–9). Earlier, writing in *Indian Philosophy*, he explained to his readers why the text was so attractive, citing 'its force of thought and majesty of vision, but also . . . its fervour of devotion and sweetness of spiritual emotion' (Radhakrishnan 1929: 522). Similarly, in the introduction to his commentary, he emphasized the importance of the text for Hindus who 'have found comfort in this great book which sets forth in precise and penetrating words the essential principles of a spiritual religion' (Radhakrishnan 1989a: 11). However, comparatively early in his career, in *Indian Philosophy*, he was describing the *Bhagavad-Gītā*'s message as 'universal in its scope', suggesting that its importance was not confined to Hindus (Radhakrishnan 1929: 521). Certainly the introductory essay to his commentary expressed the text's importance both within and outside Hinduism, whereby it embodied 'not any sect of Hinduism but Hinduism as a whole, not merely Hinduism but religion as such, in its universality' (Radhakrishnan 1989a: 12). Here, as elsewhere, he vested the greatness of the *Bhagavad-Gītā* in its capacity to accommodate widely divergent views and advance a spirituality that was practical as well as mystical.

For this reason, *Indian Philosophy* had Radhakrishnan state that the author of the *Bhagavad-Gītā* was open and inclusive in attitude, an attitude that suited him to the exposition of Hinduism since it too was typified by such openness and inclusivity (Radhakrishnan 1929: 521–2). In Radhakrishnan's view, it was the author's tolerance towards 'all forms of worship' that enabled him to express 'the spirit of Hinduism', similarly tolerant in its treatment of diverse beliefs and practices (Radhakrishnan 1929: 521–2). Just as religion in India involved a synthesis, the *Bhagavad-Gītā* attempted to synthesize disparate traditions about the nature of the self and the divine, liberation and the means to its attainment (Radhakrishnan 1929: 25, 529). The same focus on synthesis ran through the essay introducing Radhakrishnan's commentary on the *Bhagavad-Gītā*.[4] Here, referring to the variety of perspectives brought together in Kṛṣṇa's discourse, Radhakrishnan referred to the text's 'comprehensive synthesis, free and large, subtle and profound' bringing together Vedic ritual, Upaniṣadic wisdom, devotional theism and philosophical insight to form 'an organic unity' (Radhakrishnan 1989a: 13–14). He insisted that the *Bhagavad-Gītā*'s unification of seemingly antithetical ideas was in accordance with the spirit of Hinduism: thus he argued that the different commentaries on the text produced by various figures – the truth transcending any one theory – were complementary; he also argued that existing beliefs and practices were transformed and reconciled in various ways – many gods forms of the one, sacrifice an inner offering, dualism resolved into non-dualism, the Supreme Lord as the object of devotion, action and knowledge – to create an inclusive scheme for all ages and for all people (Radhakrishnan 1989a: 15, 20, 74–5).

Radhakrishnan's view of Hinduism as a religion tolerant of diversity was thus one he propounded by appeal to the *Bhagavad-Gītā*. An example of this was in *The Hindu View of Life* where he contrasted Hinduism with other religions, describing any religious ill-will as atypical on the grounds that Hinduism was characterized by an attitude of admiration and appreciation for other religions (Radhakrishnan 1927: 37). He declared that Hinduism was 'the first example in the world of a missionary religion', however, he was at pains to point out that it was not missionary in the sense of seeking converts since it was concerned with conduct rather than doctrine (Radhakrishnan 1927: 37–8). On this basis, it had been possible for Hinduism to accommodate 'worshippers of different gods and followers of different rites', just as Kṛṣṇa in the *Bhagavad-Gītā* accepted all irrespective of sex or social status (Radhakrishnan 1927: 37–8). Further, just as the *Bhagavad-Gītā* was the means by which Radhakrishnan could argue for Hindu tolerance, it was also the means by which he could argue for Hindu morality.

As Radhakrishnan made clear in *Eastern Religions and Western Thought*, the *Bhagavad-Gītā* had a crucial role in determining the nature of ethical action. He cited the *Bhagavad-Gītā* as proof that spiritual perfection had a strong activist element (Radhakrishnan 1989b: 68). Further, he justified his account of spirituality as involving action and a concern for the world by appeal to the text, stating that '[t]he man of wisdom is interested in promoting the welfare of all created beings according to the *Bhagavadgītā*' (Radhakrishnan 1989b: 98). Moreover, he quoted from the *Bhagavad-Gītā* when describing the truly liberated person in order to emphasize the commitment to the welfare of others (3.4) (Radhakrishnan 1989b: 100–1). He also alluded to the *Bhagavad-Gītā* when describing the religious life as including moral endeavour, '[c]ontemplation and action, the yoga of Kṛṣṇa and the *dhanus* [bow] of Arjuna, are two movements merged in one act', so that love for others was integral to an authentic spirituality (Radhakrishnan 1989b: 108–9). Indeed, it was by quoting from the *Bhagavad-Gītā* (possibly 6.32) that he grounded an ethical imperative in a metaphysical vision of the unity of life (Radhakrishnan 1989b: 102). In this way, the *Bhagavad-Gītā* furnished Radhakrishnan with source material to prove how moral, as well as tolerant, was Hinduism.

Radhakrishnan's interpretation of the *Bhagavad-Gītā* gave pride of place to the many paths it outlined but also addressed the ethical teaching of the text. The version of Hinduism he propounded was dominated by the same concerns, upholding Hinduism's tolerance, contrasted with the narrow dogmatism of other religions, and its morality, confronted with criticism of its moral shortcomings. Taking the *Bhagavad-Gītā* as a text representing Hinduism in its entirety and even religion itself, he stressed its value for humanity in general rather than Hindus in particular. This value lay at least in part in its presentation of many paths, supporting his claim to Hindu tolerance, and its ethical teaching, supporting his defence of Hindu morality.

Swami Sivananda Sarasvati (1887–1963) shared the neo-Vedāntic outlook articulated by Vivekananda and Radhakrishnan. Like them, he achieved some fame in the West, though perhaps this was limited largely to those interested in yoga as a spiritual discipline. His primary role was as a spiritual teacher without the exalted international career enjoyed by either Vivekananda, as an apologist for, or Radhakrishnan, as a philosopher of, Hinduism. In common with Vivekananda and Radhakrishnan, his treatment of Hinduism made great play of its open and synthetic character while upholding its moral standards founded upon a metaphysical vision of oneness. He too regarded the *Bhagavad-Gītā* as an important work, both for India and the world. Thus he advanced his argument about Hinduism by reference to the *Bhagavad-Gītā*, mandating tolerance on Kṛṣṇa's receptivity to all and action on Kṛṣṇa's own activity.

Sivananda interpreted the *Bhagavad-Gītā* in allegorical terms as having a message for all. In his *Gita Meditations*, for example, Sivananda acclaimed the text as providing a resolution to every dilemma (Sivananda 1961b: viii). He explained that just as Kṛṣṇa 'represented the True Being', Arjuna 'represented the true man' (Sivananda 1961b: viii). Moreover, he argued that the difficulties confronting Arjuna were those confronting humanity as a whole and consequently insisted that the *Bhagavad-Gītā* was 'the answer to the universal question of life' (Sivananda 1961b: viii). The introduction to Sivananda's commentary on the text also made these points, with his observation that Kṛṣṇa spoke not only for Arjuna's sake but for humanity's so that, in addressing Arjuna's situation, Kṛṣṇa was addressing the concerns of everyone (Sivananda 1969: xvi–xvii). Eulogizing the *Bhagavad-Gītā*, Sivananda indicated that '[t]he instructions that are inculcated by Lord Krishna are for the whole world' (Sivananda 1969: xvii). Although he dated the discourse to over 5,000 years previously, he stressed that the *Bhagavad Gītā* was 'meant for the generality of mankind' regarding the world as the battlefield though locating '[t]he real Kurukṣetra . . . within' (Sivananda 1969: xviii, xxxi). Elaborating on this theme, he identified Arjuna with the soul, Dhṛtarāṣṭra with ignorance, Kṛṣṇa with the indwelling divine, the chariot with the body and the horses with the senses (Sivananda 1969: xix). Consequently, the *Bhagavad-Gītā* as a symbolic work acquired a universal significance.

Further, Sivananda saw in the *Bhagavad-Gītā* many paths, often (but by no means always) treating them as equal, alternative yet complementary, routes to the same end. In *Gita Meditations*, he made mention of the different disciplines described in the text for those drawn to the various yogas, including devotion, knowledge and action (Sivananda 1961b: vi). At the same time, he was clear that the highest yoga, encompassing all yogas, was 'the Integral Yoga, the Akshara-Brahma-Yoga or the Yoga of the Imperishable Absolute', thereby indicating his Advaitin beliefs (Sivananda 1961b: 38). His account of the yogas in this context stressed their interrelatedness whereby perfection in one path entailed the acquisition of the characteristics associated with the other paths (Sivananda 1961b: 40). He was convinced that no one had the sole characteristics of emotion, insight or effort, even if one of these characteristics was dominant; in such a case one of the paths would be most appropriate as a means to spiritual progress though all culminated in realization of the impersonal absolute (Sivananda 1961b: 40).

Introducing his commentary, Sivananda also emphasized that people had different tendencies and presented the paths as suitable for different people – knowledge, devotion and action for the intellectual, emotional and practical respectively – adding that one path was as effective as any other (Sivananda 1969: xx). In this way, he focused on the three paths of knowledge, devotion and action, stating that there was no tension between them (Sivananda 1969: xx). On the model of the text's reconciliation of the paths, he declared that the ideal was a balance of personal qualities in order to achieve the highest goal conceived in Advaitin terms as 'the Self within' (Sivananda 1969: xx). He divided the *Bhagavad-Gītā* into three groups of six chapters, the first treating action, the second devotion and the third knowledge, indicating that Kṛṣṇa enabled Arjuna to understand these themes and so remove the uncertainty that had led him to despair (Sivananda 1969: xxi–xxii). Certainly Sivananda acknowledged that Kṛṣṇa taught the different paths but he reiterated that these paths were presented for the purpose of sustaining specific forms of practice and that they were of the same value and utility (Sivananda 1969: xxiv). However, elsewhere Sivananda appeared to adopt the position that the paths were ranked or ordered in such a way as to suggest that the text's inclusivity was predicated on a hierarchical conception of the religious life.

Indeed, a key to appreciating Sivananda's understanding of the *Bhagavad-Gītā* can be found in the way he sought to resolve apparent contradictions in the text by appealing to Kṛṣṇa's role as a teacher, offering guidance as appropriate to the disciple (Sivananda 1969: xxxii–xxxiii). On the grounds that 'Advaita philosophy can be grasped only by the microscopic few', Kṛṣṇa provided other teaching even if this teaching was not ultimately true (Sivananda 1969: xxxiii). Accordingly, Sivananda regarded other philosophies as lesser expressions of the truth whereby '[t]he Dvaitin and the Vishishtadvaitin eventually reach the Advaitic goal or Vedantic realisation of Oneness' (Sivananda 1969: xxxiii). Here then he made explicit the pedagogic technique of shaping the teaching to meet the needs and suit the capacities of the student.[5] This meant that he could maintain the ultimacy of Advaita while not denying that other doctrines were expounded by Kṛṣṇa, integrating these other perspectives but relegating them to Advaita with its monistic tenets and preference for knowledge.

Writing in *Gita Meditations*, Sivananda insisted that everyone had to be a karma-yogin so long as they were embodied, noting that action became a path when founded upon 'the Yoga of the understanding' and that it was on this basis that 'the activities of life can be exalted to a spiritual Yajna [sacrifice]' (Sivananda 1961b: 40–1). Introducing his commentary, he cited a verse describing karma-yoga as preferable to the renunciation of action (5.2), but did so along with verses suggesting alternative perspectives (Sivananda 1969: xxiv). In his commentary proper, he described some of the characteristics of karma-yoga: differentiating between action performed with the hope of reward that binds and action performed without hope of reward that leads to liberation, he indicated that selfless action conduced towards the acquisition of knowledge (2.48) (Sivananda 1969: 48); insisting that the wise who have knowledge should not discourage the ignorant from religious observance but encourage them to begin by performing action with the hope of reward, he recommended that the wise should instruct the ignorant in selfless action as leading to purity of heart and ultimately self-realization (3.29) (Sivananda 1969: 80–1); discussing various paths of which knowledge was described as the highest, he allowed both that practitioners of action alone ranked lowest and that progress was possible through spiritual discipline (13.24)

(Sivananda 1969: 388–9). Hence the ambivalence in Sivananda's treatment of karma-yoga since on some occasions he did seem to subordinate it to knowledge in a manner reminiscent of Śaṅkara who regarded action as the discipline appropriate for the ignorant and as a preparation for knowledge. For instance, in Sivananda's commentary, he noted the existence of two paths, action and knowledge, the former suited to the practical, the latter to the intellectual, and insisted that these were mutually exclusive but progressive (3.3) (Sivananda 1969: 66–7). The usefulness of karma-yoga, 'a means to an end', was that 'it prepares the aspirant for the reception of knowledge' (Sivananda 1969: 67). Insistent that the paths of action and knowledge could not be combined, he urged the adoption of jñāna-yoga once the heart had been purified by karma-yoga (Sivananda 1969: 67). Karma-yoga was thus to be superseded by jñāna-yoga whereas jñāna-yoga was advocated as the more direct route to realization. Such remarks as these were strikingly similar to Śaṅkara's exegesis of the text.[6]

What was evident, however, was that action was the teaching relevant to Arjuna, another observation made by Śaṅkara in reconciling the text's emphasis on action with his belief in the superiority of renunciation in the cause of knowledge. In Sivananda's view too, the message of the *Bhagavad Gītā* was action; specifically, it was liberation through performing 'the duties of life or one's Svadharma' since Kṛṣṇa had told Arjuna to act without attachment in order to attain the highest goal (3.19) (Sivananda 1969: xx–xxi). Yet Sivananda also related this to the truth of the identification of the self with ultimate reality by explaining that Arjuna was prepared by Kṛṣṇa for this knowledge (Sivananda 1969: xxi–xxii). This preparation included instruction on karma-yoga and, as the image of rungs on a ladder indicated, there was a developmental approach that culminated in self-realization (Sivananda 1969: xxi–xxii). Still, in this context where he was discussing the liberated person, he saw no necessary opposition between knowledge of the self and action in the world (Sivananda 1969: xxii). Emphasizing that the activity of the liberated person did not bind, he stated that 'the idea of doership has been destroyed by the attainment of knowledge of the Self' (Sivananda 1969: xxii). This would suggest a very different attitude from that taken by Śaṅkara for whom knowledge was incompatible with action and who accordingly espoused a renunciatory ideal, though Sivananda himself referred to Śaṅkara as a karma-yogin (Sivananda 1980: 68). In any case, action was the message appropriate to Arjuna's status and situation.

Thus in *Ethics of the Bhagavadgītā*, Sivananda underlined Arjuna's qualities and responsibilities as a warrior. A warrior was to possess intellect and insight but, above all, to be subject to the requirements of dharma and the counsel of sages (Sivananda 1957: 77). A warrior was also charged with the defence of dharma, if need be through waging war (Sivananda 1957: 77). Describing the warrior as 'the Lord of the people placed by God under his care', he defined the warrior as a part of God who assumed the divine role of sustaining good and destroying evil in order to uphold dharma (Sivananda 1957: 77–8). Moreover, he emphasized that what Arjuna required was instruction in correct action.

Adopting this position, he asked whether the setting of Kṛṣṇa's discourse was significant and, in answering this question, contended that Kṛṣṇa intended to establish the compatibility of wisdom and action (Sivananda 1957: 190). On this line of argument, any wisdom that could not meet the challenge of the battlefield was found wanting (Sivananda 1957: 190). In contrast, 'real wisdom will serve you right in the battle-field, right in a crisis, and will enable you to surmount the obstacle, resist the temptation, arise victoriously from the trial' (Sivananda 1957: 190). Therefore, there had to be an activist bias to the *Bhagavad-Gītā* because Arjuna was a warrior, his vocation to safeguard the populace entrusted to his protection, and because he was facing conflict, his need being for a teaching that was of use to him when war was imminent.

Sivananda, like Vivekananda and Radhakrishnan, was a Vedāntin and, accordingly, his account of Hinduism gave considerable prominence to Vedānta, praised as 'the most satisfactory system of philosophy', and especially Advaita Vedānta, praised as 'complete and perfect' (Sivananda 1961a: 223, 291). However, Sivananda's admiration for Vedānta did not lead him to equate Vedānta with Hinduism in the same way as Vivekananda and Radhakrishnan, despite some observations that gave Vedānta priority in morals and classified the Vedāntic triple canon as authoritative for Hinduism (Sivananda 1961a: 85, 1969: xvii). In *All About Hinduism*, he called Hinduism 'the oldest of all living religions', explaining that it was also known as 'Sanatana Dharma' and 'Vaidika Dharma' (Sivananda 1961a: 2). Hence he argued that Hinduism was 'the mother of all religions' and 'a revealed religion' (Sivananda 1961a: 2–3). Indeed, he was aware of many different formulations of Hindu identity and of the process by which it emerged, listing virtues linked with this identity including 'religious tolerance' and also 'ahimsa' and 'purity' (Sivananda 1961a: 9). Here, as elsewhere, his portrayal of Hinduism attributed to it a spirit of tolerance and a moral quality.

The tolerance of Hinduism was claimed by labelling it as 'free from religious fanaticism' at the opening of *All About Hinduism* (Sivananda 1961a: 2). Sivananda argued that Hinduism was not dogmatic or exclusive but accepted every method that would lead to liberation (Sivananda 1961a: 3). Thus Hinduism harmonized a wide range of beliefs and practices (Sivananda 1961a: 3). On the basis of this internal tolerance, he declared that Hinduism adopted the same attitude to other religions because '[i]t accepts and honours truth – wherever it may come and whatever garb it may put on' (Sivananda 1961a: 4). Although he argued that there was a fundamental unity among Hindus, he regarded the diversity of Hinduism as valuable because it provided spiritual disciplines suitable for everyone (Sivananda 1961a: 4–5). Referring to India as a spiritual nation, he also lauded it for being the most tolerant of all nations (Sivananda 1961a: 10–11). Further, his explanation for Hinduism having flourished appealed to its inclusivity; 'characterised by wide toleration, deep humanity, and high spiritual purpose', Hinduism was able to withstand the assaults of adherents of other religions (Sivananda 1961a: 12–13). Moreover, he went so far as to suggest that Hinduism had 'all the features of a universal religion' (Sivananda 1961a: 13). This was evident in the way in which it allowed for different forms of worship as progress towards the truest form, ranging from the veneration of images to meditation on the impersonal absolute where the former was not opposed, but led, to the latter (Sivananda 1961a: 163–7). Similarly, he set out four paths (karma-, bhakti-, raja- and jñāna-yogas) as applicable to individuals with different natures and as directed towards the same goal (Sivananda 1961a: 168–9). He noted that everyone was a combination of characteristics, hence that the paths could not be divided and that the ideal was a combination, 'the Yoga of Synthesis', balancing knowledge, devotion and action as truly one (Sivananda 1961a: 168–9, 179–80). Overall, he praised Hinduism as 'extremely catholic, liberal, tolerant, and elastic', a claim he supported not only by citing different forms of worship and different paths but also by identifying the number of sects, cults and schools of thought Hinduism contained (Sivananda 1961a: 181–2, 220).

Sivananda also discussed morality at some length in *All About Hinduism*, asserting that the ethics of Hinduism were inspiring and excellent (Sivananda 1961a: 13, 84). He affirmed that ethics were acknowledged as being of the greatest importance with the scriptures prescribing standards for conduct (Sivananda 1961a: 84). Insisting that Western ethics lacked a solid foundation, in contrast Hindu ethics were 'subtle, sublime, and profound' since they were founded upon the Vedāntic belief in the oneness of life whereby to harm another was to harm oneself (Sivananda 1961a: 85). Whatever the challenges of moral action, he claimed that the principle of morality was to treat others as one would wish to be treated, calling this 'the . . . essence of Karma Yoga' (Sivananda 1961a: 90, 93). He understood karma-yoga to be 'the path of disinterested service', its spirit of renunciation in action leading to the divine (Sivananda 1961a: 169). He regarded karma-yoga as discharging one's duty because it was one's duty with no thought of gain (Sivananda 1961a: 169). Doing one's duty in this way was liberating since it purified the heart and prepared for wisdom (Sivananda 1961a: 170). Nevertheless, here he was determined to deny any suggestion of the inferiority of karma-yoga (Sivananda 1961a: 170). Taking the view that 'the Yoga of Synthesis' was preferable, karma-yoga was seen as the means to remove impurity just as jñāna-yoga eliminated obscurity and bhakti-yoga eradicated disorder (Sivananda 1961a: 179). Yet, since all paths were one, karma-yoga as a spiritual discipline also promoted the qualities cultivated by the other paths for '[t]he Karma Yogin attains wisdom and devotion when his actions are wholly selfless' (Sivananda 1961a: 180). Thus, when he was describing the qualifications of those who wanted to serve Hinduism, Sivananda advocated the practice of karma-yoga (Sivananda 1961a: 353–4).

In *Practice of Karma Yoga*, Sivananda stressed that the law of action was opposed to both fatalism and determinism as it rested upon a sense of free will and as such was a firm basis for ethics (Sivananda 1980: 186–9). He argued that karma was 'an incentive to action to better one's condition' and 'a strong impetus . . . to struggle', stressing both moral agency and the oneness of all life (Sivananda 1980: 186–9). However, having established that the law of action was a force for moral good, he went further when defending action as a path with transformative potential where acting disinterestedly inspired the individual to serve others (Sivananda 1980: 67–8). Thus the karma-yogin derived 'inner spiritual strength and power' from this spiritual discipline and eventually reached a state where 'all . . . actions will be unselfish', a claim substantiated by citing examples of the selflessness of past karma-yogins (Sivananda 1980: 67–8). Thus Sivananda's view of karma-yoga was one that stressed its role in securing the welfare of others as well as the spiritual benefit to the karma-yogin.

Sivananda's own spirituality was closely connected with the *Bhagavad-Gītā* as would be expected of a Vedāntin. In the introduction to his commentary, he also recommended its study to others though he insisted that this should be conducted under the guidance of an enlightened teacher who alone could ensure that the student gained a true understanding of the text (Sivananda 1969: xix–xx). He went so far as to suggest that the *Bhagavad-Gītā* should be part of the curriculum for all Indian schools and colleges, indeed, for educational institutions worldwide, in order to supplement secular subjects with spiritual and moral education (Sivananda 1969: xxxiii). He called the *Bhagavad-Gītā* 'a sublime and soul-stirring book' (Sivananda 1969: xxxiii). In various other works, he praised the *Bhagavad-Gītā* in similarly exalted terms. In *All About Hinduism*, he called the text 'the most precious jewel of Hindu literature' and hailed it as 'rank[ing] high in the religious literature of the world' (Sivananda 1961a: 31). In *Gita Meditations*, he referred to 'the treasure-house of the Bhagavadgita', observing that '[t]he Gita is an embodiment of all sciences, scriptures and knowledges, and its word is law' (Sivananda 1961b: v, 42).

Certainly in the introduction to his commentary on the text, Sivananda stated that the *Bhagavad-Gītā* 'contains spiritual gems of incalculable value' (Sivananda 1969: xvii). He pointed to the prestige of the *Bhagavad-Gītā* in India and, more than this, he attributed Western admiration of India to the text (Sivananda 1969: xv–xxxiii). Throughout, he maintained that the *Bhagavad-Gītā* had universal significance as well as a special status in relation to Hinduism so that '[i]ts teachings do not belong to any cult, sect, creed, particular age, place or country' though the text 'expounds very lucidly the cardinal principles or the fundamentals of the Hindu religion and the Hindu Dharma' (Sivananda 1969: xviii, xv–xvi). In this way, the *Bhagavad-Gītā* was central to Sivananda's account of Hinduism as tolerant and moral, epitomizing, as he believed it did, the religion's most important truths.

This was obvious in *All About Hinduism* where Sivananda called the *Bhagavad-Gītā* 'a universal gospel', just as Hinduism satisfied the criteria to be 'a universal religion' (Sivananda 1961a: 31, cf. 13). Accordingly, when discussing Hinduism's inclusivity, he quoted the *Bhagavad-Gītā* as proof of the harmony of Hinduism, specifically Kṛṣṇa's declaration that all paths led to him (4.11) (Sivananda 1961a: 182). The text also featured in his discussion of Hinduism's ethics, quoting from it on the authority of scripture to guide behaviour (16.24) and on the complexity of action as a demanding discipline (4.16–18)

(Sivananda 1961a: 84, 90). Further, he quoted from it when setting out the avatāra ideal of divine intervention in the world (4.6–8) (Sivananda 1961a: 111). Thus, when upholding the value of karma-yoga against allegations of its inferior rank and menial nature, he referred to Kṛṣṇa's role as Arjuna's charioteer where God served humanity (Sivananda 1961a: 170). Hence the *Bhagavad-Gītā* constituted a proof text for his portrayal of Hinduism.

Sivananda's exposition of the *Bhagavad-Gītā* affirmed the existence of many paths while insisting on the importance of action. Considering Hinduism, he focused on its positive attitude towards a variety of perspectives, whether in respect of different Hindu movements or even different religions. Similarly, he addressed the issue of morality, promoting karma-yoga as an ideal of service grounded in the recognition of the unity of all life. He was extremely complimentary about the *Bhagavad-Gītā*, recommending it to all and making a close connection between the text and Hinduism as a whole. Thus the *Bhagavad-Gītā* was cited frequently in the context of his eulogizing Hinduism's tolerant character and moral calibre.

These universalist visions of the *Bhagavad-Gītā* give some impression of the power of universalist accounts of Hinduism. The *Bhagavad-Gītā* was important, not just because it was one of the texts traditionally regarded as the basis of Vedānta philosophy, but also because it contained a variety of perspectives combined with an activist element that could underwrite social service. Accordingly, it provided a textual reference to prove Hinduism's inclusivity as a religion where the ultimate goal could be reached by different means and thus other religions could be accepted as valid paths.

Vivekananda found many paths in the *Bhagavad-Gītā* as well as a call to action, enabling him to praise Hinduism as a tolerant religion with a strong ethical imperative. Radhakrishnan took very much the same neo-Vedāntic stance as he too concentrated on the *Bhagavad-Gītā*'s many paths and teaching on action when declaring that Hinduism was uniquely tolerant and defending its ethics against all detractors. Likewise, Sivananda was focused on the *Bhagavad-Gītā* as a text that set out many paths and, in some sense at least, gave priority to action while he, like Vivekananda and Radhakrishnan, appealed to the text as proof of the tolerant and ethical qualities of Hinduism.

5

ROMANTIC AND MYSTICAL INSIGHTS

Various Western writers of a romantic or mystical inclination focused on the insights of the *Bhagavad-Gītā*. Although their interpretations of the *Bhagavad-Gītā* differed markedly, they tended to share a sense of the vital importance of the text. Again, even if their accounts of Hinduism were developed differently and to different extents, they also tended to identify certain themes, ideas and experiences that could be applied more widely. This meant that the *Bhagavad-Gītā* could become part of their philosophies of life and religious outlooks; the text's association with Hinduism, however conceived, certainly constituted no bar to its acquisition.

The appeal of the *Bhagavad-Gītā* for these writers was that it seemed to support their perspectives on truth and reality, expressing such insights in a particularly powerful and profound way. What they found in the text, irrespective of what it entailed for a definition of Hinduism, was deemed significant since what it said was understood to have universal relevance. This was because the *Bhagavad-Gītā* embodied not simply exotic Oriental ideals but tenets of general validity, sometimes so general that the Hindu character of the text and the specific characteristics of Hinduism were de-emphasized.

Henry Thoreau (1817–62), a leading Transcendentalist, regarded the *Bhagavad-Gītā* as advocating the discipline of the muni (sage), preferring the cultivation of wisdom through contemplation but not excluding action in the concentration on knowledge. He did not refer to Hinduism as such but, insofar as he referred to Hindu thought (by no means always in the sense of a specific religion) or, indeed, Indian or Oriental thought, he set up a contrast with Christianity while also establishing a commonality whereby his readers could benefit from considering such ideas. Praising the *Bhagavad-Gītā* for its excellent qualities, he lauded it as an Eastern work though one valuable to him personally. Accordingly, he believed that the *Bhagavad-Gītā* epitomized the best of Eastern spirituality and at the same time he believed that there was much for the West to learn from the East.

Thoreau quoted various verses about the relationship between knowledge and action from the second to the sixth chapter of Wilkins' translation of the *Bhagavad-Gītā* (Thoreau 1985: 112–13). These verses dealt with the respective merits of knowledge and action: some suggesting the superiority of knowledge;

others the necessity for action; expressing admiration for the muni's wisdom even if expounding the performance of detached action as indicative of spiritual progress (2.47, 49, 58; 3.4–7, 19; 4.2, 18, 20, 31, 33, 36, 38; 5.4–5; 6.1) (Wilkins 1785: 40–1, 44–6, 51, 53, 55–7, 62). Still, Thoreau subordinated practicality to vision, explaining that he would sacrifice 'all the wealth of the world, and all the deeds of all the heroes, for one true vision' (Thoreau 1985: 113). That said, he did not regard the *Bhagavad-Gītā*'s teaching as wholly satisfactory, portraying it in terms of the brāhman's passivity confronted by the forces of caste, fate and time (Thoreau 1985: 113–14). Further, in his estimation, Kṛṣṇa did not make a strong case for Arjuna to fight (Thoreau 1985: 113–14). If Arjuna was won over by Kṛṣṇa's words and the Western reader was not, it was because the latter's 'judgment is *not* "formed upon the speculative doctrines of the *Sankhya Sastra*"' (Thoreau 1985: 114). Here too, and in the ongoing discussion, he was quoting from Wilkins' translation concerning the avoidance of bondage, the inferiority of action to knowledge and the importance of motive (2.39, 49) (Wilkins 1785: 39, 40). This led Thoreau to raise a series of issues about the meaning of wisdom and the nature of duty; in turn these observations provided him with a springboard for further reflection on an East–West dichotomy (Thoreau 1985: 114).

It was Thoreau's contention that the American reader had a breadth of view against which European literature appeared to be both partisan and insular (Thoreau 1985: 115). Thus he was critical of English and German intellectuals for their failure to appreciate the greatness of Indian poets and philosophers, declaring that modern Europe had ignored 'perhaps the *worthiest* of mankind and the fathers of modern thinking' (Thoreau 1985: 115–16). This recognition of the value of the East for the West was accompanied by a contrast between East and West where '[t]he former has nothing to do in this world; the latter is full of activity' though, having set up this contrast between Eastern contemplation and Western engagement, he went on to qualify it by allowing that both trends were to be found in the East as in the West (Thoreau 1985: 114). He also set up a contrast between Eastern and Western norms when discussing the role of conscience as a conservative force.

In this context, Thoreau represented Hindu thinkers as focusing on unchanging laws, the qualities of nature and the role of birth with the final goal of union with Brahman (Thoreau 1985: 110). That said, '[b]uoyancy, freedom, flexibility, variety, possibility' were lacking whereas Christianity was described as 'humane, practical, and, in a large sense radical' (Thoreau 1985: 110). The picture he painted was of Eastern sages sitting in meditation, concentrating upon the mystic syllable aum and identifying themselves with ultimate reality, wise but inert (Thoreau 1985: 110). Eventually, however, elsewhere in Asia, Christ was born, the earthly descent of Brahman to humanity (Thoreau 1985: 110). Thoreau represented the New Testament as containing practical guidance, it might not be speculative but it was sensible, indeed, its purpose was moral (Thoreau 1985: 110). Consequently, he noted that '[t]he New Testament is remarkable for its pure morality; the best of the Hindoo Scripture, for its pure intellectuality'

(Thoreau 1985: 110). However, such differences did not detract from the value of these scriptures. On the contrary, Thoreau proposed the compilation of 'the Scripture of mankind' from the sacred literature of 'the Hindoos' and others, though exempting, for the time being at least, the New Testament (Thoreau 1985: 116). This universalizing tendency was one that entailed his being able to follow the Eastern precepts for which he declared such admiration, this ability founded upon his insistence on Indian originals for Western ideas – 'our domestic thoughts have their prototypes in the thoughts of her philosophers' – and his assertion of a common human connection – '[i]n every man's brain is the Sanscrit' (Thoreau 1985: 121, 123–4).

A letter written in 1849 had Thoreau state 'rude and careless as I am, I would fain practice the *yoga* faithfully... [t]o some extent, and at rare intervals, even I am a yogi' (quoted in Christy 1932: 201). Some years previously, he had written in his journal that '[o]ne may discover the root of a Hindoo religion in his own private history, when... he does sometimes inflict on himself like austerities with a stern satisfaction' (quoted in Christy 1932: 201). In this way, Thoreau adopted for himself the yogic ideal just as he believed that it was possible for anyone to discover the wellspring of this ascetic discipline. Throughout, his account of Hinduism was prejudiced towards contemplation, consistent with his characterization of Eastern spirituality (Thoreau 1985: 122–3). Thus he was drawn to the teaching of the brāhmans, adding that their austerity was attractive (Thoreau 1985: 123). Accordingly, his praise for Eastern philosophy was predicated upon the way in which he believed it 'assigns their due rank respectively to Action and Contemplation, or rather does full justice to the latter', citing the example of the brāhmans' spiritual practice and insight (Thoreau 1985: 111). This claim was corroborated by reference to Hastings' letter of recommendation for Wilkins' translation in which Hastings commented on the brāhmans' discipline of withdrawal of the senses and development of the mind in the conduct of a contemplative life (Thoreau 1985: 111–12; cf. Hastings 1784: 9).[1] Certainly, Thoreau was deeply impressed by the *Bhagavad-Gītā* and its teachings as representing the best of Eastern thought.

Thoreau advocated that one should '[r]ead the best books first', quoting from Wilkins' translation of the *Bhagavad-Gītā* regarding different forms of worship, including the offering of wisdom with restrained senses and austere lifestyle (4.28, 31) (Thoreau 1985: 78; cf. Wilkins 1785: 54–5). More explicitly, Thoreau recommended reading of the *Bhagavad-Gītā* to anyone with an interest in sacred literature 'as a part of the sacred writings of a devout people', even suggesting that the text possessed 'a moral grandeur and sublimity' comparable with the Old Testament (Thoreau 1985: 115). Indeed he implied that the *Bhagavad-Gītā* would be of benefit to its readers, irrespective of their origins, just as the text had become important to him. Reflecting on its significance in his life, he referred to the inspiration he derived from 'the stupendous and cosmogonal philosophy of the Bhagvat Geeta', stressing its great age and profundity (Thoreau 1985: 559). Continuing, he related an imaginary visit to a well and an encounter with a brāhman's servant, mentioning Hindu gods and scriptures as he did so (Thoreau 1985: 559). In this instance too, the universalizing tendency was evident, figuratively in the mixing of the waters of Walden and the Ganges, whereby the *Bhagavad-Gītā* could command his attention and influence his thought (Thoreau 1985: 559). Hence he remarked on the *Bhagavad-Gītā*'s appeal to people in different walks of life, both 'soldiers and merchants';[2] and went on to consider the distinctive attributes of 'great poems' so that '[t]o the practical they will be common sense, and to the wise wisdom' (Thoreau 1985: 119).

Quoting from Hastings' letter of recommendation for Wilkins' translation that praised the *Bhagavad-Gītā* in often extravagant terms, Thoreau stated that the text was 'unquestionably one of the noblest and most sacred scriptures which have come down to us' (Thoreau 1985: 111). He closed his reflections on Eastern contemplation and Western engagement by quoting from Wilkins' translation on the joyful recollection of the dialogue and the promise that there would be good fortune wherever Kṛṣṇa and Arjuna were to be found (18.76–8) (Thoreau 1985: 114–15; cf. Wilkins 1785: 135). He also quoted from Wilkins' translation on the subject of conscience, in this case the divine advice to the troubled warrior to perform his duty and fight (2.18; 3.8, 29; 18.48) (Thoreau 1985: 109; cf. Wilkins 1785: 36, 45, 48, 131). Such guidance he labelled 'a sublime conservatism; as wide as the world, and as unwearied as time' and in this sense the *Bhagavad-Gītā* typified certain Eastern qualities (Thoreau 1985: 109–10). When it came to his characterization of types of scripture, he stated that '[t]he reader is nowhere raised into and sustained in a higher, purer, or *rarer* region of thought than in the Bhagvat-Geeta' (Thoreau 1985: 110–11). Thus the *Bhagavad-Gītā* furnished him with evidence for his theories on the nature of Eastern culture and civilization. Moreover, his appreciation of the *Bhagavad-Gītā* was an integral part of an outlook that saw in the East the means by which the West could become enlightened (Thoreau 1985: 116). Accordingly, he compared unfavourably even the works of Shakespeare with 'the vast and cosmogonal philosophy of the Bhagvat-Geeta', before considering the nature of poetry and concluding that the West still had much to learn from the East (Thoreau 1985: 116). The *Bhagavad-Gītā*, when located in this context, became an important aspect of the light of the East to be cast on the West, revealing something of an ancient wisdom and wonder.

Thoreau was drawn to the *Bhagavad-Gītā* as a text inculcating the contemplative path of the sage. This fitted with his exposition of Eastern wisdom and, if the term is applicable, Hinduism, though at the same time he saw this wisdom as advantageous to Westerners. The *Bhagavad-Gītā* was hailed as an important work, worthy of the widest possible readership, while its impact on his own ideas was considerable. In his version of Transcendentalism, the *Bhagavad-Gītā* illustrated and exemplified the distinctive aspects of Eastern (even Hindu on one definition) religiosity and religious literature and as such it could make a contribution towards the betterment of the West.

Annie Besant (1847–1933), a prominent Theosophist who did much to popularize the Theosophical movement, differed from Thoreau in the priority she attached to action and in the depth and detail of her examination of Hinduism. However, in common with Thoreau, she expressed admiration for the *Bhagavad-Gītā*, regarding it not just as a Hindu text. Again, like Thoreau, she subscribed to a universal vision yet, unlike him, she had a practical commitment to India as a nation. Besant focused on the two meanings of the *Bhagavad-Gītā*, the historical and the allegorical, and on the three paths, notably the message of right activity. Her account of Hinduism concentrated on its occult significance while her concern with humanity's historical evolution and India's special destiny led her to emphasize action as the means by which to serve the divine cause. She praised the *Bhagavad-Gītā* as a Hindu work offering both consolation and inspiration that had also won international prestige. Further, she quoted from the *Bhagavad-Gītā* to illustrate her exposition of Theosophy and Hinduism, the latter accorded a Theosophical treatment. Moreover, she saw the *Bhagavad-Gītā* as an activist text, inculcating a high standard of conduct in a Hindu frame of reference.

Besant's preface to her translation of the *Bhagavad-Gītā* included both its exoteric and esoteric teachings, explaining its symbolic significance whereby Arjuna represented the aspiring soul, Kurukṣetra the soul's battlefield, Dhṛtarāṣṭra's sons the soul's enemies and Kṛṣṇa the divine word within (Besant 1953: 15). It was on this basis that Besant insisted that the teachings of the *Bhagavad-Gītā* were addressed to all souls, coupling this with an assertion of the oneness of the spiritual path, 'though it has many names', and the spiritual goal, 'though they [the souls] may not realize their unity' (Besant 1953: 15). The different ways in which the *Bhagavad-Gītā* could be interpreted were investigated at much greater length in *Hints on the Study of the Bhagavad-Gītā*.

Here Besant referred to the two meanings of the *Bhagavad-Gītā*, namely, the historical and the allegorical (Besant 1906: 6). Explaining the nature and relationship of these meanings, she defined history as the outworking of the divine purpose for the future development of the world whereas allegory was its counterpart in individual experience (Besant 1906: 6–7). This was what she meant by referring to the 'double meaning' of scripture, the historical showing 'a greater Self evolving' and the allegorical relating 'the unfolding of the lesser Selves' (Besant 1906: 7–8). So the *Bhagavad-Gītā* could be read as a historical work, revealing the guiding principle of the history of the world, and as an allegorical work, revealing the prospects for the progress of the individual soul (Besant 1906: 9). In both cases, what was revealed was truth (Besant 1906: 9).

The key to Besant's response to the *Bhagavad-Gītā* was the ideal of the avatāra with Kṛṣṇa's role understood both historically and allegorically (Besant 1906: 10). Her account of Kṛṣṇa's intervention in history included the way in which Arjuna was convinced to put aside his foreboding of doom about the destruction of the old order and play his part in the divine plan as an agent of change (Besant 1906: 18–27). The allegorical interpretation of the avatāra ideal opposed Manas or the mind (Arjuna) and Kāma or the passions (Duryodhana and the Kauravas) where Kṛṣṇa was the teacher, tracing Arjuna's development from the gratification of desires to the recognition of their futility when his appeal for guidance culminated in the illumination of the mind (Besant 1906: 28–33). In both cases, she drew attention to action as well as identifying the wider implications of the text as universally applicable. Towards the close of her historical discussion, she observed 'if we can learn the spirit of the great unveiling, ... then in every struggle we can throw ourselves on the right side, and fight without doubt, without illusion, without fear, for the Warrior who really fights is doing all' (Besant 1906: 26–7). In similar vein, she concluded her allegorical discussion with the exhortation '[g]o on fighting, ... with brave and undaunted heart, and, at the end of your battle on Kurukṣheṭra, for you too shall dawn the Self in His Majesty, destroyed shall be your delusion also, and you shall see your Lord as He is' (Besant 1906: 33). Certainly this stress on action typified her exposition of the *Bhagavad-Gītā*.[3]

Writing in the prefatory essay to her translation, Besant described the dialogue as setting forth a spirituality consistent with the performance of activity in the world (Besant 1953: 11–12). This message, 'that union with the divine Life may be achieved and maintained in the midst of worldly affairs', she called the *Bhagavad-Gītā*'s 'central lesson' (Besant 1953: 12). According to her, the *Bhagavad-Gītā* was 'a scripture of Yoga', preaching union and harmony through equanimity and moderation whereby the disciple came to see everything as a divine manifestation and duty was performed in a selfless spirit as a sacrifice (Besant 1953: 12–13). This explained the answer given to Arjuna on the battlefield when confronting a conflict between his duty as a warrior to fight in a righteous cause and his duty towards his family (Besant 1953: 13–14). The answer was to do one's duty as dictated by one's social status in the knowledge that God was the author of action and that to do one's duty in an equable manner 'forges no bonds, Yoga is accomplished and the soul is free' (Besant 1953: 14–15). However, Besant was to explore the theme of action in a much fuller way in *Hints on the Study of the Bhagavad-Gita*.

Here too, calling the *Bhagavad-Gītā* 'a Scripture of Yoga', Besant interpreted the message of the text as 'right activity' (Besant 1906: 35, 46). This was 'the lesson of the *Gîṭâ*', understood as 'acting in harmony with the divine Will' (Besant 1906: 46). Yet she differentiated between 'right activity' and action – action along with knowledge and devotion being disciplines that together produced 'right activity' (Besant 1906: 47). It was her opinion, then, that knowledge, devotion and action led, and were necessary, to 'right activity' (Besant 1906: 47). Hence she insisted that this activity required a combination of 'perfect wisdom' with 'perfect devotion' and also 'perfect unattachment to the fruits of action' (Besant 1906: 47). Indeed, she placed considerable emphasis on the ultimate unity of the three paths while praising as '[t]he perfect yogî' the one who integrated the attributes associated with each individual path (Besant 1906: 60–1).

Besant indicated that '[t]he three chief means of, or paths to, yoga are also called, in a secondary sense, yoga', naming these 'the Yoga of Renunciation', 'the Yoga of Discrimination' and 'the Yoga of Sacrifice', that is, devotion, knowledge and action (Besant 1906: 66–7). However, her discussion of 'the Yoga of Sacrifice' did suggest that it had a special status, despite it being only a preparatory discipline; consequently, she claimed that on occasion it was just referred to as yoga on the grounds of its congruity with the conduct 'of the perfect yogî' (Besant 1906: 119). That said, she continued to stress the unity of the three paths of devotion, knowledge and action as directed towards the same divine focus, '[o]ne Lord, one life, one Brotherhood' (Besant 1906: 130). Even in this respect, though, using the image of the body, her comments combined a stress on unity with an activist tendency where, once the work of the present universe was completed, she looked forward to the rise of a future universe where 'we, parts of His Body, shall work with Him... more perfectly than we have worked here' (Besant 1906: 130–1). For various reasons, action seemed to be her major concern.

Besant's approach to the *Bhagavad-Gītā* as an allegorical work was related to her esoteric emphasis derived from Theosophy, an emphasis also evident in her survey of religions in general and Hinduism in particular. She described Theosophy in comparatively simple and straightforward terms in *Ancient Wisdom*, a work written with the aim of communicating Theosophical ideas to a non-specialist readership. At the beginning of this book, she declared that 'the Divine Wisdom – whether called by its ancient Sanskrit name of Brahma Vidyā, or its modern Greek name of Theosophia, Theosophy – comes to the world as at once an adequate philosophy and an all-embracing religion and ethic' (Besant 1939: 1). The starting point of her analysis of Theosophy was that different religions shared many of the same ideas (Besant 1939: 2). In seeking to account for what she regarded as a generally acknowledged truth, she offered the Theosophical explanation for such similarities, a unity underlying the apparent diversity of religions (Besant 1939: 2–3). This unity was vested in the teaching of a brotherhood of teachers whose task was to present this teaching as appropriate to their audience (Besant 1939: 3). Hence the founders of the world's religions were members of this brotherhood entrusted with the guidance of humanity (Besant 1939: 3). Since Theosophy designated the substantial commonality of religions beneath their superficial dissimilarities, she insisted that it was the foundation of every religion, opposed to none but improving all by disclosing their true significance (Besant 1939: 4–5). Further, her understanding of Theosophy meant that she did not think it necessary to renounce previous religious affiliations; instead she saw Theosophy as a means of defending religion against irreligion and at the same time recovering religion's pristine purity.

Continuing, Besant enumerated '[t]he main spiritual verities of religion': first, the oneness of ultimate reality; second, the twofold and threefold manifestation of the divine; third, this manifestation as the source of other spiritual beings; fourth, the triune nature of humanity and its essential identity with ultimate reality; and fifth, the progress of humanity through successive lives to fulfil its divine potential (Besant 1939: 5–6). She then proceeded to demonstrate how these verities were to be found in all the world's religions. Turning to Hinduism, she observed that 'the same teachings [were] embodied in the oldest Aryan religion – the Brāhmanical' (Besant 1939: 12). To substantiate her argument, she pointed to

Brahman and its character as being, consciousness and bliss, the trimūrti of Brahmā, Viṣṇu and Śiva and its role as the fountainhead of divinity, also the influence of the physical, subtle and mental bodies on the self and its transmigration and reincarnation until realization of its identity with Brahman (Besant 1939: 12–16). She was also clear that this unity of ideas in religions was matched by a unity of ethical teaching and again illustrated how Hinduism exemplified this morality in, for instance, the adherence to truth, non-violence and equanimity (Besant 1939: 32, 34). Although she insisted that the only satisfactory explanation for the common core to religions was the existence of 'the Brotherhood of the White Lodge, the Hierarchy of Adepts who watch over and guide the evolution of humanity', her more detailed exposition of Theosophical doctrine still made significant use of Sanskrit terms and Hindu concepts when setting out major themes such as the planes of existence, the nature of the soul and the destiny of humanity and the universe (Besant 1939: 41–2, 91, 197, 267, 343).

The same stress on the esoteric, a defining characteristic of Theosophy and Besant's account of Hinduism, was evident in *Four Great Religions*. Here, again in conformity with Theosophical tenets, her procedure was to examine each of the four religions she was considering 'in the light of occult knowledge' issuing from the brotherhood of spiritual masters and, on this basis, differentiating between what was fundamental and what was not – the last point particularly problematic in the case of Hinduism as a catch-all category (Besant 1897: 6–9). Throughout, it had been her intention 'to sketch each religion in its best, its purest and most occult form' (Besant 1897: 9). The first of the religions she considered was Hinduism or Brahmanism (Besant 1897: 12).

Besant's version of Hinduism was divided into three sections; 'the spiritual truths, with their later intellectual presentations'; 'the exoteric cult, detailed and wonderfully minute in its delineation of nature and of a man's relation thereto'; and 'the Science of Yoga, through which spiritual truths can alone be fully realized' (Besant 1897: 15, 17). The first section dealt with Brahman as the source of the universe and the self of every living being, bondage to the wheel of existence, the law of action and the possibility of human liberation (Besant 1897: 18–24). It also dealt with the six orthodox schools of thought as the means of articulating and communicating these teachings (Besant 1897: 25–31). The second section dealt with personal deities, various rites and observances and the classes and stages of life whereby occult knowledge was made accessible to all (Besant 1897: 32–45). The third section dealt with the paths of action, knowledge and devotion, their interrelatedness and ultimate unity, as well as the role of the teacher in securing spiritual development (Besant 1897: 45–9). Thus she surveyed 'the religion founded in immemorial antiquity, that has come down from the Rishis [seers]' (Besant 1897: 49). In any case, Besant's purpose in examining the four religions was to promote inter-religious understanding and thus prove their essential unity (Besant 1897: 5).

Although Besant's interests were esoteric, they were also historical and as such related to her understanding of India's destiny as a spiritual exemplar, in which context world renunciation was rejected in favour of work in the world for India's welfare. Certainly, in *Hints on the Study of the Bhagavad-Gita*, she accorded Kṛṣṇa's teaching a pivotal position in a long historical process (Besant 1906: 10). One avatāra, Rāma, had served as the perfect king; another, Parasurāma, had brought about the near destruction of the warriors; now yet another, Kṛṣṇa, was to ensure that India served her ordained purpose (Besant 1906: 10–12). Besant saw India as 'the world-model', politically and socially as well as religiously where her inclusivity provided teaching for peasant and philosopher alike (Besant 1906: 11). However, India was also to be the 'World Saviour' and it was to fit her for this role that Kṛṣṇa intervened in history (Besant 1906: 12). In order for India to play her part, she had to undergo humiliation and it was for this reason Kṛṣṇa killed the great armies of opposing warriors, thereby rendering India vulnerable to successive invasions (Besant 1906: 12–14). The suffering endured by India was redemptive, not just for India but for the world, since it expanded her horizons (Besant 1906: 15). So, despite Kṛṣṇa bringing doom to many, he was always acting for the good (Besant 1906: 13, 15). Accordingly, it was the work of Kṛṣṇa to subject India to suffering in order that in due course she could fulfil her global mission (Besant 1906: 15–16). Although India had this global spiritual mission, there was still an implicit, if not explicit, nationalist political tenor to her remarks.[4]

This was suggested by Besant's sense of the historical process that linked understanding to action and the impression she gave of the disjunction between the ages of Indian defeat and foreign rule and the new era where India, having learnt from her conquerors, was in a position to save all nations – a mission that surely required her to be free (Besant 1906: 14, 27). In any event, Besant was critical of a notion of spirituality, advanced by some apologists for Hinduism, that entailed withdrawal from the world and a life of seclusion notwithstanding the popularity of the renunciant ideal in modern India (Besant 1906: 39). On her developmental model, action motivated by desire was superseded by inaction once worldly objects lost their allure but this, in turn, was superseded by that combination of action and inaction constituted by action performed as duty in a selfless spirit in obedience to the divine will (Besant 1906: 40). Certainly she was prepared to state that India's decline could be attributed to the belief that action was antithetical to spirituality, associating an anti-activist ideology with India's fall from greatness (Besant 1906: 43).

Besant's Theosophical version of Hinduism was by definition a universalized treatment, both in its interpretation of Hinduism in the light of principles deemed to be basic to all religions and in its presentation of these principles as embodied in Hinduism to a wider public. The universality attributed to Hinduism was reflected in Besant's translation of the *Bhagavad-Gītā* 'dedicated to all aspirants in East and West' (Besant 1953). Her preface left no doubt of the importance she attached to the text, 'there is none so rare and precious as this', adding that Kṛṣṇa's words not only resolved Arjuna's crisis of conscience but also spoke to the distressed and despairing down through the years (Besant 1953: 11).

Besant made a very similar observation in *Hints on the Study of the Bhagavad-Gita* where she stressed the value of the text to the world at large when stating that 'in every country [it] has awakened some echo in receptive hearts' (Besant 1906: 2). The significance of the *Bhagavad-Gītā*, in her opinion, was such that it was 'worthy of the profoundest study' (Besant 1906: 2). Consequently, the *Bhagavad-Gītā* was more than Kṛṣṇa's instruction of Arjuna – it related to humanity as a whole.

In *The Ancient Wisdom*, Besant cited the *Bhagavad-Gītā* in support of the points she made about Hinduism in the light of Theosophy. Hence she quoted various verses from the text on the ethical teaching of Hinduism, setting out the ideal of equanimity (4.10; 6.27; 12.13–14) (Besant 1939: 34). Moreover, reference to the *Bhagavad-Gītā* occurred throughout the book where she discussed particular subjects: the teaching on the successive re-embodiment of the soul in her discussion of 'Devachan' (2.22) (Besant 1939: 178); the role of action in creating living beings in her discussion of 'The Law of Sacrifice' (8.3) (Besant 1939: 305); and the withdrawal from sense objects in her discussion of 'Man's Ascent' (2.59) (Besant 1939: 332).

In *Four Great Religions*, she also cited the *Bhagavad-Gītā* in her Theosophy-inspired exposition of Hinduism. In the context of 'the spiritual truths' that comprised the first section of her account of Hinduism, she quoted the text on the difficulty experienced by those who were embodied in following the path of the unmanifest in the course of explaining why the Vedānta was not taught to the population at large (12.5) (Besant 1897: 31). In the context of 'the exoteric cult' that comprised the second section of her account, she quoted the text on sacrifice given to the gods and blessings bestowed in return (3.11–12) (Besant 1897: 33–4). She also quoted verses where Kṛṣṇa declared that he would accept any offering, however humble, if made sincerely and that he was both the object of all worship and immanent in all creation to show how God could be approached in different ways (9.23, 26; 10.39) (Besant 1897: 38). She quoted other verses related to the theophany in order to illustrate that the revelation of the divine nature was in accordance with the recipient's spiritual capacity (11.31, 46) (Besant 1897: 38, 39). Oddly enough, in the context of 'the Science of Yoga' that comprised the third section of her account, her discussion of the paths did not mention the *Bhagavad-Gītā*. Here too, though, her definition of the paths, both their threeness and their oneness, was on much the same lines as her exegesis of the *Bhagavad-Gītā* (Besant 1897: 45–8). In these ways, the *Bhagavad-Gītā* enabled her to present a persuasive account of Hinduism from a Theosophical perspective, albeit in a notably Hindu Sanskritic style.

Again, when it came to advocating an activist form of Hinduism, the *Bhagavad-Gītā* was an important text for Besant. Although she acknowledged the challenging nature of the discourse in *Hints on the Study of the Bhagavad-Gita*, she noted 'a continual refrain, "fight"' (Besant 1906: 2). Kṛṣṇa's message to Arjuna was certainly to fight and thus play his part in the divine plan, hence there was no question of renouncing action as Arjuna himself had realized in resolving to join battle (Besant 1906: 20–1, 26–7). So, when condemning the current Indian antipathy towards action, Besant considered the *Bhagavad-Gītā*'s teaching to be crucial, sketching out a progression 'from step to step, action, serenity, serene action' so that in the final phase action was performed without attachment for the welfare of the world (3.25–6; 6.3) (Besant 1906: 43, 44). In this respect, too, the *Bhagavad-Gītā* was valuable to her and her argument.

Besant's understanding of the *Bhagavad-Gītā* was expressed in historical and allegorical terms as external events and internal experience respectively, with a tendency to focus on activity in relation to the three paths of knowledge, devotion and action. The same approach was taken to Hinduism, which she interpreted from an occult and also from a historical angle: the former viewing the religion through a Theosophical lens while imparting a certain Hindu tone to Theosophy; the latter pointing to India's special role as a spiritual beacon for the whole world while maintaining an activist stance in order to secure India's well-being. Acknowledging that the *Bhagavad-Gītā* was a Hindu text, she nevertheless sought to explain its message to as wide an audience as possible, hailing it for its impact in India and abroad. Thus the *Bhagavad-Gītā* featured prominently in her discussion of Theosophy and especially in her Theosophical version of Hinduism, suggesting that Hinduism was one of many expressions of the same truth yet still vitally important. Moreover, as the text preached action in the world, it was a means to provide a Hindu justification for an engaged ethic.

Aldous Huxley (1894–1963) also reflected upon the meaning and importance of the *Bhagavad-Gītā* but, unlike Besant, did not deal with the text in any depth or detail, at least in its own right. In common with Besant, he subscribed to a belief in the fundamental unity of religions though his explanation for this was different, resting on the mystical insight of others alone without offering much by way of a dedicated account of Hinduism. Also in common with Besant, he focused on there being different paths (albeit in more general terms) yet here too the emphasis was different as he regarded any stress on action as instrumental in the attainment of knowledge since his inclusivity had a strong hierarchical element. Further, Huxley's view of the *Bhagavad-Gītā* has largely to be inferred from the association of his comments with a translation of the text produced from a neo-Vedāntic standpoint for Western neo-Vedāntins. Again, though, his interests lay less in the distinctive attributes of religions than their supposed shared foundation. It was in the light of the interpretive paradigm of the Perennial Philosophy that he saw the *Bhagavad-Gītā* as having great significance. In various ways, without denying that the text was Hindu, what mattered most was the way in which it exemplified the Perennial Philosophy and as such it set out an inclusive spiritual discipline accessible to everyone.

Huxley wrote an introductory essay to the translation of the *Bhagavad-Gītā* produced by Swami Prabhavananda and Christopher Isherwood. The majority of this essay, however, did not refer directly to the text but concentrated on a more wide-ranging presentation of the Perennial Philosophy. Where Huxley did refer to the text, it was most often to illustrate aspects of the Perennial Philosophy with which he had already established Hinduism conformed (Huxley 1972: 13–17). Beyond that, he offered little by way of observation on the text itself, though he did categorize it as holding 'an intermediate position between scripture and theology; for it combines the poetical qualities of the first with the clear-cut methodicalness of the second' (Huxley 1972: 12). Yet, considering the association of his essay with a specific translation, the stance of the translators was significant. Despite the brevity of the preface, other preliminary and appended material and some biographical information provided a clear indication of the ideology with which Huxley was associating himself.

Prabhavananda's and Isherwood's preface made a number of observations about the *Bhagavad-Gītā*. Having remarked on the trend to translate the world's great literature into English, they stated that the *Bhagavad-Gītā* posed certain problems – problems of language involving issues of expression, terminology and concepts (Prabhavananda and Isherwood 1972: 9). Further, the translators proposed that it was not possible to adopt a standard style of English because the text was not unified (Prabhavananda and Isherwood 1972: 9). They then described the different aspects of the text: its place in the *Mahābhārata* making it necessary to take account of the text's epic qualities as well as its philosophical instruction; its presentation of Vedāntic thought making it necessary to take account of the text's particular cosmological premises; its prophetic nature making it necessary to take account of the text's mystical and poetic character; and its proclamation of universal truths making it necessary to communicate the text's teaching in an accessible manner (Prabhavananda and Isherwood 1972: 9–10). These considerations were what shaped the translation – the mix of prose and poetry, an interpretive rather than a literal approach, an emphasis upon its contemporary meaning rather than its ancient origins (Prabhavananda and Isherwood 1972: 10). Their insistence upon the *Bhagavad-Gītā* as 'one of the greatest religious documents of the world' was clearly important, but perhaps most relevant to the tenor of Huxley's remarks was the focus on the *Bhagavad-Gītā* as a Vedāntic and universal text (Prabhavananda and Isherwood 1972: 10).[5]

This focus was evident in the essay entitled 'Gita and Mahabharata' where Brahman as an impersonal principle was preferred to personal deity and parallels drawn between Kṛṣṇa and Christ (Prabhavananda and Isherwood 1972: 28–9). Further, the Vedāntic characteristics of the *Bhagavad-Gītā* were discussed in 'The Cosmology of the Gita', building on the basis that Brahman was ultimate reality to consider its identity with the self, its personal aspect as creator and the role of meditation in its realization before continuing with an explanation of the nature of time and matter (Prabhavananda and Isherwood 1972: 131–5). Moreover, the universal characteristics of the *Bhagavad-Gītā* were discussed in 'The Gita and War' where a lesson not only for Arjuna but for humanity as a whole was drawn from Kṛṣṇa's words of advice (Prabhavananda and Isherwood 1972: 137). The translation too had a Vedāntic tenor and its production and publication for the West implied the text's possession of a universal relevance. This was only to be expected considering that Swami Prabhavanada was the founder of The Vedanta Society of

Southern California to which Christopher Isherwood belonged. Huxley too was a member, thus he shared certain beliefs and values with the group.[6]

A book that proved to be a pivotal stage in the development of Huxley's thought was *Ends and Means*. This book sketched out the theory he was later to develop in *Perennial Philosophy*, throughout stressing that the means determined the ends while also stating that 'our metaphysical beliefs are the finally determining factor in all our actions' (Huxley 1965: 9–10). Consistent with his focus on a shared truth, Huxley did not provide a systematic or structured treatment of religions but instead adduced religious data as appropriate to his analysis. In so doing, he hailed Hinduism for its espousal of non-attachment, adherence to non-violence and tolerance of alternative perspectives – his coverage of Hinduism in this context acknowledging its diversity and, indeed, proposing that it was not one religion but several (Huxley 1965: 5, 92, 227, 246). A reason for this was that there were different paths for different people, his argument being that spiritual capacities varied with only a few being able to attain the highest goal (Huxley 1965: 226–7). Such attainment was associated with an intuition of the impersonal nature of ultimate reality transcending the personal view of the divine, again illustrated by appeal to Hinduism (Huxley 1965: 289–90). However, his exposition of such characteristics stressed the commonality of religions and simultaneously maintained the supremacy of a mystical state that combined awareness of the world with awareness of a higher order of reality (Huxley 1965: 325).

These ideas about different paths for different people, related to a theory of human nature and divine revelation, found fuller expression in Huxley's *Perennial Philosophy* where he also addressed the issue of a common core to religions, the 'Highest Common Factor' or the 'philosophia perennis' (Huxley 1969: 1). What he meant by this was a metaphysical, psychological and ethical unity, the existence of a divine reality with which the soul was identified and of which the soul sought knowledge, a reality 'immemorial and universal' (Huxley 1969: 1). Huxley argued that the Perennial Philosophy was present in all religions and thus gave an account demonstrating areas of agreement between them, evaluating any areas of disagreement as superficial in comparison (Huxley 1969: 1). His argument for this was founded on the insights of mystics who realized the truth, preferring the insight of those with experiential knowledge to academic accounts that lacked the inspiration of direct or immediate knowledge (Huxley 1969: 2–3). Accordingly, Hinduism was approached in the light of Perennial Philosophy on the grounds that this constituted '[t]he core and spiritual heart of all the higher religions' (Huxley 1969: 270). Moreover, while this book included a wealth of Hindu (perhaps more particularly Vedāntic) material, Huxley did not set out to discuss Hinduism in its own terms, rather as an instance of the Perennial Philosophy.

Among the subjects Huxley considered in his exposition of the Perennial Philosophy were the ground of being, the union of the self with this divine ground and the knowledge of this union; that he discussed these subjects in relation to the Hindu concept of the Brahman-Ātman identity and the Upaniṣadic maxim 'tat tvam asi' (that you are) demonstrated that his version of the Perennial Philosophy had a strong Vedāntic basis (Huxley 1969: 7–11). Huxley also referred to Hinduism when insisting that there were different paths for different people – action (or works), knowledge and devotion (Huxley 1969: 169–71). This was significant because it related to his ideas about humanity which, following William Sheldon, he divided into three types of physical constitution and allied temperamental characteristics: the 'endomorphic' and 'viscerotonic'; the 'mesomorphic' and 'somatotonic'; and the 'ectomorphic' and 'cerebrotonic' (Huxley 1969: 172–4). This was also significant because it related to his ideas about divinity where he upheld an impersonal over a personal conception of deity (Huxley 1969: 219). Consequently, he upheld knowledge of ultimate reality as supreme, though he did so while recognizing the role of action (Huxley 1969: 303, 312, 337). In writing his introduction to the Prabhavananda and Isherwood translation of the *Bhagavad-Gītā*, Huxley made many of the same points.

In writing this introduction, Huxley dedicated much space to an account of the Perennial Philosophy as the 'Highest Common Factor' unifying religions (Huxley 1972: 12). Here too he offered a summary of the Perennial Philosophy in the form of 'four fundamental doctrines': ultimate reality and its manifestation in material objects and living beings; the human capacity for knowledge of ultimate reality; the distinction between the empirical ego and the eternal self; and the destiny to recognize the eternality of the self and its identity with ultimate reality (Huxley 1972: 13). Demonstrating that Hinduism contained these doctrines, he pointed to Brahman as 'Divine Ground', adding that knowledge of Brahman could not be gained by 'mere learning and analytical reasoning', that Brahman was equated with 'the indwelling Atman' and that, while the objective was '[c]ontemplation of truth', 'action [was] the means' (Huxley 1972: 13–17). Having established that Hinduism, like other religions, exemplified the Perennial Philosophy, Huxley turned his attention towards the paths by which it was possible to make spiritual progress. He began with the path of knowledge but acknowledged that this path was appropriate only for a few aspirants with a particular aptitude (Huxley 1972: 17). For others, another preparatory discipline was necessary, devotion and worship, dependent upon a human incarnation of the divine (Huxley 1972: 17–18). Thus there was a link between his understanding of the paths and his understanding of humanity and divinity. In this, action too had a part to play since Huxley was definite that morality was the means to wisdom (Huxley 1972: 20).

For Huxley, Hinduism had to be located in the context of the Perennial Philosophy because he was convinced 'that the Perennial Philosophy and its ethical corollaries constitute a Highest Common Factor, present in all the major religions of the world' (Huxley 1972: 21). His references to the *Bhagavad-Gītā* thereby illustrated at one and the same time points about Hinduism and about that which unified Hinduism and all other religions – the Perennial Philosophy. As this introduction led into a translation of the *Bhagavad-Gītā*, its inclusion of Hindu references was unremarkable, but in typical perennialist manner, there were also references to a range of religious and philosophical traditions. This gave the *Bhagavad-Gītā* a prominent place in a universal theory as 'one of the clearest and most comprehensive summaries of the Perennial Philosophy ever to have been made' (Huxley 1972: 13). Thus Huxley explained the power of the text and its importance in India and abroad (Huxley 1972: 13). Although this introduction to the Prabhavananda and Isherwood translation did not so much concentrate on the text as expound the wider context in which he located it, elsewhere Huxley often chose to cite the *Bhagavad-Gītā* both in respect of Hinduism and the Perennial Philosophy.

For example, unlike *Ends and Means*, Huxley's *Perennial Philosophy* referred to the *Bhagavad-Gītā* fairly frequently along with other Hindu scriptures, notably the *Upaniṣads*. In respect of there being different paths for different people in Hinduism and in the Perennial Philosophy, Huxley observed that Kṛṣṇa taught Arjuna all three paths: 'liberation through action without attachment; liberation through knowledge of the Self and the Absolute Ground of all being with which it is identical; and liberation through intense devotion to the personal God or the divine incarnation' (Huxley 1969: 170–1). Huxley supported this contention by quoting from the *Bhagavad-Gītā* on action (3.19–20), on knowledge (4.10; possibly 5.25) and on devotion (12.5–7), illustrating the respective paths – doing what had to be done in a disinterested manner; cultivating wisdom through control of the senses and freedom from the passions; and, because the path of knowledge was so difficult, worship of the personal deity as an easier path (Huxley 1969: 171). The *Bhagavad-Gītā* also played its part in his ideas about humanity and divinity.

Having outlined Sheldon's categorization of human beings into three types, Huxley then used them to explain the three paths of the *Bhagavad-Gītā* (Huxley 1969: 174). Devotion as a path was thus appropriate for the 'viscerotonic' personality, action for the 'somatotonic' and knowledge for the 'cerebrotonic' (Huxley 1969: 175). Similarly, Huxley illustrated his view of incarnation by quoting from the *Bhagavad-Gītā*'s version of the avatāra ideal (4.7–10) (Huxley 1969: 60–1). The significance of this, and of the theophany and associated dialogue which Huxley also outlined with quotations from the text (11.3, 7, 15–16, 25, 28–9, 31–2), was that it was possible for the self to achieve union with ultimate reality – in Hindu terms the identity of Ātman with Brahman – but that this was made easier by the avatāra (Huxley 1969: 91–4). Again, Huxley cited the *Bhagavad-Gītā* when ranking different types of spiritual aspirant, allowing that those who were devoted to a personal deity would receive their reward yet acknowledging that the highest knew Brahman (7.16–23) (Huxley 1969: 303–4). This notwithstanding, as the *Bhagavad-Gītā* was quoted to prove, action performed in the right spirit, that is, sacramentally or sacrificially, was beneficial (3.9) (Huxley 1969: 312). Huxley covered some of the same ground in his introduction to the Prabhavananda and Isherwood translation from which a number of the *Bhagavad-Gītā* quotations in *Perennial Philosophy* were taken.

In this introduction, Huxley related the *Bhagavad-Gītā* to Hinduism as well as the Perennial Philosophy. He did mention one path by name, jñāna-yoga or knowledge, albeit not with reference to the text (Huxley 1972:17). However, other comments suggested something of his view about devotion and action that could be applied to the *Bhagavad-Gītā*: his view of devotion as having a preliminary role since devotion to the incarnate divine was preparatory to knowledge of reality; and his view of action as similarly preparatory since action performed in the right spirit purified the mind and thus fitted it for this knowledge (Huxley 1972: 18, 20). The link with the *Bhagavad-Gītā* was made by associating devotion with his discussion of the need for a human incarnation of the divine such as Kṛṣṇa in the *Bhagavad-Gītā*, and associating action with his discussion of morality in the pursuit of wisdom where he appealed to Śaṅkara's authority as a commentator on the *Bhagavad-Gītā* (Huxley 1972: 17, 20). There were thus different paths for different people, a teaching explained in the *Bhagavad-Gītā* where Kṛṣṇa as 'the mouthpiece of Hinduism' accepted a variety of means directed towards achievement of what appeared to be a variety of ends (Huxley 1972: 19). Here, then, Huxley was also alluding to concepts of humanity and divinity. His understanding of humanity as possessing unequal spiritual potential was illustrated by appeal to the *Bhagavad-Gītā* where such psychological variety was explained in cosmological terms by the guṇas, thereby establishing that different methods were required (Huxley 1972: 19). His understanding of divinity, as already mentioned, included ultimate reality taking human form, thereby establishing that these different methods involved seemingly different divine objects (Huxley 1972: 17). Concluding, he reiterated that the *Bhagavad-Gītā* was 'the most systematic scriptural statement of the Perennial Philosophy' (Huxley 1972: 22). As such, it was to be read not simply as a Hindu document, though of course it was this, but as a global testament.

Although some measure of inference is necessary, Huxley's interpretation of the *Bhagavad-Gītā* was framed by the neo-Vedāntic ideology that also informed his advocacy of the Perennial Philosophy. Hinduism, however significant an influence on his thought, especially as mediated by neo-Vedānta, was regarded primarily as an instance of the Perennial Philosophy. His admiration for the *Bhagavad-Gītā* showed awareness of its role in Hinduism but nevertheless stressed its universality, consistent with its being one of the best expressions of the Perennial Philosophy. The *Bhagavad-Gītā* was worthy of his admiration, then, because its teachings demonstrated how Hinduism fitted into his theory of a common core of religions and in so doing epitomized the common characteristics of the Perennial Philosophy, notably by providing for the spiritual progress of aspirants with various capacities.

The romantic and mystical insights into the *Bhagavad-Gītā* of these Western writers clearly had a universal dimension, comparable to that found in the work of many Hindu writers (and, in one case at least, owed much to the same neo-Vedāntic source). Rather than seeing the *Bhagavad-Gītā* as a fascinating glimpse into Hindu religiosity from an academic angle or as source material for the missionary's comparative theology, what it became was a part of these writers' own worldviews and spiritual outlooks. For them, the *Bhagavad-Gītā* was valuable in a personal sense and was potentially, if not actually, valuable to other Westerners.

Thoreau saw in the *Bhagavad-Gītā* a contemplative ideal typical of Eastern wisdom; by extension, this could be related to Hinduism though this concept was not in evidence in his work. Besant espoused a Theosophical style of exposition combining historical and allegorical perspectives; she found different paths with an emphasis on right activity in the *Bhagavad-Gītā* just as she found India's mission as a spiritual exemplar in Hinduism. Huxley's understanding of both the *Bhagavad-Gītā* and Hinduism was broadly neo-Vedāntic since the Perennial Philosophy was itself influenced by neo-Vedānta; hence his argument was that the text described different paths but that, as the Perennial Philosophy reflected in Hinduism indicated, these were ranked with knowledge at the apex while still according a role to action.

6

CONTEMPORARY TEACHERS AND MOVEMENTS

Some contemporary teachers and movements have also focused on the *Bhagavad-Gītā* and, since these have included teachers of Western origins and movements with many Western followers, they have further universalized the appeal of the text. Indeed, these teachers and movements, often addressing themselves to the counter-cultural community or seekers after alternative spirituality, have influenced perceptions of Hinduism, especially abroad but also in India, while paying little attention to Hinduism as a concept. Instead, they have tended to resort to other indigenous categories, such as Veda, and, on occasion, to appeal to some universal truth deemed more fundamental than Hinduism.

The 'sectarian' status of such teachers and movements obviously means that there are innumerable counter-examples where the *Bhagavad-Gītā* plays a lesser part, yet here too the text has more prominence than perhaps might be anticipated (e.g. Sai Baba 1972). Even when selecting commentators for whom the *Bhagavad-Gītā* has great importance, the diversity (and divergence from a supposed neo-Vedāntic norm) is striking. Owing their allegiance to particular traditions and lineages or affiliating themselves with prominent figures of the classical or modern period, they propose very different understandings of the nature and goal of the religious life.

However, they do have certain characteristics in common, notably an insistence upon the vital role of the teacher for an individual's spiritual progress and a strong experiential emphasis sometimes combined with a combative spirit. Insofar as these characteristics relate to Hinduism, they show that it contains a variety of perspectives in the context of specific disciplines to be applied in practice.

A.C. Bhaktivedanta Swami Prabhupada (1896–1977), previously known as Abhay Charan De, the founder of the International Society for Kṛṣṇa Consciousness (ISKCON), equated his interpretation of the *Bhagavad-Gītā* with the text itself in terms of devotion to Kṛṣṇa. He also rejected other commentaries if these were not produced by teachers whose authority and authenticity were attested by their place in the guru–disciple succession. He did not offer much by way of comment on Hinduism (though ISKCON has produced material on Hinduism and the organization's relation to it), tending to refer instead to Vedic religion or associated concepts. This he regarded as the basis of the organization he had formed while describing real religion as constituted by worship of God. He attached great significance to the *Bhagavad-Gītā* as a text epitomizing Vedic insights. Hence, in his view, the *Bhagavad-Gītā* embodied the major features of Vedic teachings including the need for a teacher, the personal nature of divinity and the primacy of devotion.

Prabhupada's commentary on the *Bhagavad-Gītā* was prefaced with a section entitled 'The Disciplic Succession' in which it was stated that Kṛṣṇa was 'the original teacher of a chain of spiritual masters which continues to the present day' (Prabhupada 1975: xxvii). Accordingly, Kṛṣṇa as the source of the teaching was placed in first position with Prabhupada himself in thirty-third (Prabhupada 1975: xxvii). In between was found: Bhaktisiddhanta Saraswati Goswami, the then head of the Gauḍiya Vaiṣṇava Mission, who had initiated Prabhupada into the religious life; Bhaktisiddhanta Saraswati Goswami's father and the founder of the mission, Bhaktivinoba Thakura; and Caitanya, a sixteenth-century Bengali saint renowned for his emotional and ecstatic devotion to Kṛṣṇa and Rādhā whose legacy the mission was founded to promote (Prabhupada 1975: xxvii).[1] The significance of this 'Disciplic Succession' was that it confirmed Prabhupada's credentials as a commentator on the *Bhagavad-Gītā* since the quality of his teaching was guaranteed by the Gauḍiya Vaiṣṇava Mission, deriving as it did from Caitanya and, ultimately, from Kṛṣṇa. For this reason, Prabhupada's introduction to his commentary on the *Bhagavad-Gītā* emphasized the importance of finding a teacher who belonged to the lineage established by Kṛṣṇa, explaining that only a member of this lineage could communicate to his disciple the truth that Kṛṣṇa, the first teacher, had taught (4.34) (Prabhupada 1975: 87).

This accounts for the title of Prabhupada's commentary where he claimed that, by virtue of his place in the 'Disciplic Succession', he could expound the true meaning of the text. This was also why he rejected other commentaries, explaining that these were written from personal opinion with no real sense of the *Bhagavad-Gītā* (Prabhupada 1975: ix). The proper attitude to the *Bhagavad-Gītā*, he asserted, was exemplified by Arjuna and, following his example, the text was to be accepted exactly as it was – literally and in its entirety (Prabhupada 1975: xvi). Thus, in his commentary, he differentiated between devotees and demons and insisted that only commentaries produced by devotees had any value (4.2–3) (Prabhupada 1975: 66). Continuing, he presented Arjuna as the model stating that 'any commentary on the *Gītā* following in the footsteps of Arjuna is real devotional service' (Prabhupada 1975: 66). Moreover, Prabhupada's commentary was characterized by an emphasis upon Kṛṣṇa as ultimate reality and devotion to him as the best path.

When discussing the true nature of divinity in the introduction to his commentary, Prabhupada upheld the supremacy of Kṛṣṇa as '[t]he Lord, the Supreme Personality of Godhead' (Prabhupada 1975: xii). In so doing, he upheld the personal deity, Kṛṣṇa, over the impersonal absolute, Brahman (Prabhupada 1975: xv). Further, he was definite that the name Kṛṣṇa was not sectarian in character; indeed, Kṛṣṇa was the original Viṣṇu (Prabhupada 1975: xix, xxvi). Such themes as these ran through Prabhupada's commentary: Kṛṣṇa himself declared his supremacy and that he could be understood through study of his own words in the *Bhagavad-Gītā* and *Bhāgavata Purāṇa* (10.2) (Prabhupada 1975: 170); the devotee went beyond identification with the impersonal absolute in the experience of serving Kṛṣṇa (18.50–4) (Prabhupada 1975: 274); and Kṛṣṇa was not one of many incarnations but their common origin (11.1) (Prabhupada 1975: 185). Throughout, Prabhupada maintained that the divine was personal, that an impersonal conception of divinity was a less adequate understanding of the true nature of the divine and that Kṛṣṇa was the source and ground of all existence.

Interrelated with this was Prabhupada's stress on bhakti. After all, Kṛṣṇa taught Arjuna because Arjuna was a devotee, an observation made by Prabhupada in the introduction to his commentary where he asked '[h]ow, then, can a human being know Kṛṣṇa unless he is a devotee?' (Prabhupada 1975: x–xi). The purpose of bhakti was clear – as living beings have been badly affected by their association with matter, it was essential to purify activity so that consciousness shifted from material objects to the Supreme Lord (Prabhupada 1975: xiv). Hence, while Prabhupada acknowledged that there were other paths, devotion was the best course (Prabhupada 1975: xxiv–xxv). Consequently, he pointed out that everyone could hear about Kṛṣṇa irrespective of their social status or sex and so that God's promise was that devotion to Kṛṣṇa was enough (Prabhupada 1975: xxv). Championing devotional service to the Supreme Lord, Prabhupada described it as 'the sum and substance of *Bhagavad-gītā*' (Prabhupada 1975: xxv). So it was that he called 11.55, where Kṛṣṇa assured Arjuna that anyone who served him would come to him, the text's essence (Prabhupada 1975: 198). Similarly, in respect of another verse extolling service of Kṛṣṇa, he declared that this was superior to all other methods of achieving spiritual fulfilment (12.20) (Prabhupada 1975: 209). This meant that Prabhupada's account of the paths subordinated them all to bhakti.

In Prabhupada's judgement, action was work for, and knowledge was knowledge of, Kṛṣṇa. This was made clear in his commentary where he defined both action and knowledge in relation to Kṛṣṇa consciousness. Thus '[a] person acting in Kṛṣṇa consciousness...with his body, mind, intelligence and words, is liberated' and '[a] Kṛṣṇa conscious person has realized knowledge...because he is satisfied with pure devotional service' (5.11; 6.6) (Prabhupada 1975: 97, 110). However, action and knowledge in and of themselves could detract from devotion to Kṛṣṇa, the easiest and most effective path leading not only to liberation but also the blissful enjoyment of a loving relationship with Kṛṣṇa. Although there were a number of yogas, not just action, knowledge and devotion, all other paths subserved and led to devotion (6.46–7) (Prabhupada 1975: 122–3). So, for Prabhupada, bhakti-yoga was the culmination of spiritual practice leading to Kṛṣṇa consciousness and, accordingly, action and knowledge were given a devotional meaning consistent with the primacy of devotion to God. Hence, when he defined '[d]irect Kṛṣṇa consciousness' as bhakti-yoga, he observed that it meant '[t]o work with the complete knowledge of the Lord' (5.26–9) (Prabhupada 1975: 104).

In this way, Kṛṣṇa consciousness was established as the goal since Kṛṣṇa was the Supreme Lord to whom devotional service should be offered.[2]

The themes Prabhupada addressed in his commentary on the *Bhagavad-Gītā* ran through his speeches and writings. However, these speeches and writings did not demonstrate much interest in Hinduism even though ISKCON as an organization has recognized the need to position itself in relation to the religion, whether to act as a specialist educational provider or refute the allegations made by the Anti-Cult Movement. In both instances, this has necessitated an emphasis on the ancient origins and Vedic nature of ISKCON as an authentic part of Hinduism (e.g. ISKCON n.d.a,b,c; Subhananda dasa 1978). Speaking in America in 1968, Prabhupada had also explained that ISKCON had an ancient heritage with Vedic roots. The Kṛṣṇa consciousness movement, he related, could be traced back 500 years to Caitanya, even 5,000 years to Kṛṣṇa, and could be identified in the Vedic scriptures (Prabhupada 1997: 229). On other occasions, he described the movement in terms of devotional service to Kṛṣṇa in accordance with scriptural injunctions and stated categorically that the movement was legitimate because it was based on Vedic texts (Prabhupada 1997: 35, 233).

In the introduction to his commentary on the *Bhagavad-Gītā*, for example, Prabhupada stressed that Vedic knowledge was 'infallible' and 'above all doubts and errors' (Prabhupada 1975: xvi). He indicated that study of Vedic literature was to be undertaken in order to understand Kṛṣṇa and to turn the mind to higher things (15.1; 17.16) (Prabhupada 1975: 233, 258). Nevertheless, sometimes he mentioned Sanātana Dharma and even Hinduism in the course of advancing his argument about religion. It is interesting that he did not equate Sanātana Dharma, 'the eternal religion', either with Hinduism in particular or with religion in general (Prabhupada 1975: xviii). Instead, he set up a contrast between religion as changeable and Sanātana Dharma as changeless (Prabhupada 1975: xviii). Whereas a religion had some historical point of origin, Sanātana Dharma stood outside history (Prabhupada 1975: xviii). Again, while a person's affiliation with a specific faith, including Hinduism, might change, true religion consisted in service (Prabhupada 1975: xix). His insistence on the fundamental truth that living beings were created by the Supreme Lord to render him devotional service was thus the basis of his understanding of religion (Prabhupada 1975: xix).

So, in his commentary, Prabhupada offered an interpretation of the *Vedas* in which they specified 'the principles of religion' in order to promote 'complete surrender' to God (4.7) (Prabhupada 1975: 70–1). Further, in *Elevation to Kṛṣṇa Consciousness*, he argued that, whether Hindu, Muslim or Christian, a person of faith believed in 'a supreme controller of this universe' whom he identified as Kṛṣṇa (Prabhupada 1973: 45). Moreover, in *The Quest for Enlightenment*, he rejected the idea that religion involved the adoption of a label, be it Hindu, Muslim or Christian, rather it was 'to know that God is great' and hence acknowledge Kṛṣṇa (Prabhupada 1997: 82–3). In these books too, he emphasized the Vedic heritage and devotion to the divine in the light of which conventional religious labels seemed irrelevant. For example, he referred to '[t]he Vedic religion, or *varṇāśrama dharma*' (duty of classes and stages of life) as having no historical point of origin but being 'the eternal religion of the living entity' (Prabhupada 1973: 7). He also rejected the translation of '*dharma*' as religion in the sense of a specific faith, regarding the latter as chosen, the former as natural, at the same time indicating that the role of religion was to inculcate 'love of Godhead' so that 'God's service is *dharma*' (Prabhupada 1973: 87–9). Or again, he regarded self-identification as a Hindu as a cause of dissension and a denial of the oneness of humanity and hence maintained that 'real *dharma*, or religion' was 'to surrender to God' (Prabhupada 1997: 81–2). As he focused on being 'a lover of God', he treated religious affiliation as comparatively trivial while advocating 'hearing about Kṛṣṇa and chanting about Kṛṣṇa' to those who had yet to develop love for the divine (Prabhupada 1997: 221).

Certainly Prabhupada concentrated on the same themes, the vital part played by a teacher, the supremacy of Kṛṣṇa and the efficacy of devotion, when speaking or writing more generally as is evident from *Elevation to Kṛṣṇa Consciousness* and *The Quest for Enlightenment*. He urged remembrance of the instructions given by Kṛṣṇa and one's teacher in an effort to lessen any sense of separation (Prabhupada 1973: 57). He also stressed that one's teacher should belong to the lineage established by Kṛṣṇa and receive respect as Kṛṣṇa's representative (Prabhupada 1997: 89–90). He cited the testimony of esteemed teachers as evidence of Kṛṣṇa's status as Supreme Lord with both personality and form (Prabhupada 1973: 52). Indeed, following Caitanya, he insisted that only devotion could restore the proper relationship with Kṛṣṇa (Prabhupada 1997: 111).

In Prahbhupada's various publications, the *Bhagavad-Gītā* featured alongside other texts. The relationship between these texts was sometimes seen as progressive, beginning with the *Bhagavad-Gītā As It Is* as 'the entrance examination', continuing with the *Bhāgavata Purāṇa* as 'the graduate course' and succeeded by the *Caitanya caritāmṛta* as 'the postgraduate level' (Prabhupada 1997: 232–3). Nevertheless, Prabhupada upheld the importance of the *Bhagavad-Gītā* as spoken by Kṛṣṇa himself (Prabhupada 1997: 117). The importance of the text thus derived from its divine origin as well as its embodiment of the tenets of Kṛṣṇa consciousness (Prabhupada 1997: 2).

Indeed, Prabhupada made some of these points in the introduction to his commentary on the *Bhagavad-Gītā* (Prabhupada 1975: xxiii). Similarly, in his commentary, he extolled the text as a revelation of Kṛṣṇa though this did not obviate the need to approach the *Bhagavad-Gītā* with the proper attitude since to do otherwise detracted from the authority of the text (2.12) (Prabhupada 1975: 25). It was Arjuna, to whom Kṛṣṇa delivered the *Bhagavad-Gītā*, who served as exemplar for understanding the text as 'the perfect theistic science... directly spoken by the Supreme Personality of Godhead' (1.1) (Prabhupada 1975: 1–2). One way in which Prabhupada set out the special significance of the *Bhagavad-Gītā* was by describing it as epitomizing Vedic ideals.

In the introduction to his commentary, Prabhupada hailed the *Bhagavad-Gītā* as 'the essence of Vedic knowledge and one of the most important *Upaniṣads* in

Vedic literature', insisting that 'one who simply reads *Bhagavad-gītā* need not read any other Vedic literature' (Prabhupada 1975: ix, xxv). During his commentary, he repeatedly mentioned such Vedic credentials. Thus, for instance, Arjuna was the recipient of 'Vedic truth' (2.12) (Prabhupada 1975: 24). Further, while the *Vedas* prescribed the principles of religion, it was the *Bhagavad-Gītā* that declared the highest of these principles to be surrender to the Supreme Lord (4.7) (Prabhupada 1975: 71). Consequently, Kṛṣṇa's teaching concerning devotional service was described as 'the substance of all revealed scriptures' when commenting on a verse that Prabhupada translated as referring to 'the most confidential part of the Vedic scriptures' (15.20) (Prabhupada 1975: 239–40). Since he saw the *Bhagavad-Gītā* as epitomizing Vedic ideals, he believed that 'the last instruction of the *Gītā* is the last word of all morality and religion: surrender unto Kṛṣṇa' (18.77–8) (Prabhupada 1975: 281–2). On these grounds, Prabhupada appealed to the *Bhagavad-Gītā* when outlining the beliefs and practices of Kṛṣṇa consciousness.

In *Elevation to Kṛṣṇa Consciousness*, Prabhupada referred to the *Bhagavad-Gītā* to prove the necessity of being subject to authority, here citing the account of Kṛṣṇa's inauguration of a lineage of teachers (4.1) (Prabhupada 1973: 3). Discussing the divine nature, he also referred to the text in order to demonstrate Kṛṣṇa's supremacy as the origin of all the gods and the source of Brahman (7.7; 10.8; 14.27) (Prabhupada 1973: 48, 51, 55). Similarly, he referred to the text when stressing the role of devotion, specifically Kṛṣṇa's promise that his devotee would come to him (18.65) (Prabhupada 1973: 40). Other instances can be found in *The Quest for Enlightenment*. So, in insisting upon the aspirant's requirement to have a teacher and to submit to that teacher to approach God, Prabhupada quoted from the *Bhagavad-Gītā* on the role of the teacher (4.34) (Prabhupada 1997: 100). When it came to acceptance of Kṛṣṇa as Supreme Lord, he quoted Arjuna's acclamation of Kṛṣṇa (10.12) (Prabhupada 1997: 94–5). Again, when recommending devotion, he quoted from the text on the devotee of Kṛṣṇa as the best of all yogins (6.47) (Prabhupada 1997: 106–7). Clearly, Prabhupada cited the *Bhagavad-Gītā* fairly frequently, along with selected other texts, when setting out the beliefs and practices associated with Kṛṣṇa consciousness.

Prabhupada's approach to the *Bhagavad-Gītā* was determined by his insistence on what he called the 'Disciplic Succession' whereby the validity of an exposition of the text rested on a spiritual lineage traced back to Kṛṣṇa. Since his allegiance was to the Gauḍiya Vaiṣṇava tradition, this meant that he understood the *Bhagavad-Gītā* in terms of devotion to Kṛṣṇa. Insofar as he discussed Hinduism, he tended to reject or at least relativize the term, preferring to mention Vedic ideals while proposing an alternative definition of religion centred on worship of God. For him, the *Bhagavad-Gītā* was of foundational significance as containing Vedic insights. Accordingly, when setting out Vedic teachings, he often quoted from the *Bhagavad-Gītā* to support his arguments.

Sri Krishna Prem (1889–1965), once known as Ronald Nixon, was also affiliated with the Gauḍiya Vaiṣṇava tradition, in his case through initiation by Monica

Chakravarti which was subsequently confirmed by her becoming a renunciant in the Gauḍiya Vaiṣṇava saṃpradāya (lineage) as, following her example, he was also to do. However, while Prabhupada's association with this tradition was generally orthodox, Krishna Prem's was not, even if Prabhupada established an innovative structure for ISKCON by designating 11 gurus of Western origin just as Krishna Prem eventually succeeded his own guru as head of the ashram thus inaugurating a line of Western gurus.[3] In any event, Prabhupada had travelled from India to the West to preach the message of Kṛṣṇa consciousness, Krishna Prem had travelled from the West to India in search of spiritual wisdom. Krishna Prem shared Prabhupada's antipathy towards academic treatments of the *Bhagavad-Gītā* and, like him, insisted on the need for a teacher with authentic insight. Although he did give prominence to a personal conception of deity in Kṛṣṇa and devotion as a path, his emphasis was rather different. Hinduism did not seem to be much of an issue. In his view, all religions rested on the same truth while his writings returned again and again to the subjects of the guru, Kṛṣṇa and devotion. Indeed, in his capacity as guru, his view of religion was often expressed in terms of devotion to Kṛṣṇa. He was full of praise for the *Bhagavad-Gītā*, its importance extending beyond India to the world at large. He thus cited the *Bhagavad-Gītā* in support of various points but also asserted that the text was an Indian representation of universal reality.

Referring to the variety of interpretations of the *Bhagavad-Gītā* in the introduction to his own commentary, Krishna Prem was critical both of the partiality of Indian commentators who were more concerned with advocating a particular perspective than with determining the text's meaning and of Western scholars whose academic methodology led them to concentrate on the text's supposed contradictions (Krishna Prem 1988: xiii). In contrast, he maintained that 'the Gita is based on direct knowledge of Reality', as such neither sectarian affiliation nor critical questions had any importance (Krishna Prem 1988: xiv). His insistence that '[t]hose who know Reality belong to a Race apart' was consistent with the claim that spiritual progress depended upon having a teacher who knew the truth (Krishna Prem 1988: xiv). Accordingly, his commentary on the *Bhagavad-Gītā* was dedicated to his own guru, Sri Yashoda Mai (Krishna Prem 1988). The reason for his belief in the guru was explained in his commentary in terms of needing to find a teacher who embodied the teacher in the heart (4.34) (Krishna Prem 1988: 34). This was because, without the guidance of a human teacher, the counsel of the inner voice was all too easily ignored or mistaken (4.34) (Krishna Prem 1988: 35). He added his assurance that such a teacher could always be found, though only when one was prepared to dedicate oneself to the religious life (4.34) (Krishna Prem 1988: 35).

For Krishna Prem, the focus of the religious life was Kṛṣṇa. One aspect of his portrayal of Kṛṣṇa was shaped by his symbolic reading of the *Mahābhārata* as outlined in the prologomena to his commentary (Krishna Prem 1988: xx). When describing Arjuna's relationship with Kṛṣṇa, he stated that 'the inseparable friends, are in fact well known to represent *Nara* and *Nārāyaṇa*, the human soul and the Divine Soul, the *jīva* and *Ātman*' (Krishna Prem 1988: xxii). As well as offering an allegorical account of Kṛṣṇa, his commentary upheld Kṛṣṇa's supremacy. For example, he characterized Kṛṣṇa as 'beyond the opposites of personality and impersonality, form and formlessness, He is the highest and most excellent of all' (15.18) (Krishna Prem 1988: 154). Although favouring a personal conception of deity, in this way he did give consideration to other dimensions of ultimate reality, albeit identified with Kṛṣṇa, as was also evident in his treatment of the paths.

When it came to the paths, Krishna Prem attached great importance to devotion. He stated that '[l]ove is . . . the power by which we rise, whether that love be of the True or of the Beautiful or, best of all, of the One *Ātman*, Krishna' (8.22) (Krishna Prem 1988: 74–5). However, he had to deal with the relative merits of different paths to decide if devotion to the manifested divine delimited the prospects for spiritual fulfilment (12.1) (Krishna Prem 1988: 112–13). According to him, Kṛṣṇa's answer to this question was that both worshippers of the manifested and the unmanifested divine reached him (12.2) (Krishna Prem 1988: 113). The advocacy of devotion to the manifested divine was, then, inspired by the difficulty of concentrating on the unmanifested divine and the danger of succumbing to spiritual error through a failure of comprehension and an absence of love (12.4–5) (Krishna Prem 1988: 113–15). In contrast, devotion to the manifested divine was recommended as suiting human nature with its strong emotional quality, typified by love to which was attributed a transformative power (12.6–7) (Krishna Prem 1988: 114–15). Krishna Prem went on to explain Kṛṣṇa's instructions in respect of meditation, initially on his human form as that appealed to the disciple's heart, advising that if the performance of meditation proved too much the disciple should serve Kṛṣṇa in action inspired by love and, should this still be beyond the disciple's capacity, perform action selflessly as duty (12.8–12) (Krishna Prem 1988: 116–18). Krishna Prem maintained, therefore, that the fullness of Kṛṣṇa could be reached by no other means than devotion so that he referred to 'the innermost treasure of man, Sri Krishna's richest and intensest being, approachable alone through personal surrender and personal love' (18.66) (Krishna Prem 1988: 186–7). Despite giving some prominence to knowledge, Krishna Prem was clear that it led only to experience of Kṛṣṇa as Brahman, an incomplete revelation when compared with that of Kṛṣṇa's true nature, his revelation as personal divine in the human heart (18.66) (Krishna Prem 1988: 186–8).

Strikingly, Krishna Prem related that he had written his commentary on the *Bhagavad-Gītā* on the basis that it was 'a textbook of Yoga, a guide to the treading of the Path' (Krishna Prem 1988: xiv). In this context, he stressed not the individual paths but the one inner path that was their origin and source (Krishna Prem 1988: xiv). Hence the individual paths were understood to be partial expressions of the one path (4.3) (Krishna Prem 1988: 30). This stance meant that he hailed the yogin as the one who possessed the qualities of all the paths (6.46) (Krishna Prem 1988: 57–8). With Kṛṣṇa promising union with him to one who was dedicated to him in thought, feeling and deed, the disciple was urged to adopt a balanced approach 'avoiding any one-sided intellectualism, emotionalism, or activity, head, heart and hands all fixed on Him, filled with Him, transmuted to His nature' (9.34) (Krishna Prem 1988: 88–9). In such ways, Krishna Prem stressed the fundamental unity, interrelatedness and integration of the paths resting upon the oneness of the path from which they all derived.

It was this notion of the one path that set the tone for Krishna Prem's treatment of religion. The introduction to his commentary proclaimed that '[t]he Path is not the special property of Hinduism, nor indeed of any religion', proposing that it was present in all religions and even beyond their boundaries (Krishna Prem 1988: xv). His view was that this path was not the property of any religion because it was their common basis (Krishna Prem 1988: xvi). It was not Oriental in nature and thus inaccessible to the Occidental; rather it was available to anyone (Krishna Prem 1988: xvi). However, the aspirant who came to the path through a specific tradition would have to reject any notion of the uniqueness of his religion and the authority of its scriptures (Krishna Prem 1988: xvi). What was required was introspection since '[t]he only authority is within the Soul itself', a radical claim that could entail a rejection of religious precepts (Krishna Prem 1988: xvi). In general, Krishna Prem's view relativized all religions, including Hinduism, in comparison to the one path that informed and underlay them.

Krishna Prem made many of the same points in *Initiation into Yoga* with much the same effect. Here too, his argument relativized religions, including Hinduism, notably in his account of the attitude taken towards scripture. He began by stating that '[o]ne of the greatest obstacles to the finding of Truth is the belief current among religious people that Truth is written down in some book or books' (Krishna Prem 1976: 31). Instances of this included Hindu reverence for the *Vedas* as divinely composed when they were the work of human seers, and attribution to Vyāsa of a vast quantity of Purāṇic and Epic literature of various persuasions (Krishna Prem 1988: 31–2). Without devaluing such texts, his concern was to combat an uncritical acceptance of scriptures that obstructed spiritual progress (Krishna Prem 1988: 31). Explaining why it was necessary to be critical about scriptures, he argued that their authorship was unknown, their content subject to change through transmission, and also that it was necessary to distinguish between the experience and its expression as appropriate to a particular audience (Krishna Prem 1976: 31–2). The study of scripture could be beneficial, as it had been to him, but discernment was essential (Krishna Prem 1976: 32). In any case, the ultimate test of scriptures was the truth in the heart (Krishna Prem 1976: 33). Overall, on the premise that '[t]he Truth is within us', he envisaged books as being of use to the extent that 'they crystallize and make manifest what is... only obscurely known' (Krishna Prem 1976: 34–5). In this way, Krishna Prem appealed to a source of authority within the individual, rather than prioritizing the traditional sources of authority associated with religious orthodoxy.

In *Initiation into Yoga*, Krishna Prem also explained that there was 'a Path the treading of which leads to full knowledge of the Truth' (Krishna Prem 1976: 40). This path was present at all times and in all places, albeit known by different names and knowledge of it was preserved in various forms (Krishna Prem 1976: 40). Although the path could be suppressed by official opposition to its tenets, circumscribed by an elite view of religious experience or diminished by a scientific style of explanation, it was still in existence (Krishna Prem 1976: 41). Again, he made the point that the path was the foundation of all religions without having a real connection to any religion (Krishna Prem 1976: 41). The effect of this argument was to subordinate all religions to a more basic truth from which they sprang while denying any religion monopoly over this truth. This was how he accounted for the poor treatment meted out to teachers of the path by the established religious order (Krishna Prem 1976: 41). Taking 'the term Yoga... as a synonym for this Path', he emphasized its capacity for transformation though it did demand great effort and commitment (Krishna Prem 1976: 41–2).

Despite the fact that in works like this Krishna Prem was not seeking to expound Hinduism or even religion, his discussion of topics such as a reality, universally present and potentially knowable, had its impact on views of Hinduism in terms of the centrality of experience and the aim of spiritual realization. Key to this was his emphasis on the teacher. In *Initiation into Yoga*, for instance, he rejected the belief that all spiritual progress depended on having a human guru, however possibly beneficial (Krishna Prem 1976: 35). Progress could be made without a human teacher because '[t]he Guru is the pure Consciousness itself dwelling in the heart of every living being' (Krishna Prem 1976: 35). Yet a human guru could be of assistance in enabling the disciple to attend to the true teacher within and not the promptings of desire (Krishna Prem 1976: 36). In this there was no question of compulsion because the disciple had to make the choice to follow the path and, even before so doing, had to begin to practise self-control (Krishna Prem 1976: 37). Only when some measure of self-restraint had been achieved was the disciple prepared for the guidance of the human guru whereupon that guru would appear (Krishna Prem 1976: 37). Moreover, 'those who tread that Path exist and form a brotherhood,... perhaps the only true brotherhood' (Krishna Prem 1976: 41). Here, then, he extolled guruship but not in a sectarian context since the truth was not the preserve of any religion.[4]

Of course, as he wrote in a letter to his friend Dilip Kumar Roy, Krishna Prem's view of religion not only equated it with yoga but also defined it in terms of devotion to Kṛṣṇa where religion was 'the utter and entire giving of oneself to Sri Krishna' (Roy, D.K. 1968: 134). Another letter to the same correspondent, though referring to the existence of one yoga, also concentrated on Kṛṣṇa, advising Roy that '[a]ll else but Him is nothing, absolutely nothing' (Roy, D.K. 1968: 173, 175). Statements such as these show that Krishna Prem combined an advocacy of the ultimacy of Kṛṣṇa with the oneness of truth or reality.

The same universalizing tendency was evident when Krishna Prem explained the significance of the *Bhagavad-Gītā*. He noted the text's authority in India where 'it is revered by Hindus of all schools of thought' and its popularity in the West where '[m]any have come to value it as one of the world's great spiritual classics and not a few take it as their guide to the inner life' (Krishna Prem 1988: xiii).

Just as the path was not particular to Hinduism or any other religion, the *Bhagavad-Gītā* was both 'a definitely Hindu book' and 'capable of being a guide to seekers all over the world' (Krishna Prem 1988: xv). Certainly the *Bhagavad-Gītā* portrayed the path in an Indian form but the path was universal (Krishna Prem 1988: xv–xvi). Likewise, as truth was eternal, the *Bhagavad-Gītā* could be interpreted without reference to the past (Krishna Prem 1988: xiv). Accordingly, Krishna Prem's commentary was written by a seeker for other seekers, the text retaining its relevance to spiritual aspirants in all ages and from all backgrounds (Krishna Prem 1988: xiv).

Therefore, the *Bhagavad-Gītā* was a point of reference in Krishna Prem's letters and other works. On the theme of yoga, writing to Roy, he quoted from the text the statement that '[e]ven the seeker after Yoga transcends the *Vedas*' (Roy, D.K. 1968: 115). On much the same lines, he wrote in *Initiation into Yoga* that the one prepared to embark upon the spiritual life could be confident that 'as Sri Krishna teaches in the Gitā, even the seeker after yoga goes far beyond the hopes and fears of ordinary religion' (Krishna Prem 1976: 54). There again, in his commentary on the *Bhagavad-Gītā*, he denied that the text was either disordered or selective, stating that '[i]t aims at setting forth the Yoga or Path to the Goal as a coherent whole' (3.1) (Krishna Prem 1988: 19–20). The significance of this was set out in Kṛṣṇa's declaration that what he was teaching Arjuna he had taught previously (4.1) (Krishna Prem 1988: 29). It was a form of the 'Eternal Wisdom', the criterion by which all teaching was to be assessed and the source of all religions, identified with Kṛṣṇa as its incarnation revealing 'that which is hidden in all mere "teaching," the ultimate Mystery of His own Divine Being' (4.1, 3) (Krishna Prem 1988: 30). In this way, citing the *Bhagavad-Gītā* enabled Krishna Prem to substantiate his arguments, expounding the text in the light of his general theories hence as both universal in scope and connected with Kṛṣṇa.

Krishna Prem had an experiential emphasis consistent with his view of the teacher's vital role as well as a focus upon devotion to Kṛṣṇa as a personal deity, albeit with some variety in his account of Kṛṣṇa and the paths. Without concentrating on Hinduism, he described all religions as deriving from one source and being essentially the same. Yet, on occasion, he defined religion as devotion to Kṛṣṇa. For him, the *Bhagavad-Gītā* was a Hindu text of universal value. There was one path to one truth, as the *Bhagavad-Gītā* proved, equating Kṛṣṇa with ultimate reality.

Sri Chinmoy (1931–), named by his parents as Chinmoy Kumar Ghose, differed from Krishna Prem since he was Indian, not Western, by birth and his ministry was in the West, not in India. Moreover, notwithstanding other tendencies, Krishna Prem was affiliated with the Gauḍiya Vaiṣṇava tradition while Chinmoy's religious background and education was in the Sri Aurobindo Ashram.[5] In common with Krishna Prem, Chinmoy attached great importance to the *Bhagavad-Gītā* and relativized the significance of conventional religious labels such as Hinduism. More generally, he adopted an unorthodox approach to the religious life, embracing creativity and physical fitness expressed in the arts and athletic prowess respectively. Chinmoy was unimpressed by an academic approach to the *Bhagavad-Gītā* because its teaching was to be lived under a teacher's guidance. When interpreting the *Bhagavad-Gītā*, he did give some prominence to devotion to Kṛṣṇa as a personal deity though he did not exclude impersonal notions of divinity or other paths. Discussing religion, he maintained that religions were one, just as the divine was one, though he subordinated religion to spirituality. Thus, for him, Hinduism as an identity had to be transcended. He praised the *Bhagavad-Gītā* as both Hindu in origin and significant to humanity as a whole, going so far as to describe it as unique. Consequently, he regarded the *Bhagavad-Gītā* as embodying the insights of other scriptures and epitomizing spiritual realization.

One of the 'Stories from the Gita' indicated Chinmoy's attitude towards academic knowledge of the text. In 'The Scholar Came to His Senses', he told of the encounter between a brāhman and a scholar in which the latter offered his help to the former who was crying and clasping a copy of the *Bhagavad-Gītā* (Chinmoy 1973: 159). The scholar had supposed that the brāhman's reaction was due to his inability to understand the text and that he could be of some assistance but the brāhman explained that he was crying because 'I see my Lord in all the pages' (Chinmoy 1973: 159). In response to this, the scholar, in the words of the story's title, came to his senses.

Such an anti-academic bias was accompanied by a stress on the guru, notably Kṛṣṇa as guru. In another of the stories that were published along with his commentary on the *Bhagavad-Gītā*, 'Krishna, the Eternal Mystery', Chinmoy began by describing Kṛṣṇa as a teacher; as the counsellor of the Pāṇḍavas, Kṛṣṇa not only urged Arjuna to take part in the battle but instructed him in 'the spiritual life' (Chinmoy 1973: 140, 144). It was in this context that Chinmoy referred to Kṛṣṇa's declaration that he would incarnate himself whenever evil was on the rise and good was on the decline as among the key verses of the *Bhagavad-Gītā* (4.7) (Chinmoy 1973: 144–5). Such points as these were made in Chinmoy's commentary on the *Bhagavad-Gītā* too. For instance, while scholars argued over academic theories, he insisted that the real aspirant 'prays to the Lord Krishna to have the Gita as his personal experience' (13) (Chinmoy 1973: 97). Continuing, he asserted that '[t]he devotee needs a Guru', just as Arjuna needed Kṛṣṇa, also stressing that in the final analysis the true guru was God (13) (Chinmoy 1973: 98). This already indicates something of his focus on the personal nature of deity through devotion and the devotee's personal relationship with the divine.

Chinmoy explained that Arjuna knew Kṛṣṇa in different capacities – as his cousin, his friend, his teacher and his Lord (4) (Chinmoy 1973: 35). He stated that Kṛṣṇa was a full avatāra, an incarnation in whom ultimate reality was fully manifested (4) (Chinmoy 1973: 38). Kṛṣṇa as the supreme being was beyond the opposites of form and formlessness, personality and impersonality (15) (Chinmoy 1973: 106–7). Dealing with the respective merits of two paths, meditation and devotion, the former directed towards the impersonal, the latter towards the personal, divine, Chinmoy cited Kṛṣṇa's answer to Arjuna's question that both paths led to the same goal but that meditation was more difficult than devotion (12) (Chinmoy 1973: 90–1). Explaining this, he emphasized the difficulty of focusing the mind for meditation when its object was not manifested, far easier to be devoted to the manifested though eventually love of form should be superseded (12) (Chinmoy 1973: 91–2).

On this basis, Chinmoy's support for devotion can be understood. He stated that all of Kṛṣṇa's teachings were aimed at the achievement of the same goal but, because human beings differed in temperament, this complicated Arjuna's choice of path (5) (Chinmoy 1973: 45). However, the greater ease and accessibility of devotion as a path led him to extol this path: he wrote that devotion alone was sufficient (8) (Chinmoy 1973: 67); he wrote that the closest relationship was between devotee and deity (10) (Chinmoy 1973: 77); and he also wrote that devotion was the only way to win Kṛṣṇa (11) (Chinmoy 1973: 89). This commentary was but one of many works of various kinds including commentaries on the *Vedas* and *Upaniṣads*, added to which Chinmoy gave interviews and made other public pronouncements. His interpretation of the *Bhagavad-Gītā* featured in these works as an integral part of his ideas about Hindu scripture, Hinduism and associated subjects.

A volume that collected together commentaries on the *Vedas*, the *Upaniṣads* and the *Bhagavad-Gītā*, its title describing them as '[t]he Three Branches of India's Life-Tree', was prefaced with a short verse that subordinated scriptural study to God-realization (Chinmoy 1996). This matched Chinmoy's own priorities since to realize God was to embody the scriptures. Scriptures were important, though what mattered more was experience. Indeed, when commenting on the *Vedas* and the *Upaniṣads*, he made more general observations about openness and inclusivity transgressing the boundaries of religions. For instance, from 'Intuition-Light from the Vedas' he derived the message of the truth as one yet known in different ways by different aspirants, a message he regarded as representative of Indian religiosity in its acceptance of other religions as valid paths to the goal (*Ṛg Veda* 1.164.46) (Chinmoy 1996: 30–31). This stress on tolerance and respect that eschewed exclusive truth claims was also evident in a discussion of the *Upaniṣads* entitled 'The Crown of India's Soul' where he illustrated spiritual qualities associated with the *Upaniṣads*, not just with Hindu saints and sages, but with Jesus Christ and the Buddha (Chinmoy 1996: 80). There was no sense, then, in which Hinduism had a monopoly over spiritual greatness.

This probably accounted for Chinmoy's ambivalence about Hinduism. Hence, when interviewed by *Hinduism Today*, he responded to the question whether he was a Hindu with some reservation, affirming that he was a Hindu in the sense of an ordinary affiliation but denying it in the sense of an ultimate ambition (Chinmoy 1994). The answer he gave to his interviewer was that 'Hinduism is a home' while 'real religion is the heart home', so from the standpoint of the supreme spiritual quest he was not a Hindu, rather 'a seeker of Truth, a lover of God' (Chinmoy 1994). Moreover, he likened all religions to homes, places where one lives, and prayer and meditation to a school one attends under the tutorship of the divine (Chinmoy 1994).

Chinmoy's official website contains further information on a range of topics. Exploring the meaning and relationship of 'Religion and Spirituality', Chinmoy argued that God was one though apprehended differently (Chinmoy 2002e). On this basis, he asserted that all religions were true, each expressing the truth in its own terms (Chinmoy 2002e). In his view, religions shared the same objective of realizing the truth and, while there might be disagreements as to which was best, these would be resolved on reaching the final goal (Chinmoy 2002e). Moreover, he insisted that '[i]n Truth there is no conflict; Truth or God-realisation transcends all religions' (Chinmoy 2002e). In the process, he distinguished between what he called true and false religion, the former characterized by its universality and tolerance, the latter by its exclusivity and intolerance (Chinmoy 2002e). This distinction was drawn on the grounds that all religions were worshipping the same God, aimed at the same target, even if this reality was not recognized by all religions (Chinmoy 2002e). However, in order to come to the understanding that all religions were true, spirituality was required since spirituality facilitated the identification with, as well as the vision of, reality (Chinmoy 2002e). Religion thus informed by spirituality lost any sectarian spirit, accordingly, '[w]hen a religion comes to realise that all religions form one eternal religion, . . . then that religion is perfect' (Chinmoy 2002e). Indeed, he judged such an outlook had God's approval (Chinmoy 2002e). Further, other observations about spirituality on his webpages, a term apparently preferable to religion, echoed many of the ideas Chinmoy expressed in his commentary on the *Bhagavad-Gītā*.

For example, Chinmoy explained the advantages of having a guru, observing that it was sensible to learn from another 'the easiest, safest and most effective path to the goal' (Chinmoy 2002b). Further, when he described the divine, he did so in terms of the personal images of parenthood, 'our Divine Father and our Divine Mother', and the associated qualities, both masculine such as wisdom and feminine such as love (Chinmoy 2002a). Although he was clear that the personal and impersonal were aspects of the same God who encompassed both, he reiterated that 'it is easier to approach God in His personal aspect' and at the same time insisted that it was a mistake to esteem the formless more highly than the form (Chinmoy 2002d). Moreover, in like manner, he emphasized that '[o]ur path is basically the path of the heart and not the path of the mind', on the grounds that the mind was subject to doubt and confusion whereas the heart was full of love (Chinmoy 2002c). These web pages show that Chinmoy's commentary on the *Bhagavad-Gītā*, at least in respect of the guru, the personal deity and devotion, was typical of his general stance.[6]

In the introduction to Chinmoy's commentary on the *Bhagavad-Gītā*, he hailed the text, among other things, as 'God's Vision immediate' and 'God's Reality direct' (Chinmoy 1973: xi). Contrasting perspectives on the text, he attributed to others the belief that the *Bhagavad-Gītā* was 'a Hindu book' while in his opinion it was 'the Light of Divinity in humanity' (Chinmoy 1973: xi). In poetic language, he described '[t]he inspiration of Hinduism' as 'the Soul-Concern of the Gita', '[t]he aspiration of Hinduism' as 'the Blessing-Dawn of the Gita' and '[t]he emancipation of Hinduism' as 'the Compassion-Light of the Gita' (Chinmoy 1973: xv). However, this did not mean that the *Bhagavad-Gītā* belonged solely to Hinduism (Chinmoy 1973: xv). On the contrary, it belonged to the world and, just as the New Testament was the West's gift to the East, the *Bhagavad-Gītā* was the East's gift to the West (Chinmoy 1973: xv).

Within a Hindu context, Chinmoy referred to the *Bhagavad-Gītā* as 'the epitome of the Vedas' and 'the purest milk drawn from the udders of the most illumining Upanishads' (Chinmoy 1973: xvii). In a wider context, he described the *Bhagavad-Gītā* as 'unique' and 'the Scripture of scriptures' because it upheld the value of true devotion (Chinmoy 1973: xvi). Thus he praised the *Bhagavad-Gītā* both as containing the essence of the *Vedas* and the *Upaniṣads* and as constituting the best of scriptures. The *Bhagavad-Gītā* was also extolled as a declaration of Kṛṣṇa, a guide to realization and an account of spirituality.

In 'The King', a series of short spiritual sayings appended to his commentary on the *Bhagavad-Gītā*, Chinmoy showed how the text revealed Kṛṣṇa as divine and provided for humanity's growth and progress. Using the image of a door for Kṛṣṇa, the *Bhagavad-Gītā* was the key to the door (Chinmoy 1973: 124). Moreover, the *Bhagavad-Gītā* offered solutions to the problems of life and helped to raise the consciousness of bliss (Chinmoy 1973: 125). Writing in the introduction to his commentary, Chinmoy related that the *Bhagavad-Gītā* set forth yoga which he defined as 'the union of the finite with the infinite', proclaiming that the text contained 'the soul-wisdom, the heart-love, the mind-knowledge, the vital-dynamism and the body-action' (Chinmoy 1973: xviii). Thus the significance of the *Bhagavad-Gītā* lay in large part in the manner in which it promoted spiritual transformation (Chinmoy 1973: xviii). Turning to the main text of his commentary, he began by examining the meanings of dharma and, on the grounds that one of these meanings was religion, he emphasized that there was only one religion because religion was concerned with realization of the self and the divine, which in any case were synonymous (1) (Chinmoy 1973: 1–2). Accordingly, he referred to the *Bhagavad-Gītā* as 'an ocean of spirituality' and 'the revelation of spirituality' (15; 18) (Chinmoy 1973: 104, 119). The importance of the *Bhagavad-Gītā* was, then, established by reference to Hinduism through its scriptures and by appeal to the text's broader audience as well as by the presence of themes that ran through all his works.

Chinmoy did not approve of a scholarly perspective on the *Bhagavad-Gītā*, advocating instead that it should be the focus of spiritual development best secured by having a guru. Devotion to Kṛṣṇa as a personal deity had pride of place in his commentary on the grounds that this was easier than approaching the divine as impersonal through the power of the mind, all the while allowing for a range of views and a variety of paths. Perhaps typically, he tended to regard religion as essentially one; however, in some instances he contrasted true and false religion and, notably, religion and spirituality. Insofar as this had a bearing on Hinduism, he was ambivalent about a Hindu identity since it did not relate to the true religious quest. He saw the *Bhagavad-Gītā* as important for Hinduism and for humanity as a whole. His commentary on the *Bhagavad-Gītā*, together with prefatory and appended sections, not only located the text in the context of the *Vedas* and *Upaniṣads* but also in the wider context of a teaching to the world. Indeed, when upholding the *Bhagavad-Gītā*'s importance, he did so in terms of Kṛṣṇa's divinity and the way in which it satisfied humanity's needs as well as by addressing the issues of realization and spirituality.

Maharishi Mahesh Yogi (1917 [alt. 1911 or 1918]–), earlier known as Mahesh Prasad Varma (or alternatively, J.N. Srivastava), was, like Chinmoy, an Indian by birth with a ministry to the West. However, his religious background was in the Advaitin tradition of Śaṅkara as a disciple of Swami Brahmananda Saraswati, the Śaṅkarācarya of Jyothir Math.[7] His commentary on the *Bhagavad-Gītā*, covering only the first third of the text, facilitated a more monistic, more knowledge-centred, interpretation than that advanced by Chinmoy and, indeed, Krishna Prem and Prabhupada. Further, rather than just being an exponent of a spiritual philosophy, he was associated with a spiritual technique, Transcendental Meditation, that was represented as the fulfilment of all religions. Maharishi was very critical of other commentaries on the *Bhagavad-Gītā* for failing to give a faithful account of its true meaning, taking as his model Śaṅkara whose ideas, he insisted, had been misinterpreted. He too underlined the importance of having a teacher though, reflecting his Advaitin credentials, he gave more prominence to the impersonal absolute and also to knowledge. Nevertheless, if his assertion of the superiority of the impersonal absolute over the personal deity was classically Advaitin, his understanding of knowledge and its relationship with action and devotion was markedly different from conventional readings of Śaṅkara's philosophy. He concentrated on religions having a common core, attaching little significance to differences between religions or different religious labels such as 'Hindu'. His own teaching, Transcendental Meditation, was advocated as fulfilling all religions but, when working within a Hindu frame of reference, he did refer to Vedic wisdom and the six orthodox schools of thought. He also discussed the role of the guru, the impersonal nature of the divine and the proper understanding of the process of spiritual development. He observed that the *Bhagavad-Gītā* was of value to everyone as a guide to life. Calling it a 'Scripture of Yoga', he found in it the solution to humanity's spiritual crisis that summed up the *Vedas*, traditional Indian philosophical systems and also Transcendental Meditation.

In the introduction to his commentary, Maharishi acknowledged that the *Bhagavad-Gītā* had inspired more commentaries than any other scripture but asserted that no commentary had yet done it justice (Maharishi 1990: 19). Alleging that past commentators had not identified 'the very essence of this ancient wisdom' linked with 'one simple technique', he observed that he had written his commentary 'to present that key to mankind and preserve it for generations to come' (Maharishi 1990: 20). He argued that it was necessary to expound the *Bhagavad-Gītā* in relation to the four levels of consciousness, ranging from ordinary consciousness through transcendental and cosmic levels of awareness to God-consciousness, and also in relation to the six systems, Nyāya, Vaiśeṣika, Sāṃkhya, Yoga, Karma Mīmāṃsā and Vedānta (Maharishi 1990: 20–1). Thus Maharishi advocated that there should be 24 commentaries – a number generated by requiring that four commentaries were written as appropriate to the different levels of consciousness and that each of these was commented upon by each of the six different systems (Maharishi 1990: 20–1). Only when the *Bhagavad-Gītā* was interpreted in the light of the four levels of consciousness could it 'present a straight path to the seeker and bring him the profound wisdom of this practical philosophy' (Maharishi 1990: 20). Only when these commentaries were themselves interpreted in the light of the six systems was it possible to explain 'the complete significance of the Bhagavad-Gita' (Maharishi 1990: 21). This commentary was to serve as the basis for these other commentaries and, though he expressed the intention of writing these should there be sufficient time to do so, he explained that the spiritual need was too great to brook delay in publishing his present work (Maharishi 1990: 21). Moreover, Maharishi stressed that this commentary was composed after its technique of spiritual regeneration had proved beneficial to people from all backgrounds, hence a truth accessible to all whatever their religion or culture (Maharishi 1990: 21).

Nevertheless, this universal truth was basically predicated upon Advaitin teachings so that Maharishi described his commentary on the *Bhagavad-Gītā* as a supplement to Śaṅkara's commentary (Maharishi 1990: 21). Moreover, Maharishi's commentary was dedicated to his own teacher, Swami Brahmananda Saraswati, who stood in the lineage of Śaṅkara and was described in the preface as the inspiration of the commentary as well as the embodiment of Śaṅkara's 'head and heart' (Maharishi 1990: 16). One reason for this focus upon Swami Brahmananda Saraswati was Maharishi's insistence that the authentic insights of Śaṅkara had been lost but that his guru had been able to revive Śaṅkara's true teaching (Maharishi 1990: 16). Thus Maharishi could declare that his commentary was concerned to reveal the real meaning and implications of the *Bhagavad-Gītā* (Maharishi 1990: 17). He made this declaration on the grounds that his commentary was informed by his own guru's instruction, itself a return to Śaṅkara's original teaching, entailing the recovery of Śaṅkara's unified vision from the false and fragmentary account so often given of his philosophy (Maharishi 1990: 16).

Maharishi's commentary on the *Bhagavad-Gītā* reiterated the importance of lineage in the transmission of teaching and also the relationship between guru and disciple. For example, Maharishi related how Kṛṣṇa telling Arjuna that previously the same instruction had been given to Vivasvat was enough to assure Arjuna of its origin (4.1) (Maharishi 1990: 254–5). Or again, when Arjuna asked Kṛṣṇa to instruct him, Maharishi stated that, as soon as Arjuna was ready to become a disciple, Kṛṣṇa became his guru (2.7) (Maharishi 1990: 84–5). The claim that Maharishi's own commentary had a special status arising out of its link to Śaṅkara through Maharishi's guru, the then Śaṅkarācarya, was therefore made in a context that upheld the teacher as a decisive influence on the individual's spiritual growth. The significance of Śaṅkara, albeit understood in an unconventional manner that rejected most accounts of his philosophy, was reflected in Maharishi's discussion of the nature of divinity and the conduct of the religious life.

Maharishi's understanding of the nature of divinity emerged when he explored the theme of spiritual development from transcendental to cosmic to God-consciousness (6.29–32) (Maharishi 1990: 441–50). Here he referred to Brahman both in terms of unity and diversity, observed that the relationship between the unmanifested and the manifested would become clear, pointed to the harmony between the impersonal absolute and the personal deity and, in respect of the ultimate level of consciousness, stated that the influence of devotion to the personal deity was superseded by the sense of the identification of the self with the divine (6.29–32) (Maharishi 1990: 442, 444, 448). He suggested that the highest form of spiritual realization was realization of 'the supreme oneness of life in terms of one's own Self' (6.32) (Maharishi 1990: 449). Here were strong echoes of the Brahman-Ātman identity though he did hold together the personal and impersonal conceptions of godhead.

Maharishi's understanding of the conduct of the religious life was one in which knowledge was central but, just as he combined the personal and the impersonal, he emphasized the complementarity of knowledge and action and the integration of knowledge with devotion. Commenting on Kṛṣṇa's mention of two paths for two types of people, knowledge for the contemplative and action for the active, Maharishi explained that 'the state of transcendental consciousness, or Yoga' developing into cosmic consciousness through thought was the path of knowledge and through work was the path of action (3.3) (Maharishi 1990: 183). Indeed, in one respect knowledge too could be defined in terms of action, though in this case the action was mental (Maharishi 1990: 184). Certainly knowledge and action were regarded as equally effective, albeit suited to specific lifestyles, that of the renunciant and householder respectively (Maharishi 1990: 185). Maharishi explained the part played by devotion when describing the transition from cosmic to God-consciousness. In this context, he indicated that Kṛṣṇa stressed 'the importance of gaining knowledge of Unity in God-consciousness which results from devotion in the state of cosmic consciousness' (4.35) (Maharishi 1990: 306). This development involved a transition from duality to unity, the former associated with the distinction between the self and action, the latter with the experience of everything in God, effected by devotion and constituted by knowledge of identity of the self and the divine (4.35) (Maharishi 1990: 306–7). Continuing, Maharishi differentiated between two states, seeing all beings in the self and then seeing the self in the divine (4.35) (Maharishi 1990: 307). The culmination of spiritual progress was thus 'when life is dominated by the light of knowledge, the light of awareness of life's Unity in God-consciousness, which establishes eternity in the ephemeral world' (4.35) (Maharishi 1990: 307–8). Such an account, rejecting the separation of knowledge and devotion and preference for a renunciant over an activist ethic, suggested something of the approach he took towards Śaṅkara's ideas as having been misunderstood.

Maharishi's perspective on Śaṅkara also related to the view he took about religion and the religions. Writing in *The Science of Being and the Art of Living*, he asserted that '[r]eligion provides a practical way to the realisation of the supreme reality brought to light by philosophy' (Maharishi 1966: 255). However, he was critical of the failure of religions to live up to their own teachings, presenting an unflattering comparison between a lifeless corpse and the current state of religion when its true spirit had been lost (Maharishi 1966: 256). For him, what was at the centre of religion was an experience of fulfilment and this was where he believed that Transcendental Meditation was useful since through its practise members of all religions could attain God-consciousness (Maharishi 1966: 257). He referred to Transcendental Meditation as 'the fulfilment of every religion', maintaining that it was an original part of each religion that had been lost over time (Maharishi 1966: 259). Attaching priority to realization from which everything else would flow, he regarded this as the basis of the religious life (Maharishi 1966: 259). He advocated that people belonging to all religions should practise Transcendental Meditation, being of the view that they could do so while retaining their existing religious affiliations since Transcendental Meditation was the essence of every faith (Maharishi 1966: 260).

Overall, Maharishi's argument was that religious affiliation was irrelevant – what was relevant was the true principle of religion (Maharishi 1966: 261). Accordingly, he attached no importance to labels such as Hindu from the perspective of God-consciousness, arguing that the aim was 'a life of complete integration' and that this could be achieved through practising Transcendental Meditation (Maharishi 1966: 261). He was convinced that Transcendental Meditation was consistent with and promotive of all religions, the means by which the highest state of realization could be achieved and thereby the consummation of the religious quest (Maharishi 1966: 262). Of course, much of what he wrote did relate to Hinduism, whether or not he used the term, but he aligned Transcendental Meditation with the true interpretation of the Advaitin tradition taught by his own guru (Maharishi 1990: 16).

In the preface to his commentary, Maharishi explained the significance of Śaṅkara in a broad historical survey.[8] He began with the *Vedas* and their message concerning ultimate reality, the nature of the world and the prospects for spiritual progress (Maharishi 1990: 9). In the course of time, however, this Vedic revelation needed to be renewed. Thus Kṛṣṇa delivered his teaching to Arjuna in the *Bhagavad-Gītā* but his message about the conduct of the integrated spiritual life was also obscured by misinterpretation (Maharishi 1990: 9–10). This was why the Buddha was needed, though again his followers failed to appreciate the true nature of his teaching when they isolated action from realization (Maharishi 1990: 10–11). The subsequent revival of the truth was brought about by Śaṅkara who 'restored the wisdom of the Absolute and established it in the daily life of the people' (Maharishi 1990: 11). As such, Maharishi regarded Śaṅkara's message as essentially the same as that proclaimed by Kṛṣṇa and the *Vedas* and, in common with these earlier revelations, his teaching was distorted by a renunciant stress on knowledge (Maharishi 1990: 11–13). This loss of holism led to the view that knowledge and devotion were distinct paths, thereby promoting the rise of devotional sects, and that the spiritual ideal was renunciation, thereby producing a confusion in which the path of action was deprived of its basis in realization (Maharishi 1990: 13–15).

This was all the more important because, in Maharishi's judgement, Śaṅkara's teaching was acknowledged to constitute 'the centre of Indian culture' (Maharishi 1990: 15). The implications of a failure to remain faithful to Śaṅkara's legacy were thus far-reaching, encompassing religion and philosophy as a whole (Maharishi 1990: 15–16). This was why Swami Brahmananda Saraswati, his own guru, had a pivotal part to play as an authentic exponent of Śaṅkara's ideas 'able to revive the philosophy of the integrated life in all its truth and fullness' (Maharishi 1990: 16). Moreover, Maharishi appealed to Indian culture and civilization, calling India a country that prized truth and Indians a people who cherished the divine, witness to repeated revivals of the truth (Maharishi 1990: 16–17). Transcendental Meditation was, then, one in a long line of movements in Indian history 'aiming at the revival of true life and living' (Maharishi 1990: 17). Throughout, Maharishi associated Transcendental Meditation with Śaṅkara's Advaita Vedānta, albeit a distinctive version of that philosophy.

However, Transcendental Meditation's frame of reference was far wider than Hinduism since, despite its association with Śaṅkara's Advaita Vedānta, it was the shared basis of all religions. Notwithstanding this, insofar as Maharishi did use Hindu terminology and concepts, especially as a commentator on the *Bhagavad-Gītā*, he referred to Vedic wisdom and the six orthodox schools of thought. For example, he noted that 'Vedic wisdom comprises various expressions of Reality, as seen from different points of view and taught by different schools of thought' (2.53) (Maharishi 1990: 147). More generally, the beliefs and practices that he recommended in accounts of Transcendental Meditation could also be read as applicable to Hinduism. Thus, in *The Science of Being and Art of Living*, when setting out the principles of Transcendental Meditation, he declared that it was necessary to receive instruction from a teacher who had mastered the technique and who had been authorized to teach by his own movement (Maharishi 1966: 58–9). In the same volume, he expressed his gratitude for the teaching he had received from his own teacher (Maharishi 1966: 270). More strikingly, he discussed at some length the nature of the godhead in relation to the paths by which God was realized.

Discussing God, Maharishi identified both the impersonal and the personal conceptions of divinity (Maharishi 1966: 271): the former was described as being 'without attributes, qualities or features, because all attributes, qualities and features belong to the relative field of life, and the impersonal God is of absolute nature' (Maharishi 1966: 272); whereas the latter 'necessarily has form, qualities, features and likes and dislikes; and, having the ability to command the entire existence of the cosmos, the process of evolution and all in creation, the personal God is Almighty' (Maharishi 1966: 276). Thus God-realization could mean realization of either the impersonal or personal divine though there was no doubt that the impersonal was higher than the personal and, consequently, realization of the impersonal divine was at the level of transcendental consciousness while realization of the personal divine was at the level of ordinary consciousness (Maharishi 1966: 280). In this respect, Maharishi's debt to Śaṅkara was evident since he upheld the impersonal absolute over personal deity.

When Maharishi enumerated five paths by which the aspirant could achieve God-consciousness, his debt to Śaṅkara as conventionally interpreted was less evident for the obvious reason that he was critical of the partial and selective take on Śaṅkara's philosophy. Certainly, knowledge was included as one of the paths to realization of the impersonal divine, '[t]he psychological or intellectual approach', but there were other paths to this goal (Maharishi 1966: 281–2). These other paths were '[t]he emotional approach', '[t]he physiological approach', '[t]he mechanical approach' and '[t]he psycho-physiological approach' (Maharishi 1966: 282). What was more, he observed that to follow one of these paths would be enough as they were appropriate for people of different temperaments (Maharishi 1966: 282). His account of the intellectual path was progressive, beginning with discrimination of the real from the unreal, developing into reflection on the unchanging substratum of the changing creation and concluding with expression of the eternal principle of oneness in one's life (Maharishi 1966: 287). This was the first path he considered and at much greater length than the alternative approaches, but he was aware that it was not suitable for householders and alive to the problems caused by adopting this approach when still actively engaged in the world (Maharishi 1966: 289). Nevertheless, there was no sense in which knowledge was less effective than devotion or that these paths aimed at apparently different objects. Moreover, whatever path was taken, he maintained that Transcendental Meditation would prove to be beneficial (e.g. Maharishi 1966: 304).

Maharishi's commentary on the *Bhagavad-Gītā* addressed many of these issues. The view he expressed of the nature and implications of the *Bhagavad-Gītā* was certainly in line with his emphasis on realization. In the introduction to his commentary, he described the *Bhagavad-Gītā* as an eternal work of universal significance, providing guidance for life that brought individual fulfilment and social welfare (Maharishi 1990: 19). Calling the text 'the Scripture of Yoga, the Scripture of Divine Union', Maharishi defined its role as facilitating God-consciousness through providing teaching appropriate to every stage of spiritual progress (Maharishi 1990: 20). This emphasis on realization, which he believed characterized the *Bhagavad-Gītā*, was reiterated throughout his commentary where he emphasized the text's nature and purpose as a work of yoga (e.g. 1.28; 3.12) (e.g. Maharishi 1990: 50, 199). Furthermore, his treatment of the *Bhagavad-Gītā* related it, not only to his understanding of religion as concerned with realization, but also to Hindu ideas and institutions and the technique of Transcendental Meditation.

The relationship between the *Bhagavad-Gītā* and Hinduism, though not a concern of Maharishi's, can be deduced from his discussion of Vedic wisdom and the six orthodox schools of thought. Thus he explained that the *Vedas* set forth the means of attaining liberation including both action and knowledge, disciplines to which Kṛṣṇa referred in the *Bhagavad-Gītā* (2.42) (Maharishi 1990: 122–3). On this basis, he concluded that the *Bhagavad-Gītā* was 'the essence of the Vedas and the highway to the fulfilment of the Vedic way of life' (2.42) (Maharishi 1990: 123–4). There again, in his commentary on the text, he defined Yoga as the method of experiencing reality while Sāṃkhya was the theoretical formulation of reality, identifying the methodological and theoretical facets of knowing reality in Kṛṣṇa's teaching (2.39, cf. 2.12–15, 45–8) (Maharishi 1990: 116–17). Hence Maharishi observed that '[t]he Sankhya of the Bhagavad-Gita presents the principles of all the six systems of Indian philosophy, while the Yoga of the Bhagavad-Gita presents their practical aspects' (Maharishi 1990: 116–17). Just as the *Bhagavad-Gītā* could be related to Vedic wisdom and the six orthodox schools of thought and, by extension, to Hinduism, it could also be related to Transcendental Meditation, itself in some respects not easily separable from Hinduism or even from Hindu texts and philosophies.

References to Transcendental Meditation also ran through Maharishi's commentary on the *Bhagavad-Gītā*. For instance, he mentioned the teaching that it was through practising Transcendental Meditation that one could develop transcendental consciousness and, subsequently, cosmic and God-consciousness (6.45) (Maharishi 1990: 465). Another example, in a footnote to one of the appended sections, explained that Transcendental Meditation as a technique for realization constituted the text's main teaching (Maharishi 1990: 473). In such ways as these, the *Bhagavad-Gītā* was a key to the true understanding and conduct of the religious life.

Maharishi claimed to be offering an authentic interpretation of the *Bhagavad-Gītā* following in the tradition of Śaṅkara when properly understood, as it was under the guidance of his own teacher. He accepted neither the primacy of the personal deity nor that of the path of devotion; rather he extolled the impersonal absolute and refused to subordinate knowledge as a path. When it came to religion, what mattered most was realization. In comparison with this, specific traditions were of minor importance. Transcendental Meditation, he taught, was the fulfilment of all religions though his comments on Vedic wisdom and the six orthodox schools of thought had a bearing on views of Hinduism. In a more general sense, so did his advocacy of the role of the teacher and his discussion of the divine and the means by which humanity can achieve God-consciousness. For him, the *Bhagavad-Gītā* was of supreme significance, not simply for Hindus but for humanity. Its significance lay in its being a 'Scripture of Yoga' with a relationship to the *Vedas*, Indian philosophies and the technique of Transcendental Meditation at the core of all religions.

For all that there are commonalities between these contemporary teachers and movements – all recognize the *Bhagavad-Gītā* as important and none vests much significance in the category of Hinduism – the diversity of their thought underlines the dynamism and vitality of the tradition. Running contrary to the tendency to interpret modern Hinduism in accordance with neo-Vedāntic principles, only one of these figures is affiliated with Vedānta and even then in an unconventional sense. Moreover, the continuities with earlier teachers and movements are such that any attempt to marginalize or disparage them has much wider implications. On the contrary, not least in the involvement of Westerners, they represent significant trends in the universalizing of Hinduism in particular or religion in general.

Prabhupada focused on the *Bhagavad-Gītā* as a work praising Kṛṣṇa, its fundamental role signalled by his hailing it as Vedic in character; Vedic ideals, rather than Hinduism, framed his argument in which he defined religion in terms of the worship of God. Krishna Prem also regarded the *Bhagavad-Gītā* as a devotional and theistic work, albeit with a different emphasis; while sometimes he represented religion as worship of Kṛṣṇa, he stressed that all religions were fundamentally the same. Chinmoy adopted much the same position, favouring the personal conception of the divine and the devotional path; he too saw religions as basically unified and so had little interest in Hinduism. Maharishi was different in his focus upon the impersonal absolute and the importance he attached to knowledge; he located the unity of religions in Transcendental Meditation at the same time as referring to Vedic wisdom and Indian philosophies.

CONCLUSION

The role and importance of the *Bhagavad-Gītā* – global presence and contemporary media

Globalization is a much discussed feature of today's world where technological innovation, including improved communications technology, has facilitated an internationalization of culture alongside the internationalizing of economic interests, social trends and political developments. Although this internationalization is often equated with Westernization or even Americanization, the reality is much more diverse at least in its religious aspects. The presence of the *Bhagavad-Gītā* in a range of global contexts testifies to this, notably its prominence in published literature and various other contemporary media such as film, television and the internet, taking it far beyond its traditional place and portrayal.

Certainly the *Bhagavad-Gītā* has figured in the works of some major Western poets and writers over the last 200 years or so. For example, William Blake (1757–1827) knew Charles Wilkins' translation of the text and a strong case can be made out for the *Bhagavad-Gītā*'s teaching on the guṇas and the varṇas, coupled with the injunction to abide by one's own dharma, as having shaped the 'Bard's Song', a section of *Milton* likewise sung during an interregnum in epic action (Lindop forthcoming: 6–11). Samuel Taylor Coleridge (1772–1834) was also familiar with Wilkins' translation, as is evident from his unpublished writings and public speeches but, additionally, the influence of the *Bhagavad-Gītā* has been detected in poems such as 'On a Homeward Journey Upon Hearing of the Birth of a Son', 'Eolian Harp', 'Religious Musings' and 'Dejection: An Ode' (Muirhead 1930: 224–5, 283–4; Srivastava 2002: 198–202, 216–46). The narrative poem, *The Curse of Kehama*, by Robert Southey (1774–1843) quotes from Wilkins' translation in its preface when considering the depiction of the divine and in a number of footnotes on the nature of the soul, death and an end to reincarnation, memorial rites for the ancestors etc., but arguably its indebtedness to the *Bhagavad-Gītā* is more general (Southey 1844: 548, 553, 563, 594; Srivastava 2002: 259–74). Ralph Waldo Emerson (1803–82) was aware of both Wilkins' translation and Southey's poem and, if his reflections on the *Bhagavad-Gītā* tend to be found in his private papers, his poem 'Brahma' is strongly reminiscent of the text and, indeed, the parallel passage in the *Kaṭha Upaniṣad* (Packer 1985: 137–8; Sharpe 1985: 25; Srivastava 2002: 4).

Then again, T.S. Eliot (1888–1965) was fascinated by Kṛṣṇa's message of disinterested action, a theme examined in 'The Dry Salvages', one of his *Four Quartets*, and possibly also alluded to at the close of 'To the Indians who Died in Africa' (Donoghue 1969: 219–21; Eliot 1974: 231; Gardiner 1978: 56–7). Similarly, E.M. Forster (1899–1966) focused on the disinterested performance of action, linking this with the glorious vision of the divine in offering his own interpretation of the *Bhagavad-Gītā* in 'Hymn Before Action' (Das 1979: 210–12; Forster 1940: 328–30). Moreover, this rich and complex literary heritage has more recent counterparts.

A famous example of an artistic interpretation of the *Bhagavad-Gītā* occurs in Peter Brook's staging (and subsequent filming and televising) of the *Mahābhārata*. Brook's version of the *Mahābhārata* is based on a play by Jean-Claude Carrière that he translated into English for Anglophone performance. This play lasted about nine hours but he also produced a five-hour television film (now available on video and DVD, see Brook 1989) and a three-hour film for cinema release (O'Connor 1990: 24). In his foreword to the English version of the stage play, Brook recounts how the Sanskrit scholar, Philippe Lavastine, had told him and his collaborator, Carrière, stories from the epic (Brook 1988: xiii–xiv). This, as Brook recalls, led them to commit themselves to 'find a way of bringing this material into our world and sharing these stories with an audience in the West' (Brook 1988: xiv). Such statements as this point up the central tension in the project – the universal versus the Indian – reflected in many of Brook's pronouncements. Typical of this is his account of the aim of presenting the epic as being 'to celebrate a work which only India could have created but which carries echoes for all mankind' (Brook 1988: xvi). Thus, at the beginning of the play, Vyāsa tells the boy that his story is 'the poetical history of mankind' (Carrière and Brook 1988: 3), a declaration matched by an international polyglot cast and cross-cultural mode of performance that nevertheless sought to be evocative of India. However, the success of this undertaking has been challenged, not least by allegations of neo-colonialism levelled against the production on the grounds that this was an act of cultural appropriation or Orientalist misrepresentation of an Indian epic (Williams 1991: 24).

Criticisms of Brook's adaptation of the *Mahābhārata* often focus on the *Bhagavad-Gītā*. Indeed, considering that the *Bhagavad-Gītā*'s importance to Hindus and its significance to the ongoing action meant that it had to be included, 'Brook's elliptical treatment of the sequence has elicited a strong critical response' (Shevtsova 1991: 212). Rustom Bharucha, for instance, deplores 'a five-minute encapsulation of the *Bhagavad Gita*' that impoverishes the appreciation of Kṛṣṇa's teaching so that '[w]hat could have been a moment of revelation was reduced to banality' (Bharucha 1991: 232). Similarly, Gautam Dasgupta rejects the reduction of the epic to 'a compendium of martial legends' that leads to the *Bhagavad-Gītā* being 'rendered into whispered words never revealed to the audience' (Dasgupta 1991: 264). As these remarks suggest, the resulting dialogue is much shorter than the standard version with much of the instruction murmured by Kṛṣṇa in Arjuna's ear (Carrière and Brook 1988: 159–61). Hence there are only brief allusions to some of the *Bhagavad-Gītā*'s main themes (a passing reference to the paths of knowledge and action), demonstrating a marked preference for the epic and dramatic aspects of the dialogue, respectively associated with its martial setting (the injunction to fight underlined by the presence of the warriors on the battlefield) and the divine revelation (the theophany described by Arjuna followed by Kṛṣṇa's self-description) (Carrière and Brook 1988: 158–61). As well as cutting the greater proportion of the dialogue, that which remains is often reordered and rearranged giving a very different impression of the meaning and implications of the *Bhagavad-Gītā*; the overall effect is to foreground acting without attachment, confident that one can neither kill nor be killed and assured of Kṛṣṇa's love (Carrière and Brook 1988: 158–61). The result of such a reworking of the *Bhagavad-Gītā* has been hotly debated, yet for Brook, in his search for a universal theatre, it was a creative expression of a universal vision.

An even more radical transposition of the *Bhagavad-Gītā* for a Western audience is Steven Pressfield's 1995 novel, *The Legend of Bagger Vance: A Novel of Golf and the Game of Life*. This novel is set at an exhibition match held in 1931 on the Links at Krewe Island, Georgia. Playing in this match, together with the two greatest golfers of the period, is a local champion, Rannulph Junah (R. Junah, representing Arjuna), assisted by his caddie, Bagger Vance (Bhagavān, representing Kṛṣṇa). In this novel, Bagger Vance explains that '[t]he game [of golf] is a metaphor for the soul's search for its true ground and identity' where '[t]he search for the Authentic Swing is a parallel to the search for the Self' (Pressfield 1995: 127). Even so, a direct connection with the *Bhagavad-Gītā* is made only on a preliminary page of the novel by a quotation from the text that has Dhṛtarāṣṭra request Saṃjaya to tell him of the events that occurred when the Kauravas and the Pāṇḍavas met on the field of battle (Pressfield 1995).

Giving rise to a sense of familiarity is the martial dimension of the novel: not only is Junah a hero of the Great War whom Vance served as a driver, alluding to Kṛṣṇa's role as Arjuna's charioteer, but the golf course itself is described as the site of an ancient battle in which the protagonists had fought aeons earlier and Junah had begged Vance for mercy towards his enemies and allies alike but had been sent forth into the fight (Pressfield 1995: 38–9, 78–9, 151, 190–1, 265). More generally, Junah's feeling of futility and his appeal to Vance for guidance are reminiscent of Arjuna's desolation and his close friendship with Kṛṣṇa (Pressfield 1995: 99–102). Other parallels with the *Bhagavad-Gītā* can be found in the novel's central concerns. Accordingly, Vance asks Junah a series of questions about his identity intended to promote Junah's realization of his true nature, albeit couched in terms of playing golf (Pressfield 1995: 118–23). Most striking of all, perhaps, are Vance's proclamation of his mission, recalling Kṛṣṇa's declaration of the avatāra ideal, and Vance's exposition of three paths, recalling Kṛṣṇa's discourse on the paths of action, knowledge and devotion (Pressfield 1995: 76–7). As to the substitution of golf for spirituality, Vance himself explains that he does so on the grounds that '[i]n the East, men are not embarrassed to speak openly of the Self' whereas 'in the West, such piety makes people uncomfortable' hence '[t]hat is where golf comes in' (Pressfield 1995: 73). Certainly, in interviews, Pressfield has stated that the novel is an attempt to offer a contemporary version of the *Bhagavad-Gītā* (Rosen 2000: 18).

Pressfield's novel has inspired *Gita on the Green: The Mystical Tradition Behind Bagger Vance* by Steven Rosen, a book that makes explicit the Hindu religious element. Thus Rosen comments that 'for the real deal behind the Bagger Vance story, one would do well to go to the source – *Bhagavad-gita* – the original', continuing by calling the *Bhagavad-Gītā* 'the Holy One's hole in one' (Rosen 2000: 26). Rosen's book can, then, be seen as a form of commentary on the *Bhagavad-Gītā* that, following the lead of *The Legend of Bagger Vance*, explores its themes through golf. Identifying various links between golf and the Hindu tradition, the association of the deity Viṣṇu with the invention of the modern golf ball for instance, he also makes connections between golf and the *Bhagavad-Gītā* including the 18 holes of the golf course and the 18 chapters of the text (Rosen 2000: 15–16). He pursues deeper connections too. Not only does he refer to the *Bhagavad-Gītā* as '[t]he Song of the Perfect Caddie-Master' (and, indeed, the *Mahābhārata* as '[t]he Ultimate Playing Field') but he also describes his personal quest for truth leading him to the teachings of Prabhupada as '[m]y Search for "the Authentic Swing"', and expresses his criticism of commentators other than Prabhupada in terms of 'not seeing the Authentic Swing for the Inauthentic Field' (Rosen 2000: 27, 40–1, 52, 70). The result is a book that has been hailed by some reviewers as an innovative and entertaining take on the *Bhagavad-Gītā*, the review by Tamal Krishna Goswami quoted on the back cover likening its popularizing project to the popularizing of Zen Buddhism by Robert Pursig's *Zen and the Art of Motorcycle Maintenance*.

Pressfield's novel has also been turned into a film directed by Robert Redford that eschews explicit appeal to the Hindu tradition. Reviews of the film variously made little, if any, mention of a spiritual message (Lawrenson 2001), interpreted this message in a broad religious or philosophical sense (Ebert 2000; Turan 2000) or even expressed relief that the film did not reproduce what was regarded as the novel's New Age ethos as a variation on the theme of the *Bhagavad-Gītā* (Travers 2003). Redford's comments on the film, however, indicate that he was drawn to the story's mystical dimension and was aware of its mythological scope (Redford 2002). Yet, on the evidence of his production notes, Redford's acknowledgement of the spiritual aspect of the story did not extend to a discussion of the *Bhagavad-Gītā* as the basis for Pressfield's novel, preferring instead to emphasize how the golf match symbolized the universal human experience (Redford 2002).

A significant change is the portrayal of Vance as Junah's spiritual guide whom Redford decides to present in a trickster persona (Redford 2002). Other changes affect the relationship between Vance and Junah since Redford has them meet for the first time just before the golf match and, accordingly, their relationship lacks the sense of eternity, the cyclical nature of time and the shared destiny of the main characters through repeated reincarnations that characterize the novel

(Redford 2000). Still, there are resonances with the novel such as the use of special effects to convey an appreciation of nature and the oneness of existence as well as some new scenes that seem to echo the sentiments of the *Bhagavad-Gītā*, perhaps most forcefully when Junah rebukes a young boy for being ashamed that his father is sweeping the streets where the father's honour and integrity are a powerful testament to duty (Redford 2000). Yet, at times, in the absence of any indication to the contrary and consistent with the religious profile of the southern states of America, the film could be viewed in a Christian light (Redford 2000). Pressfield's novel has thus provoked very different responses, a book of spiritual exploration with a renewed stress on the *Bhagavad-Gītā* and a film adaptation from which the *Bhagavad-Gītā* has for the most part been excluded, both aimed at a Western audience.

The *Bhagavad-Gītā* has also acquired a position in a broader Western context, be it as an object of study in the curriculum or a source for New Age spirituality. The *Bhagavad-Gītā* has an important place in higher education as a set text for learning Sanskrit and a reference work for central concepts in Hinduism. In Britain, where Religious Education is compulsory in state schools, the School Curriculum and Assessment Authority's (now Qualifications and Curriculum Authority's) model syllabus *Living Faiths Today* features the *Bhagavad-Gītā* at key stages 3 (pupils aged 11–13 years) and 4 (pupils aged 14–16 years). At key stage 3, pupils are expected to consider the nature and role of Hindu sacred literature, in which context the syllabus lists the *Bhagavad-Gītā* before the *Mahābhārata* and the *Vedas*, and '[e]xplore some of Krishna's teaching on yoga within the Bhagavad Gita' as well as '[r]elate their own questions of meaning to teachings within the Bhagavad Gita' (SCAA 1994: 49). At key stage 4, the distinction between śruti and smṛti literature is drawn, citing the *Bhagavad-Gītā* as belonging to the latter category, and pupils are invited to '[i]nterview Hindus about their favourite passages within the Bhagavad Gita, and explore why it is so popular amongst Hindus' (SCAA 1994: 63). This syllabus clearly reflects the priority of the *Bhagavad-Gītā* in a textualized version of the tradition and illustrates that its popularity is taken for granted.

The *Bhagavad-Gītā* also plays a part in New Age belief and practice. One vehicle of its dissemination has been interest in yoga since this has exposed people to the teachings of the *Bhagavad-Gītā* as well as other yogic treatises. Further, Alice Bailey, an iconic New Age figure who channelled a Tibetan teacher, Djwahl Khul, recommended study of the *Bhagavad-Gītā* to a disciple in need of guidance (Bailey and Khul 1998a), also mentioning the text in a discussion of spiritual methods where it was described as having 'embodied... superlatively' what was called 'the way of the heart' and 'the Way of Love' (Bailey and Khul 1998b). Moreover, Wayne Dyer's classic New Age book, *Real Magic: Creating Miracles in Everyday Life*, includes the advice that readers should consult the *Bhagavad-Gītā* as a guide to 'real magic' (Dyer 1992: 17). Instances such as these demonstrate how the *Bhagavad-Gītā* has served as a source of inspiration in this individualized and eclectic form of spirituality.

Of course, the *Bhagavad-Gītā* has had historical importance in India and for Hindus as a focus for meditation and contemplation and an object of philosophical and theological thought, the anniversary of its advent thousands of years ago marked by the Gītā-jayānti festival celebrated on the eleventh day of the bright half of the month of Mārgaśirṣa. That said, there has been much development in the modern period – new insights, new observances and new representations. One aspect of this is the rise of visual representations of the *Bhagavad-Gītā* from the mid-eighteenth century onwards, located in the context of the text's transition from elite status to popular work (King, U. 1982: 150–2; 1987: 168–70). Illustrations of the *Bhagavad-Gītā* were first produced by painters in the court studios of North India (King, U. 1982: 150), an innovation speculatively explained by reference to the appeal of Arjuna as a warrior to Hindu princes seeking to define themselves as distinct from their Mughal rulers (King, U. 1987: 168). In any case, there is continuity between the imagery of the early manuscripts and later iconographic forms; these later forms also mirror the ideas and imperatives of their time, notably as representations of an activist ideology though there are also devotional and didactic trends (King, U. 1982: 157–9). Indeed, alongside their increase in number, there has been a proliferation in the type and purpose of illustrations, ranging from those found in publications of and about the *Bhagavad-Gītā* to devotional art and Gītā temples to greetings cards and ornaments and even to commercial advertisements (King, U. 1987: 174–9). The result has been a growing independence of the iconography (King, U. 1982: 160) where it features in both sacred and secular settings (King, U. 1987: 186).

Among the contemporary visual representations of the *Bhagavad-Gītā* are children's comics and storybooks. The most famous comics are probably those published in the *Amar Chitra Katha* ('immortal illustrated story') series established by Anant Pai of India Book House (Pritchett 1995: 76). This series has been characterized by an idealized version of India's past, a social conscience and a political vision of a unified multicultural India (Pritchett 1995: 105). It displays a great interest in the *Mahābhārata* as well as a decided preference for Kṛṣṇa with illustrations of Arjuna kneeling at Kṛṣṇa's feet on the field of battle prominent in the *Mahābhārata* mini-series (Pritchett 1995: 85, 96–7).

The *Amar Chitra Katha* version of the *Bhagavad-Gītā* is prefaced with a commendation by Swami Chinmayananda that endorses the comic genre as the means by which children can be influenced in positive ways, hailing Kṛṣṇa's teaching of Arjuna as ensuring material success and spiritual perfection (Chinmayananda 1977). The comic gives considerable weight to the epic context of the narrative and hence its martial qualities (Pai and Mulik 1977: 1–11, 22–3, 31). It also provides a fairly full rendition of the discourse within the limitations of its format; there are footnotes identifying jñāna-, bhakti- and karma-yogas, for example (Pai and Mulik 1977: 18, 21, 25). However, it excludes certain themes, such as the distinct duties of the four classes, and moves others, such as the declaration of the avatāra ideal that occurs here just before the theophany (Pai and

Mulik 1977: 14, 26–7). Something of the national significance of the *Bhagavad-Gītā* is suggested on the final page of the comic where there are pictures of great Indians past and present, encompassing religious figures from earlier eras as well as modern social activists and political leaders (Pai and Mulik 1977: 32).

Children's storybooks are other sources of knowledge and understanding of the *Bhagavad-Gītā*. Attractively illustrated and clearly expressed accounts, in much the same way as comics they tend to add interest and excitement by bringing the battle to the fore while expounding complex philosophical and theological concepts in an accessible way. Certain general trends do emerge, the distinction between soul and body, the quality of equanimity and the role of detached action among them. However, storybooks can exploit longer wordage than comics and so can explore ideas in more depth while still adopting a flexible attitude towards order and structure. Alongside the importance attached to building the character of their young readership, what becomes apparent, notwithstanding individual differences of emphasis and interpretation, is that there is often a juxtaposition of the Indian and the universal. Such a juxtaposition is evident in two examples, *The Gita* (*The Song of the Supreme Being*) published by Anada and *The Bhagwad-Gita* published by Dreamland: the preface to the former quotes both Mahatma Gandhi's and Aldous Huxley's praise for the text, describing the *Bhagavad-Gītā* as 'an ancient Indian classic of dynamic philosophy of eternal significance' (Nayak *et al.* 1984); the introductory sections of the latter not only relate the text to the *Upaniṣads* but also to seekers of different faiths, calling the *Bhagavad-Gītā* 'the divine gospel given in India for the world to all human-beings at all times and in all climes' (Gupta *et al.* 1977: 5–6). Comics and storybooks like these are part of Hindu religious nurture, inculcating pride in a rich cultural heritage, explaining fundamental norms and values and instilling a respect and reverence for the *Bhagavad-Gītā* in national, even global, terms.

Another way in which the *Bhagavad-Gītā* has been communicated to a mass Indian audience is in the context of B.R. and R. Chopra's serialization of the *Mahābhārata*. This series, following the serialization of India's other great epic, the *Rāmāyaṇa*, on Indian national television, devotes three episodes to the *Bhagavad-Gītā* (Malinar 1995: 442). As such, the *Bhagavad-Gītā* is presented as an integral part of the *Mahābhārata* rather than as an independent work, important in its own right as well as central to the story (Malinar 1995: 443, 447). Characterized throughout by selectivity and reinterpretation, the bias of this adaptation of the *Bhagavad-Gītā* is signalled by those sections delivered in Sanskrit, showing a preference for the early chapters of the dialogue and stressing action, the welfare of the world and sacrifice (Malinar 1995: 456, 458–9). Indeed, while the comparatively lengthy exposition of the dialogue with its martial ideology serves a contemporary conservative cause in upholding the traditional social order, the *Bhagavad-Gītā* is also seen as having a universal scope since Arjuna's questions are not asked by him alone, rather they are relevant to humanity in general (Malinar 1995: 449 n.15, 460, 461 n.50, 463–6). The overtly traditional style of presentation underlines the Indian nature of the series yet marketing of the DVD (15-hour format) underlines its international reach as well as the special status of the *Bhagavad-Gītā*; hence the DVD's box eulogizes the *Mahābhārata* as 'India's Greatest Epic', stressing that subsequently the series had been broadcast across the world while advertizing the inclusion of the *Bhagavad-Gītā* (Chopra and Chopra 2003).

The *Bhagavad-Gītā* has also been presented to an elite audience through the medium of film. G.V. Iyer (1917–2003), known as the 'bare-foot director' and famous for his films on spiritual subjects both mythological and historical, directed an award winning version of the *Bhagavad-Gītā*, remarkable in that it is a Sanskrit feature (Bhattacharya 1998; Deccan Herald 2003; Rajadhyaksha and Willemen 1999: 110). Although he came from a family of temple priests and espoused an orthodox agenda, his reason for making this film was the universality of the *Bhagavad-Gītā*'s message, stressing that it is not solely concerned with the war or with Kṛṣṇa's instruction of Arjuna but with human evolution (Gokulsing and Dissanayake 1998: 57; Rajadhyaksha and Willemin 1999: 110). Accordingly, the war becomes an inner battle and Arjuna an everyman, the film an allegory of the cultivation of a higher consciousness (Bhattacharya 1998). Thus, even expressed in a classical Indian language, there is a sense of the *Bhagavad-Gītā*'s wider relevance and application.

The *Bhagavad-Gītā* obviously plays an important part in Hindu life. Hence the powerful image of Kṛṣṇa, portrayed on the battlefield, calling Arjuna, the reluctant warrior, to arms has been exploited by the Hindu radical right (Bhatt and Mukta 2000: 427). The association of the *Bhagavad-Gītā* with this ideology is made clear in the 1998 Hindi film, *Satya*, where the villain, a leading Mumbai politician, is shown standing in front of a wall panel depicting Kṛṣṇa and Arjuna in the war chariot from the *Bhagavad-Gītā* (Smith, D. 2003: 181). A very different role for the *Bhagavad-Gītā* is in death rituals where Kṛṣṇa's declaration of the eternality of the soul, putting on and casting off bodies the same way that a person changes clothes, is recited in funerals (Narayanan 2003: 52). Indeed, in the diaspora, the *Bhagavad-Gītā* continues to be valued so, just as in India, the text is chanted to assist the dying to focus on the divine (Firth 1991: 60–2).

Moreover, the diaspora offers an opportunity to reflect on the significance of the *Bhagavad-Gītā* for Hindus in conjunction with the attitude taken towards its significance by host societies. In Britain, a tendency labelled 'generic levelling', prioritizing the 'great tradition', has been identified where the *Bhagavad-Gītā* and the *Vedas* are regarded as constituting 'the central texts of tradition' (Knott 1982: 83). That the British establishment and officialdom have come to accept the primacy of the *Bhagavad-Gītā* is clear in the legal system where, for example, jurors taking oaths can choose to do so on one of a number of holy books, the Hindu version sworn on the *Bhagavad-Gītā* formulated as follows: 'I swear by the Gita that I will faithfully try the defendant and give a true verdict according to the evidence' (Court Service 2004).

What bearing does this have on the Hindu tradition? Here are some cases in point. The conventional notion of the three paths of the *Bhagavad-Gītā* can be cited by liberal-minded Western teachers of Religious Education to prove that the Hindu tradition accepts the existence of many paths to one goal, attributing to it virtues of tolerance and inclusivity that can sustain wider claims about interreligious relations. Regarded by some Western seekers as a source of Eastern wisdom or eternal truths, the *Bhagavad-Gītā* can be read as proving that the Hindu tradition is more experiential and less dogmatic than Western faiths. There again, the *Bhagavad-Gītā*'s prominence in the imagery of Indian nationalism leaves a militant and violent impression of the Hindu tradition that qualifies other more pacifist perceptions also related to the text by certain commentators. The recitation or reading of the *Bhagavad-Gītā* in life cycle rites, however, emphasizes the theistic and devotional character of the Hindu tradition in popular practice. Overall, there is ample evidence that the *Bhagavad-Gītā* has assumed an exalted position among Hindu scriptures, all the more notable when the religion is itself defined in literary terms. In some multireligious contexts, the *Bhagavad-Gītā* has even been deemed to function for Hindus as the equivalent to the Bible for Christians.

Certainly the ways in which interpretations of the *Bhagavad-Gītā* influence images of the Hindu tradition cast some light on both modernity and post-modernity in global perspective. Definitions of these concepts are contested but Paul Heelas analyses them in relation to two themes, differentiation and dedifferentiation. He suggests that if modernity is marked by differentiation, be it political, economic, social or religious, it is also characterized by dedifferentiation including a perennialism endorsing an essential truth underlying its diverse expressions (Heelas 1997: 2–4). Similarly, if a feature of post-modernity is dedifferentiation, in this instance religious deregulation combined with cultural freedom, then differentiation still figures because variety remains at the level of a plurality of discourses (Heelas 1997: 4–7). The demarcation of the Hindu tradition as a distinct religion alongside the *Bhagavad-Gītā*'s emergence as the Hindu scripture illustrate modern differentiation. However, the assertion of the unity of the Hindu tradition with other religions and the relevance of the *Bhagavad-Gītā* to humanity as a whole illustrate modern dedifferentiation. Likewise, approaching the Hindu tradition and other religions as resources for developing a personal spirituality and the *Bhagavad-Gītā* as a spiritual classic providing guidance for all aspirants typifies post-modern dedifferentiation. On the other hand, reinforcing the religious and cultural specificity of the Hindu tradition and the particular philosophical and practical teaching of the *Bhagavad-Gītā* typifies post-modern differentiation.

In any case, what has been demonstrated is that the multivalence of the *Bhagavad-Gītā*, suggesting or supporting many meanings, gives rise to alternative versions of, or at least different emphases in, the Hindu tradition. The range of interpretations of the *Bhagavad-Gītā* – to offer an academic assessment, to justify activism rather than renunciation, to judge its merits by Christian criteria, to advocate universalism against exclusivity, to articulate mystical insights or to instruct disciples in the truths it contains – relate to diverse images of the Hindu tradition – defining the tradition as a scholarly artefact, identifying its rationale for social and political engagement, determining its relationship with Christianity, representing it as uniquely tolerant and open, appealing to it as embodying eternal verities of value to all or stressing its continuing dynamism and vitality as a vehicle of realization. The significance of the different interpretations of the *Bhagavad-Gītā* is thus that they have proved to be particularly influential on images of the Hindu tradition. This reflects the primacy accorded to the *Bhagavad-Gītā* in the construction of the Hindu tradition in the modern period and indicates, whatever changes have occurred, that the *Bhagavad-Gītā* is still central to its character in the contemporary world.

NOTES

INTRODUCTION

1 There is, of course, a relationship between translations and commentaries, not only because the two are often combined but also since commentaries often depend upon translations. The decision to concentrate on commentaries was made both because a high level of linguistic expertise is required to appreciate the interpretive element of translations and because the nature of commentaries means that the interpretive element is explicit, even while acknowledging that many commentaries have also been read in translation.

2 This is in line with recent trends in textual scholarship summed up by O'Flaherty who writes that 'the ultimate task of the textual critic is the interpretation and understanding of the text in its context' (O'Flaherty 1979: xiii). Accordingly, contemporary textual scholarship has reacted against an earlier textual bias and the subsequent stress upon non-textual methodologies by treating texts seriously yet not vesting them with a foundational role or ignoring alternative sources of information.

3 It should be noted that the *Bhagavadgītāparvan*, or Book of the *Bhagavad-Gītā*, of the *Mahābhārata* contains not only the text of the *Bhagavad-Gītā* but also a significant proportion of other material (van Buitenen 1981: xi).

4 However, though in the *Mahābhārata* the dominant characterization of Kṛṣṇa is as a hero, there are some references to, and demonstrations of, his divinity. Moreover, even if Arjuna's characterization in the *Bhagavad-Gītā* seems to be at odds with his epic reputation as a great warrior, the predicament in which he finds himself lends credibility and poignancy to his refusal to fight.

5 These questions are contentious, especially when conclusions challenge cherished notions about the text. Garbe's thesis that the *Bhagavad-Gītā* was initially a monotheistic work in praise of Kṛṣṇa founded upon Sāṃkhya-Yoga that subsequently received a pantheistic Vedāntic treatment (Garbe 1909: 2.536b) provoked much controversy. S.C. Roy wrote his book on the *Bhagavad-Gītā* partly to refute Garbe's ideas about interpolations, rejecting Garbe's analysis that there were contradictions in the text only explicable in terms of an earlier and later version with different theological-cum-philosophical perspectives (Roy, S.C. 1941: ix). Instead, Roy insists upon the integrity and coherence of the *Bhagavad-Gītā* which, far from having a sectarian character, has a universal message as a poetical attempt to reconcile diverse religious and cultural standpoints (Roy, S.C. 1941: 248–50).

6 This account can be contested at least in part. For instance, the assertion that the *Bhagavad-Gītā* has few textual variants has been disputed by Belvalkar, the editor responsible for the critical edition of the *Mahābhārata* (Belvalkar 1947: IX). Or again, it could be suggested that the *Bhagavad-Gītā* is ambivalent in its attitude towards śruti

(16.23–4, cf. 2.46), laying claim to an alternative source of authority (4.1) (Sharma 1986: xiv). Nevertheless, other points can be made in favour of this account. For example, the text of the *Bhagavad-Gītā* quotes from the *Kaṭha Upaniṣad* 2.19 (Zaehner 1966b: 174). This then establishes a clear connection between the *Bhagavad-Gītā* and the *Upaniṣads* which is also made by the oft-quoted verse of the *Vaiṣṇavīya Tantrasāra* that describes the *Upaniṣads* as cows, Kṛṣṇa as the milker, Arjuna as the calf, the wise one as the drinker and the *Bhagavad-Gītā* as the milk (cf. Radhakrishnan 1989a: 13 n.3). This is certainly the opinion of Edgerton who argues for such a connection on the basis that the *Bhagavad-Gītā* deals with the issues that he identified as the subject matter of the *Upaniṣads* (Edgerton 1972: 108).

7 Van Buitenen notes that śruti is defined as eternal, authorless and self-validating but, while acknowledging that the *Bhagavad-Gītā* does not satisfy these criteria since it is delivered at the time of the Mahābhārata War by Kṛṣṇa who authenticates its teaching, vests the śruti-like authority of the *Bhagavad-Gītā* precisely in its divergence from these norms as 'personal, historic, and original' with a new message (van Buitenen 1981: 7, 9, 12–13).

8 The different schools of thought on the nature and provenance of 'Hinduism' are represented in the contrasting opinions expressed by Hawley and Hiltebeitel. Hawley, suggesting that the category, not just the terminology, might be modern and Western, comments that 'Hindus had a concept of India as sacred space and they had histories and epics that established their complex common ancestry, but they never developed a concept of themselves as a society unified by religion' (Hawley 1991: 20, 24). In contrast, Hiltebeitel criticizes the notion that 'Hinduism' is a modern Western creation, claiming that, '[i]n Hinduism, we are faced with a deep and diverse tradition, one that cannot be expected to rethink the name it wants to call itself, no matter how recent the name may be' (Hiltebeitel 1991: 26). Those opinions are typical of contributions to the current debate.

9 For an alternative perspective, see Lorenzen 1999. It is Lorenzen's claim that what he calls 'the loose family resemblance among the variegated beliefs and practices of Hindus' can be dated as far back as 300–600 CE (Lorenzen 1999: 655). Mughal rule, in his judgement, was crucial for the development among Hindus of 'a consciousness of a shared religious identity' founded upon this family resemblance (Lorenzen 1999: 655). Accordingly, he insists that 'the rapid changes of early colonial times never had such an overwhelming impact that they could have led to the invention of Hinduism' (Lorenzen 1999: 655). To this, it may be responded that the thesis of the construction of 'Hinduism' does not mean that 'Hinduism' was constructed out of nothing since this concept is a specific ordering and arrangement of extant traditions. In addition, it may be asserted that the colonial period, however inappropriate the terminology for the Indian instance, not only had earlier origins and broader manifestations but was also associated with some significant shifts in knowledge and understanding. Further, it may be suggested that encounter with Muslims promoted a sense of difference between 'Hindus' and Muslims that did not necessarily resolve into 'Hindus' perceiving a religious unity among themselves. Moreover, it may even be queried whether the evidence adduced to support the case advanced by Lorenzen seems convincing precisely because it is all too easy to read back the later notion of 'Hinduism' into earlier statements though these need not have been informed or inspired by this notion. Certainly there is sufficient ethnographic material to indicate that even in modern India many people did not subscribe to normative definitions of 'Hinduism' or, indeed, view 'Hinduism' and Islam as separate entities: many 'Hindus' visited Muslim shrines and many Muslims observed 'Hindu' life-cycle rites (Oberoi 1997: 3–4); some people declared themselves to be 'Mohammedan Hindus' and others were Muslim by faith but retained 'Hindu' names (Oberoi 1997: 11–12); moreover, there was a heritage of

mutual influence in religious biography and popular cults that challenged any division of the population into exclusive communities (Oberoi 1997: 17–18).

10 Al-Birūnī's thought is not easy to interpret in either respect. For example, von Steitencron regards him as having distinguished a number of 'religions', Ernst regards him as having depicted 'Hindus' as a religious group opposed to Muslims and Lorenzen regards him as having described the 'Hindu religion' (von Stietencron 1995: 77; Ernst 1992: 24; Lorenzen 1999: 653–4). Similar disputes surround other scholars' contributions. Certainly Thapar is sceptical of the notion of 'two monolithic religions, Hinduism and Islam, coming face to face in the second millennium A.D.' that she attributes to a misinterpretation of Muslim court chronicles (Thapar 1989: 233). Her view is that such chronicles referred to 'Hindus' in a variety of senses – ethnic, geographic and, sometimes, religious 'as followers of a non-Islamic religion' (Thapar 1989: 224). This accounts for her advocacy that references to 'Hindus' be analysed for their particular meaning and not generally be assumed to denote membership of the 'Hindu religion' (Thapar 1989: 224).

11 It is interesting that at the outset the native population did not use the label Muslim for the incomers: 'The term used was either ethnic, Turuṣka, referring to the Turks, or geographical, Yavana, or cultural, *mleccha*' (Thapar 1989: 223). This re-emphasizes that the religious aspect of identity, at least in the sense that is now familiar, was not primary in the past. On the contrary, it was part of a more general conflict between the native civilization of the subcontinent and the incoming Islamic civilization. As Thapar explains 'the perception which groups subscribing to Hindu and Islamic symbols had of each other was not in terms of a monolithic religion, but more in terms of distinct and disparate castes and sects along a social continuum' (Thapar 1989: 225). Much the same conclusion is drawn by Talbot in her work on Andhra Pradesh from the fourteenth to seventeenth centuries (Talbot 1995: 700). Based on her examination of inscriptions, she dates what she believes to be the earliest use of the word 'Hindu' in any Indian language to the mid-fourteenth century and interprets it 'as a sign of an incipient Indic ethnicity – incorporating territorial associations, language, a common past and customs, as well as religious affiliation' (Talbot 1995: 700). She downplays the religious aspect so that, even where religious rhetoric came to the fore, she sees appeals to religious images as a means of strengthening community solidarity (Talbot 1995: 720). Nevertheless, the compositions of fifteenth- and sixteenth-century poet-saints such as Kabir and Eknath are cited as proof that 'Hindu' did have a sense of belonging to the 'Hindu' religion (e.g. Lorenzen 1999: 648–52; Oddie 2003: 160–1). However, research in this area has yet to resolve questions about the importance of the religious aspect of 'Hindu' identity in comparison with ethnic and cultural factors and the extent to which any religious identity achieved a positive unity vested in certain criteria and transcending areas of disagreement between 'Hindu' religious groups (e.g. Gokhale 1984: 155–6, 158, 160–1).

12 In this context, it is perhaps significant that some of the earliest examples of Western use of the word 'Hindu' employ it as a synonym for 'Pagan' or 'Gentile' and hence it has the same sense of 'Heathen' or 'Idolater' as the word 'Gentoo'.

13 Although he cited the fourfold classification at the outset, Ziegenbalg's study of the Malabar Indians would seem to be a transitional work in that it was informed by knowledge of indigenous beliefs and practices as well as by a sense of India as a geographical entity (Caland 1926: 9, 23). Referring to 'Tschiwasáimeiam' (Śaivism) and 'Wischtnusameiam' (Vaiṣṇavism) as sects of 'Malabarian Heathenism' (Caland 1926: 23), his account anticipated the development of the concept of 'Hinduism' in terms of Indian 'Heathen' having their own 'religion'. Sweetman, however, is sceptical of von Stietencron's reading of Ziegenbalg's *Malabarisches Heidenthum* in terms of a missionary assumption that there was but one 'Heathen religion' with a number

of 'sects' (Sweetman 2001: 216, 218). Also drawing on evidence from Ziegenbalg's *Malabarischen Götter* (see Germann 1867), Sweetman's reasons for scepticism include the interchangeability of the terms 'religion' and 'sect' in Ziegenbalg's writing so that there are references to Śaivism and Vaiṣṇavism as 'religions' (Sweetman 2001: 215–18). Sweetman may well be correct in criticizing the tendency to read back into Ziegenbalg's writings, and those of other early authors, a later concept of 'religion' but, as he demonstrates, Ziegenbalg did regard Śaivism and Vaiṣṇavism as 'sects' when examining 'Malabarian Heathenism' as a whole (Sweetman 2001: 216, 218).

14 This analysis involves drawing rather different conclusions from von Stietencron's discussion than he does. He attaches no significance to the shift in terms from 'Gentoo' to 'Hindu' and instead states that the term 'Hindu' supplanted 'Gentoo' without a change in meaning as both appealed to a notion of the fundamental unity of Indian 'religion' (von Stietencron 1991: 13). Consequently, he stresses continuity between the earlier category of 'Heathenism' as a worldwide phenomenon, albeit regionally inflected, and the later category of 'Hinduism' since they shared the assumption that Indian 'religion' was unified (von Stietencron 1995: 72). However, there is a marked contrast between 'Heathenism' as one 'religion' with many 'sects' and 'Hinduism' as one 'religion' in its own right with many 'sects' of its own, the language employed signalling a growing awareness of the distinctiveness of the Indian case. Here the argument advanced is closer to R. King's in emphasizing the dissimilarity between 'Heathenism' and 'Hinduism' while noting trends in terminology (King, R. 1999: 99–100).

15 Again, this account can be criticized. D. Smith, for example, disavows any imperial ambitions on the part of individual scholars and distinguishes between imperial ideology and general cultural assumptions (Smith, D. 2003: 88, 101). However, a number of other issues are involved, including how Indology is defined (and this could be extended beyond the study of language and literature) and the environment in which Indology is pursued as well as the uses to which it is put. As for the relationship between Indology and Christian missionary effort, this needs to be viewed in the light of claims that Indology was instrumental in enabling 'Hindus' to rediscover their own heritage and Christianity in prompting 'Hindus' to reform their own tradition (Andrews 1912: 11, 106–7, 146).

16 Something of the complexity of the nature of 'Hinduism' has been reflected in the constitution of independent India and in responses to its practical consequences. The legal system includes Sikhs, Buddhists, Jains as well as 'Hindus' under the heading of 'Hinduism' (Sugirtharajah 2003: xi), a claim that causes some considerable offence to members of such religious groups (Embree 1990: 113–14). At the same time, the legal system provides for the protection of minority religious belief and practice while retaining the right to reform the belief and practice of the notional 'Hindu' majority (Embree 1990: 76–7), a situation that led the Ramakrishna Mission to proclaim itself a minority 'religion' in an effort to prevent government interference in its affairs (Young 1993: 201).

17 Nevertheless, in an article on the construction of 'Hinduism', B.K. Smith articulates some ambivalence about this thesis (Smith, B.K. 1998: 315–19). While allowing that it has some strengths, he nevertheless questions its presuppositions and repercussions (Smith, B.K. 1998: 317–18, 321, 330). He disputes the representation of 'Hinduism' that is attributed to past scholarship, identifying Orientalist and Indological tendencies, not towards a 'monolithic and essentialist position', but towards a 'peculiarly unbounded and nondescript entity' (Smith, B.K. 1998: 319–21). Here he has in mind the prevalence of the style of definition that elsewhere he terms 'inchoate' (Smith, B.K. 1989: 7–8). Yet, though such definitions do feature prominently, there are other

styles, perhaps as popular, that are more prescriptive in nature, characterized by reference to normative criteria. Further, it is not clear why any lack of boundary, associated as it has been with conventional claims of inclusiveness and tolerance, has not served as some sort of unifying factor along the lines of a 'unity in diversity'. He also denounces the way in which 'the postmodern critique of any monolithic conceptualization of "Hinduism"' entails the delegitimizing of 'anyone who claims to speak for a singular "Hinduism"' (Smith, B.K. 1998: 321–30). Here he has in mind the role of the brāhmans as sacred specialists that elsewhere he regards as demarcating 'the mainline Hindu traditions' (Smith, B.K. 1989: 14). However, without underestimating the influence of Brāhmaṇic orthodoxy, this appears to treat it as equivalent to 'Hinduism' though the latter contains many more traditions, some unrelated, others actively opposed. Indeed, it fails fully to appreciate the danger of replicating established hierarchies that uphold Brāhmaṇic orthodoxy at the cost of depriving other groups of agency and other perspectives of authenticity.

18 If it is possible to point to a large measure of agreement about the status of 'religion' in the sense of the term having no counterpart in reality, it is not so easy to find such agreement as to whether 'religion' should be retained or rejected. On this point, J.Z. Smith's support for retaining 'religion' as a useful analytical and classificatory tool can be contrasted with Fitzgerald's rejection of 'religion' as a category since in his judgement this amounts to a theological claim (Smith, J.Z. 1998; cf. Fitzgerald 2000).

19 The modern Western ways of thinking that produced the concept of 'religion' were influenced by certain Christian ideas. However, 'religion' was associated with the process of secularization whereby the concept gained an increasing measure of independence from Christian institutions (Preus 1987: x, xiv). 'Religion' was treated as a natural object susceptible to rational and empirical methods of scientific enquiry, yet the concept owed much to Christianity, notably the heritage of the Reformation (Harrison 1990: 5, 7).

20 Max Müller refers to both of these etymologies of '*religio*' (Müller 1891: 11–12, n.1). However, Müller, unlike most modern scholars, favoured '*relegere*' over '*religare*' though he emphasized that the meaning of 'religion' had changed over time (Müller 1891: 11–12).

21 W.C. Smith has been credited with pioneering a non-essentialist approach to 'religion' though he has been criticized both for his proposed solution to the problem he identified (the distinction between '[personal] faith' and '[cumulative] tradition') and, more generally, for not pursuing to its logical conclusion the thrust of his own argument (Fitzgerald 2000: 21; McCutcheon 1997: 128).

22 Roman usage has been defined: '(1) as a quality of persons, *scrupulousness, conscientious exactness*: a primarily, *respect for what is sacred, religious scruple, awe*:... b *strict observance of religious ceremonial*:...(2) as a quality of gods and religious objects, *sanctity*' (Simpson 1966: 511). It is noteworthy that the *Oxford English Dictionary*'s definition of 'religion' reflects previous Christian usage, both in referring to rites (definition 3a) and religious orders (definitions 1 and 2) (Simpson and Weiner 1989: XIII.568–9).

23 Among the uses of the suffix '-ism' is '[f]orming the name of a system of theory or practice, religious, ecclesiastical, philosophical, political, social, etc' (Simpson and Weiner 1989: VIII.113). Instances of this usage include 'religions' such as 'Brahmanism' (though not 'Hinduism') (Simpson and Weiner 1989: VIII.113). It is noticeable that this *Oxford English Dictionary* definition derives the names of systems from their founders rather than their followers (contra Smith, W.C. 1978: 62).

24 Said's study on Orientalism has been acclaimed as ground-breaking and, accordingly, has been subjected to intense scrutiny, generating some telling criticisms concerning

the homogeneity of his notion of Orientalism, the positing of Asia as Europe's 'Other' and the insistence on the relationship between knowledge and power. Rocher is critical of the way in which 'it creates a single discourse, undifferentiated in space and time and across political, social, and intellectual identities' (Rocher 1993: 215); Tuck argues against Said that 'it is equally the case that the urge to find parallels, to see Asia as a mirror has been at work' (Tuck 1990: 8); and Clarke asserts against Said that 'the association of orientalism with colonising power can represent only one part of the story' (Clarke 1997: 26). Thus Rocher accuses Said of advancing his thesis with primary reference to the Middle East and Islam and only including India and 'Hinduism' as another instance of the same process based on limited evidence (Rocher 1993: 215). Further, Tuck points out that, in concentrating on the antithetical relationship between Europe and Asia, Said ignores the search for common origins and cultural links that has been a significant trend in Indology (Tuck 1990: 7–8). Moreover, Clarke rejects Said's equation of Orientalism and imperialism even during the heyday of empire by citing the contribution to Indology made by German scholars though Germany had no imperial interests in India (Clarke 1997: 26–7). Other criticisms of Said's works emphasize the diverse agendas of different commentators such as travellers, missionaries and officials, the idealization of the East as a source of the West's reform and renewal and the fascination of the West for the East in a period predating the age of empire. Nevertheless, much of this criticism seems to be directed towards qualifying or modifying Said's theory rather than a wholesale repudiation of its premises. Even so, Western impact on the East was not without its counterpart, Eastern influence over the West. This is the thesis advanced by Schwab who proposes that there was an 'Oriental Renaissance' – 'the revival of an atmosphere in the nineteenth century brought about by the arrival of Sanskrit texts in Europe, which produced an effect equal to that produced in the fifteenth century by the arrival of Greek manuscripts and Byzantine commentators after the fall of Constantinople' (Schwab 1984: 11). Similarly, Clarke refers to an 'Oriental Enlightenment' – 'throughout the modern period…, the East has exercised a strong fascination over Western minds, and has entered into Western cultural and intellectual life in ways which are of considerably more than passing significance within the history of Western ideas' (Clarke 1997: 5). Their analyses suggest that any transformation of the East wrought by Western ideas (Orientalism in Said's sense) had a parallel in the changes made in the West in response to Eastern beliefs and values even if these changes could themselves be seen as Orientalist in character. However, whether regarded as complements or correctives to Said's theory, both Schwab and Clarke are perhaps vulnerable to a charge of overstatement on the grounds that the West was not transformed by the East in a breadth or depth equivalent to the East's transformation by the West.

25 The impact of Said's theory on the study of 'Hinduism' and the post-Orientalist perspectives it has inspired have been criticized by Pollock on the grounds that they explain inequalities in Indian society as imperial inventions (Pollock 1993: 96–7). Against this, he argues for an account of traditional India marked by inequalities that he proposes prefigure the imperial period so that such inequalities can be considered 'a preform of orientalism' (Pollock 1993: 76–7). He sees significant continuities between pre-imperial and imperial India, identifying how 'indigenous discourses of power intersected with the colonial variety' and indicating 'the pre-existence of a shared ideological base among indigenous and colonial elites' (Pollock 1993: 100–1). He even suggests that the similarities between Indian and British attitudes may have been part of the reason for the successful establishment of the raj (Pollock 1993: 101). According to Pollock, then, the association of knowledge and power to which post-Orientalist scholarship points was evident earlier in India's history and hence was not a product of imperial rule (Pollock 1993: 115).

26 Staal and Balagangadhara can be criticized for claiming that 'Hinduism' is not a 'religion' on the grounds that their criticism rests on precisely those Christian assumptions that such scholars identify as shaping the concept of 'religion' and thus in practice perpetuate the Christian bias that in other respects they oppose. This criticism has been made by Sweetman (2003), developing his earlier argument against R. King and von Stietencron that their rejection of 'Hinduism' as a 'religion' rests on 'a particular monothetic definition of a religion' (Sweetman 2001: 219). This is an important point but it was because the dominant concept of religion was shaped by Christian assumptions that these assumptions proved extremely influential in the construction of other 'religions'. In turn, this produced a norm from which other 'religions' deviated to a greater or lesser extent, very much the former in the case of 'Hinduism'. Yet there was also a strong tendency to claim that 'Hinduism' was a 'religion' nevertheless; in what sense was either not examined at all or expressed in essentialist terms that posed equally intractable problems. Perhaps, then, the argument that 'Hinduism' is not a 'religion' has some validity in historiographic perspective where past scholars, less prone to theorize categories, implicitly or explicitly worked within a Christian paradigm of 'religion' yet simultaneously wanted to demand for 'Hinduism' the status of a 'religion'. Of course, this might only establish the proposition that 'Hinduism' is not like Christianity and hence indicate that, if 'religion' has a Christian paradigm, then it is difficult to accommodate 'Hinduism'. However, it might also contribute to a more critical attitude towards 'religion' as a concept associated historically with Christian ideals and values and towards 'Hinduism' as a concept informed by this understanding of 'religion' despite its divergent characteristics.

27 Of course, it can be claimed that this idea does not so much solve the problem of defining 'Hinduism' as a 'religion' as transfer and, indeed, exacerbate the problem by defining particular movements as 'religions' themselves. Even so, the suggestion that there are several 'Hindu religions' rather than one 'Hindu religion' has some precedent as other commentators have been unable to reconcile the evident diversity of belief and practice with the conventional model of 'Hinduism', and so have conceded some measure of plurality.

28 Tiele's other category was 'nature religions', classifying what might now be categorized as 'sects' of 'Hinduism' under this heading too – '[t]he non-Aryan (Dravidian) religions of India' as 'therianthropic polytheism' and '[t]he ancient Vaidic religion' as 'anthropomorphic polytheism' (Tiele 1886: 20.369–70).

29 Tiele's definition of 'nomistic or nomothetic communities', however, was that these 'religions' were based on 'law or Holy Scripture' so, for him, that was not the unique property of 'universal or world religions' (Tiele 1886: 20.368, cf. 1877: 3).

30 For this reason, scholars have differed in their assessment of the cross-cultural utility of the concept of 'scripture'. Coburn argues that 'scripture' should be abandoned because of its association with writing though, in contrast, W.C. Smith argues for 'scripture' as a relational concept in which a community is decisive in turning a text into a 'scripture' (Coburn 1984: 463; cf. Smith, W.C. 1993: 18). Even those who are content to keep the concept differ as to how it should be interpreted with Levering supporting and Timm opposing a generic definition of 'scripture' (Levering 1989: 11; cf. Timm 1992: 3).

31 Some impression of these developments can be gained from the *Oxford English Dictionary*, which documents 'scripture' in both the plural and the singular to designate the Bible as well as the extension of the term to designate the texts of other traditions (definition 1) (Simpson and Weiner 1989: XIV.742).

32 The primacy of 'scripture' was clearly stated in Müller's lectures on the Science of Religion where he described 'scripture' as being of 'the utmost importance' and

devoted much attention to those 'religions' that had 'sacred and canonical books' (Müller 1873: 102, 104). He did not, though, suggest that the study of 'scripture' was sufficient, both because he recognized 'scripture' had to be approached critically as a source of knowledge about a specific 'religion' and because he realized some, indeed many, 'religions' were without 'scripture' necessitating an alternative methodology (Müller 1873: 102–3, 116–22).

33 Certainly Müller stressed that the division of 'religions' into 'revealed' and 'natural', leading to Christianity (and possibly Judaism) being regarded as 'revealed' and all other 'religions' as 'natural', was of no utility for the Science of Religion (Müller 1873: 128). He insisted 'that the claims to a revealed authority are urged far more strongly and elaborately by the believers in the Veda, than by the apologetical theologians among the Jews and Christians' (Müller 1873: 128). Here, however, his concern was to demonstrate that the 'revealed' – 'natural' dichotomy was unsatisfactory (Müller 1873: 127–8).

34 Folkert's comments on *The Sacred Books of the East* are instructive: 'The very title of the series (including its reference to the "East") is an index of the problem that wants addressing: the widespread use of a general notion of a sacred book, and the unhesitating extension of this notion into the earliest stages of collection, editing, and translating of the literature of major traditions' (Folkert 1989: 171). To pick up a point he makes in passing, it is clear that the term East, and of course its counterpart West, is problematic and as such invites comment. Yet while recognizing the ideological nature of the East–West divide, these terms are used in this study as convenient shorthand, especially for denoting historical controversies, and as consistent with scholarly practice in this subject area. Clarke, for instance, defends the use of such terminology on the grounds of ease and economy while also treating it with some suspicion (Clarke 1997: 10–11).

35 While the programme of translation for *The Sacred Books of the East*, together with the subsequent publication of English versions of the 'scriptures' of 'Hinduism' and also Buddhism, Jainism, Confucianism, Taoism, Zoroastrianism and Islam (Winternitz 1910: xv–xvi), did describe the East in religious terms, it is recorded that Müller favoured the inclusion of the Old and New Testaments though he was unable to overcome objections to this proposal and finally ceded the point to secure the future of the series. Recalling these events some years later, he referred to the opposition of Dr Pusey whose approval was conditional on the omission of the Old and New Testaments and whom he was unable to persuade to his point of view (Müller 1899: 76). This raises some intriguing possibilities about Judaism and Christianity as Eastern 'religions', quite cogent if their origins in the Near East are considered, despite the now more common labelling of Judaism and Christianity along with Islam as Western 'religions'. Of course, the exclusion of the Old and New Testaments can be attributed, not to a disagreement about the boundaries of the East, but to an affirmation of the uniqueness of the Judaeo-Christian tradition.

36 Eder refers to Telang as the only non-Western contributor to *The Sacred Books of the East* (Eder 2003: 171). Certainly Western scholars dominated the list of translators and, where 'Hindu scriptures' were concerned, Telang was the only non-Western translator but a scholar named Junjiro Takakusu did contribute to volume 49 on Buddhist Māhāyaṇa texts (Winternitz 1910: xv).

37 An interesting area of debate is the impact of writing on texts. Ong has noted how 'writing restructures consciousness' in an account stressing that writing distances the knower and the known (Ong 1982: 78, 103). The conclusion he draws is that '[w]riting makes possible the great introspective religious traditions' (Ong 1982: 105). Taking issue with this analysis as it relates to 'Hinduism', C.M. Brown disputes the connection made between the quality of introspection and literacy (Brown, C.M.

1986: 84–5). In Brown's judgement, Ong is not well enough informed about the 'Hindu' case because he fails fully to acknowledge the oral transmission of the *Vedas*, even asking '[w]ithout a [written] text, how could a given hymn – not to mention the totality of hymns in the collections – be stabilized word for word, and that over many generations?' (Ong 1982: 65–6). Brown points out that there is evidence for this stabilization having occurred and that a written text was an inadequate medium of transmission since it did not display the accents essential to recitation (Brown, C.M. 1986: 84, n.68). Goody's argument is similar to Ong's in that he differentiates between the features of the literate and non-literate 'religions', emphasizing the role of 'scripture' or 'scriptures' albeit with some recognition of the disparity between East and West (Goody 1986: 4–7). Consequently, he argues that literate religions are associated with universalism, itself linked with conversion where membership is not solely determined by birth and also with generalizability where abstract norms are accorded priority (Goody 1986: 10–13). However, here too questions might be asked about the treatment of 'Hinduism'. For example, though referring to his brāhman neighbour's daily recitation from the *Ṛg Veda* , he claims that '[w]riting is surely critical in the fact that Hinduism . . . exists in recognizably similar forms throughout the sub-continent' when the orality of the *Vedas* is paramount (Goody 1986: 7). Further, if his analysis concerning how 'literate religions influence the normative structure of a social system towards universalism' is meant to apply to 'Hinduism', then an issue arises about the relevance of conversion considering the hold of the caste system and also perhaps the extent of generalizability considering the particularity and plurality of dharmic norms (Goody 1986: 12).

38 For an alternative view on the *Mahābhārata* to that espoused by Brockington, see Hiltebeitel 2003. Whereas Brockington envisages a period of transmission by bards preceding the epic's authorship by the brāhmans (Brockington 1998: 19), Hiltebeitel postulates a transmission starting with brāhmans and then passing to bards (Hiltebeitel 2003: 123). For Hiltebeitel, Ugraśravas' declaration illustrates the bards' role in disseminating the epic differentiated from the brāhmans' role in composing it, and the relationship between Vyāsa and Gaṇeśa explains the mixed genres of the epic by equating the act of composition with the creation of a written text through dictation (Hiltebeitel 2003: 122–3).

39 The following account is based on Sharpe 1985 with supplementary references indicated in the main text.

40 Indeed, in 1984, the International Gita Society was established in America with aims including to '[s]pread the basic Non-sectarian Universal teachings of Srimad Bhagavad-Gita and other Vedic scriptures' and to '[p]ublish and distribute, free if possible, The Bhagavad-Gita in simple and easy to understand languages' (International Gita Society 2003). Its website appeals for help in achieving its objectives such as the supply of copies of its version of the *Bhagavad-Gītā* in hotel rooms and public places across the world (International Gita Society 2003). This shows that the prominence of the *Bhagavad-Gītā* continues to be reflected and reinforced in contemporary campaigns.

41 For a more detailed account of the Gītā Press, albeit concentrated on the magazine *Kalyāṇ* that she describes as the main motivation for its foundation, see Horstmann 1995.

42 This development, whereby the *Bhagavad-Gītā* was regarded as forming part of a shared human heritage, has not been without its critics. Bharati is far from complimentary when offering his opinion of the text. On the contrary, he laments how the *Bhagavad-Gītā* 'has been too much popularized, too often translated, and hence too banalized' so that, in common with other books so treated, 'it has become an epitome of profoundly "different" thought for the escapists in the West who must be tickled by the

mysteries of the East' (Bharati 1980: 131). Indeed, coining the pejorative term 'pizza effect' for the exportation of cultural artefacts from their homeland and re-importation of these artefacts with a revised sense of their significance based on their reception abroad, he cites the *Bhagavad-Gītā* as a possible instance (Bharati 1971: 88–90). He explains '[t]he fact that the *Bhagavadgītā* has assumed an ideological importance far beyond its traditional place may be due to a concatenation of literary and historical events commencing with Wilkins' translation' (Bharati 1971: 90).

43 Brodbeck's new introduction to the re-issue of Mascaró's translation of the *Bhagavad-Gītā* discusses some of the themes that characterize Mascaró's approach to the text. As well as identifying Mascaró's use of Vedāntic terminology with its Upaniṣadic basis and his allegorical take on the martial setting that he shared with Gandhi, Brodbeck demonstrates how Mascaró 'stands the *Bhagavad Gita* alongside the Greek and English literary classics, and introduces ideas derived from Christian morality…, from European mysticism, and from post-Enlightenment rationalism' (Brodbeck 2003: xxviii). This underlines the way in which Mascaró views the *Bhagavad-Gītā* from a cross-cultural vantage point, reading the text in the light of various ethical, religious and philosophical principles.

44 The data contained in these surveys is not wholly consistent even in respect of English translations. However, both illustrate general trends in publishing on and about the *Bhagavad-Gītā* since 1785.

1 ACADEMIC AND SCHOLARLY WRITING

1 David Hume's *The Natural History of Religion* (1757) posited that the oldest form of religion was polytheistic and idolatrous; this was the religion of primitive savages that was in time superseded by the monotheistic and iconoclastic religion of the civilized (Wollheim 1963: 33). Alternatively, Lord Herbert of Cherbury (1582–1648) described a universal religion defined by belief in one God; underlying and unifying all historical religions, it was based on the exercise of reason and independent of revelation but had been obscured and obfuscated by later institutionalization (Preus 1987: 23, 28). However different from Hume's theory of the origin of religion, this too conduced towards an appreciation of monotheism.

2 In more detail, Müller delineated three periods in the development of thought and language. The first, labelled rhematic, was characterized by the invention of words for necessary concepts. The second, the dialectic period, involved the separation of language groups and the establishment of grammatical forms. The third period was named the mythological or mythopoetic and denoted the process by which the dawn, for instance, became personified as 'she of the dawn' (Sharpe 1975: 41–2).

3 It is possible to find Müller suggesting that Vedic religion had passed from childhood, through manhood and into old age in the *Veda saṃhitās*, the *Brāhmaṇas* and *Upaniṣads* respectively. Yet he indicated that the latter did not supersede or supplant the earlier but all were preserved (Müller 1891: 370). Even so, it is difficult to decide what this meant for contemporary Indian religion (Müller 1891: 379–80). Something of the ambivalence that frustrates analysis is present in the articulation of his hopes for a future form of religion. His inclusivism is evident in his expectation that this religion would draw upon diverse expressions of truth, the best quality of each tradition, yet his hierarchizing of these expressions privileged Christianity, at least in its ideal form, as the highest religion (Müller 1891: 385–6). Indeed, he went so far as to suggest that the Science of Religion would establish the superiority of Christianity since he insisted that a comparative approach would reveal its unique properties (Müller 1868: xx, xxvii–xxviii). Hence, when ranking religions, he ranked missionary religions such as

Christianity over non-missionary religions such as Brahmanism with the confidence to assert that Christianity alone proclaimed divine love for humanity and to argue that this assured Christianity's ultimate triumph (Müller 1875: 258–9, 263–4, 278).

4 Commenting on Monier-Williams' work on the *Bhagavad-Gītā*, Sharpe suggests that his interest was inspired by the text's devotional theistic emphasis, even that he saw in the text a kind of Protestantism centred on bhakti and Kṛṣṇa (Sharpe 1985: 54–5). This is a persuasive explanation as far as it goes but it must be borne in mind that Monier-Williams regarded such devotion to the divine in Hinduism as flawed by its ultimate reducibility to absolutistic pantheism – a significant difference from Christianity and one that by his criteria established the superiority of Christianity over Hinduism.

5 In this context, Monier-Williams described four stages of development in which Vedism preceded Brahmanism, and in which Śaivism then emerged from Brahmanism and Vaiṣṇavism from Śaivism (Monier-Williams 1882).

6 In examining Otto's works, it is necessary to remember that they have been translated into English from German and so, although it is important to consider his ideas, some aspects of the discussion (insofar as they relate to terminology) may reflect decisions made by a translator.

7 Sharpe surveys some of the responses Otto's book provoked, including the unenthusiastic response of Sanskritists who questioned his linguistic expertise and competence to undertake a literary analysis of the text. For different reasons altogether, many Hindu commentators were similarly dubious of his conclusions about the heterogeneity of the *Bhagavad-Gītā* (Sharpe 1985: 125–6).

8 Indeed, referring to Otto's ideas about an original form of the *Bhagavad-Gītā*, Zaehner explained that the text was more unified than many scholars thought and that this was his motivation for producing yet another version of it (Zaehner 1973: 1–2). Further, though Zaehner's career began with a specialization in Zoroastrianism, it developed in the direction of Hinduism, especially its literature, and also Taoist, Confucian and Buddhist texts (Zaehner 1957: xiv, cf. 1970: 19). It is also noteworthy that Zaehner was aware of Otto's work on comparative mysticism and, though critical of it in certain respects, rather more positive about it than about Otto's deconstructive strategy towards the complexities of the *Bhagavad-Gītā* (Zaehner 1957: 182).

9 Insofar as terminology was concerned, Zaehner suggested that Brahmanism was a synonym for Hinduism (Zaehner 1966a: 5). Conceptually, he compared Hinduism with Hellenism and Judaism, the former a culture, the latter an ethnic religion, concluding that Hinduism was both though he also contrasted it with Judaism on the grounds that Judaism rested on certain definite theological premises (Zaehner 1966a: 1).

2 SOCIAL AND POLITICAL ACTIVISM

1 As M.J. Harvey has demonstrated, Tilak reinterpreted the key terms karma, yoga and dharma: karma was defined as action conducive to the achievement of release; yoga as skilful means; and dharma as both the duty of this world and the duty beyond this world (Harvey, M.J. 1986: 325–9). Attaching priority to the former meaning of dharma, Tilak's definition of Karma-yoga Dharma was 'skilful use of action in the world' (Harvey, M.J. 1986: 328–9). On this basis, Tilak gave a strongly this-worldly activist interpretation of the *Bhagavad-Gītā*.

2 D.M. Brown outlines the problems that Tilak had to overcome when appealing to the *Bhagavad-Gītā* as a Hindu rationale for political and social action. These included the extension of Arjuna's duty as a warrior to all members of society, irrespective of their varṇa (class) and associated dharma (duty). However, in doing so Tilak had to put in

place safeguards, which were the references to a state of crisis as requiring special measures and to guidance offered by leaders of society (Brown, D.M. 1958: 201–2).

3 Sharma terms Gandhi's approach as 'individual, ethical and allegorical' whereas Tilak's was 'national, political and metaphorical', underlining the fact that for Gandhi the martial aspects of the *Bhagavad-Gītā* were but the means to convey a deeper spiritual truth about an inner battle (Sharma 1983: 45–6).

4 Richards discusses the relationship between truth and non-violence as follows: 'Ahiṁsā could be described as the means leading to the realization of Truth as the end or goal, but since means and ends are convertible terms in Gandhi's philosophy of life, to practise ahiṁsā is to realize Truth and to realize Truth is to practise ahiṁsā. That is, as far as Gandhi is concerned, the attainment of one involves also the realization of the other' (Richards 1982: 31).

5 Minor explains how and why Ghose's ideas about the *Bhagavad-Gītā* and its importance altered over time (Minor 1991: 87). Although omitting consideration of the first phase, the following account is indebted to Minor's analysis and periodization of Ghose's work. It discusses the supporting role of the *Bhagavad-Gītā* in his nationalist heyday and its greater significance after his imprisonment, illustrated by reference to *Bande Mataram* and *Karmayogin* respectively. It then discusses the part played by the *Bhagavad-Gītā* after he ceased to be actively involved in nationalism, illustrated by reference to *Essays on the Gita* and *The Synthesis of Yoga*. Finally it discusses the eclipse of the *Bhagavad-Gītā* for his own spiritual purposes, illustrated by reference to *The Life Divine*. In so doing, it accepts Minor's thesis concerning the nature and implications of religious experience until eventually for Ghose '[t]he experiential authority asserted itself beyond all other authorities' whereby '[t]he *Gita*-yogin had transcended the *Gita*' (Minor 1991: 87).

6 Sharma asserts that, for Ghose, Kurukṣetra was 'existential, martial and typical' (Sharma 1983: 45). That it was martial and typical is clear, it is less obvious in what sense it was existential.

3 CHRISTIAN THEOLOGICAL AND MISSIONARY CRITIQUES

1 Sharpe describes Griffith's essay as 'the earliest missionary evaluation of the Gita', noting that it appeared fifty years before the 'Neo-Kṛishṇa movement' (Farquhar 1977: 294) occupied centre stage (Sharpe 1985: 35).

2 As Sharpe so astutely observes, this was 'a most remarkable exaggeration' even making allowance for the fact that at that time the *Bhagavad-Gītā* had yet to be hailed as embodying the whole of Hinduism so that its major role was restricted to devotional Vaiṣṇavism (Sharpe 1985: 36–7).

3 Despite the interregnum between the two, Sharpe refers to Farquhar as 'the first to attempt an independent interpretation of the Gita since Griffith' (Sharpe 1985: 96).

4 Sharpe does make the point that for Farquhar the focus was on Christ over Christianity, also that Farquhar's expertise as an exponent of Hinduism probably overshadowed his skills as a Christian theologian (Sharpe 1977: 23–4, 28–9).

5 Griffiths was convinced that he had a call to India, travelling to the subcontinent where at first hand he encountered Hindu belief and practice and embarked upon an experiment in Christian monasticism in an Indian setting. He acknowledged his predecessors and colleagues in the enculturation of [Catholic] Christianity in India and its reconciliation with Hinduism, citing Roberto de Nobili for his linguistic skills and renunciant lifestyle, Fathers Johanns and Danday for their theological explorations of Hindu thought, especially Vedānta, and Fathers Monchanin and Le Saux for their espousal of an ascetic and contemplative way of life (Griffiths 1966: 59–64).

6 Trapnell demarcates the characteristics of the earlier and later periods of Griffiths' career, chronicling the shift from the position in which '[g]race is universal, but one way to salvation and one way of knowledge alone lead to the final truth who is Christ' to that in which 'the Truth who is Christ may only be fully known if he is met in the wisdom of the other religions as well as Christianity' (Trapnell 2001: 104, 185).

4 UNIVERSALIST VISIONS

1 As French indicates, there was a dichotomy in Vivekananda's discourse on the *Bhagavad-Gītā*, tending to be more traditional in approach when talking to Westerners and more critical in approach when talking to Indians. French's explanation for this is that Vivekananda knew that Westerners were less knowledgeable than Indians about such sacred literature (French 1991: 134). An alternative explanation would be that he was offering Westerners a glimpse of an eternal truth of universal relevance but instructing Indians in the issues that preoccupied Western scholars, that is, the relationship between the *Bhagavad-Gītā* and the *Mahābhārata*, the origin and development of the Kṛṣṇa cult, the existence of the war fought by the Pāṇḍavas and the historicity of Arjuna (Vivekananda 1985: 102–5). In either case, as French observes, little, if any, information was provided as to his sources and his writings and speeches were not supported by scholarly apparatus (French 1991: 134).

2 Many scholars have noted that Vivekananda had rather different messages for the West and for India (e.g. French 1991). In the West, he emphasized Indian spirituality; in India, the need for practical activity. Some impression of the contrasting attitude adopted in addressing Hindu audiences can be gained from his observations on 'Vedanta in its Application to Indian Life' when he attached priority to physical culture over religion, provocatively asserting that '[y]ou will be nearer to Heaven through football than through the study of the Gita' on the grounds that the *Bhagavad-Gītā* could be better understood by the strong (Vivekananda 1995b: 242).

3 As Minor observes, during his career, Radhakrishnan produced commentaries on the *Upaniṣads*, *Vedānta Sūtra* and the *Bhagavad-Gītā* in the manner of traditional Vedāntic philosophers and theologians (Minor 1991: 161; cf. Radhakrishnan 1989a: 16).

4 In the preface to his commentary on the *Bhagavad-Gītā*, Radhakrishnan differentiated between two aspects of a scripture, 'one temporary and perishable, belonging to the ideas of the people of the period and the country in which it is produced, and the other eternal and imperishable, and applicable to all ages and countries' (Radhakrishnan 1989a). Explaining that the *Bhagavad-Gītā* addressed his contemporaries as it had past generations, he identified the major issue then facing the world as global unity and claimed that the text was appropriate to this cause because it united diverse, even seemingly contradictory, religious perspectives (Radhakrishnan 1989a).

5 As Miller suggests, such a technique might account not only for apparent contradictions in Kṛṣṇa's instruction of Arjuna but also for the impression of inconsistency given by Sivananda's own attempts to instruct his disciples and assist them to make progress from different starting-points (Miller 1991: 178).

6 Miller examines the complexities of Sivananda's treatment of karma-yoga, observing Sivananda's tendencies to demote this path and also to see it as an alternative path to knowledge while emphasizing its particular applicability to Arjuna on the battlefield (Miller 1991: 194–5).

5 ROMANTIC AND MYSTICAL INSIGHTS

1 Richardson suggests that Thoreau's interpretation of Hindu scriptures during 1849–50 focused on the themes of 'withdrawal' and 'liberation': finding in the *Vedas*, the restraint of passions; in the *Harivaṃśa*, the path to release; in the *Sāṃkhya Kārikā*, the primacy of knowledge over action; and in the *Viṣṇu Purāṇa*, the supercession of duality by unity (Richardson 1986: 206–7). He notes how Thoreau's interest in Hindu scriptures changed from an earlier emphasis on the *Laws of Manu* associated with 'concepts of cosmic order and universal law' to a preoccupation with 'a practical path to individual freedom', addressing the issue that had troubled him in his treatment of the *Bhagavad-Gītā*, namely, the inadequacy of the argument advanced to persuade Arjuna to fight (Richardson 1986: 206).

2 Sharpe takes this to be a mistaken reference to Warren Hastings and Charles Wilkins (mistaken because Hastings was not a soldier) though another possibility, perhaps not to be excluded entirely, would be a reference to the class system set out in the *Bhagavad-Gītā* (Sharpe 1985: 28).

3 As Neufeldt explains, action is doing what needs to be done without attachment, predicated upon the identification of the many with the one, entailing a transcendence of the conventional categories of good and evil as arising out of ignorance and involving a realization of the unity of reality (Neufeldt 1991: 27).

4 This is in line with Sharpe's interpretation of Besant's ideas as articulated in *Hints on the Study of the Bhagavad Gita* where Sharpe insists that at the time, with the rise of nationalist consciousness, the exhortation to action would be understood to apply to contemporary Indians (Sharpe 1985: 108).

5 Larson analyses different translations of the *Bhagavad-Gītā* under four headings – the '[s]tylistic', '[p]edagogical', '[i]nterpretive' and '[m]otivational' continua (Larson 1981). He describes the Prabhavananda and Isherwood translation in the following terms: stylistically, attractive, if very free; pedagogically, addressed to Western adherents of neo-Vedānta; interpretively, influenced by Śaṅkara's Advaitin philosophy if in a general, rather than a particularly Indian, sense; motivationally, a confessional work written by and for neo-Vedāntins (Larson 1981: 524–5).

6 The link with The Vedanta Society, according to Holmes, was through Trabuco College, which The Vedanta Society sponsored and where Huxley and others established a monastic community as an experiment in the conduct of a simple, disciplined spiritual life (Holmes 1970: 139–41). It should be noted, however, that in Woodcock's opinion, Huxley's association with The Vedanta Society was characterized by scepticism (Woodcock 1972: 239).

6 CONTEMPORARY TEACHERS AND MOVEMENTS

1 As Kim Knott observes, the man then known as Abhay Charan De was entrusted by his own spiritual master with the task of communicating the mission's message to an English-speaking audience, a task that involved him in an enormous publishing effort, especially after he renounced the world, and eventually in travel to the West where he preached the message of Kṛṣṇa consciousness (Knott 1986: 28–9).

2 As Rawlinson indicates, Prabhupada regarded devotional service (including worship of the form, eating blessed food, reading literature extolling Kṛṣṇa and chanting Kṛṣṇa's name) as itself constituting liberation rather than only leading to it (Rawlinson 1997: 481).

3 An editorial in *Vaishnava News* hails Ronald Nixon as '[t]he First Western Vaishnava' (Parivrajak 1999). Rawlinson relates how the former fighter pilot took up a lectureship at Lucknow University before being initiated by Monica Chakravarti, wife of the

university's vice-chancellor, into the Gauḍiya Vaiṣṇava tradition. After his guru renounced the world, receiving vairāginī status in the Gauḍiya Vaiṣṇava saṃpradāya under the authority of Acharya Sri Balkrishna Goswami and taking the name Sri Yashoda Mai, he took his own vows whereupon he became known as Sri Krishna Prem (Rawlinson 1997: 380). The approach taken by Krishna Prem to the Gauḍiya Vaiṣṇava tradition was characterized, especially latterly, by a certain freedom and independence in respect of orthodox belief and practice (Ginsburg 2003). His successor, Sri Madhava Ashish, testified that Krishna Prem's move away from orthodoxy was motivated by his differentiation between the essential and the inessential in the religious life and by his recognition of changing attitudes in both East and West (Madhava Ashish 1976: 28–9). One aspect of his unorthodoxy, perhaps too an aspect of continuity with his earlier life in terms of his interest in Theosophy, was his authorship of a commentary on the *Stanzas of Dzyan*, the source material of Madame Blavatsky's *The Secret Doctrine*, published as *Man: The Measure of All Things* and *Man: Son of Man* (Kaul 1980: x). Significantly, as Rawlinson points out, the lineage of Krishna Prem, Madhava Ashish and Dev constitutes a branch of the Gauḍiya Vaiṣṇava tradition in India led by Western gurus (Rawlinson 1997: 381).

4 Here then was the ambivalence of Krishna Prem – he was a Hindu guru but not all of his ideas or actions conform to this image. One explanation for any possible divergence is chronological: perhaps his earlier insistence on strict observance of orthodoxy was inspired by his respect for his predecessors and his consequent readiness to follow the path they had followed to reach the goal; whereas later he had the confidence to change the norms established by his own guru, dispensing with many aspects of orthodoxy whether in his teachings or in his conduct (Rawlinson 1997: 381, n.3; cf. Madhava Ashish 1976: 23, 28–9).

5 Despite his links with the Sri Aurobindo Ashram, Chinmoy did not see himself as continuing the beliefs and practices associated with Aurobindo since, despite his admiration for Aurobindo, he took a more independent line (Anon. 1994). In the course of his commentary on the *Bhagavad-Gītā*, Chinmoy did refer to other teachers, among them Krishna Prem whom he quoted with approval (11.15–31; 17) (Chinmoy 1973: 86–7, 114). No reference was made to either Bhaktivedanta Swami Prabhupada or Maharishi Mahesh Yogi but other contemporary teachers were mentioned at various points to illustrate and substantiate his argument. The effect of this was to link his commentary to the spiritual wisdom expounded by many other Hindu figures whereas numerous references to Western material underlined the universality of the *Bhagavad-Gītā*.

6 To some extent, the interpretation Chinmoy offered of the *Bhagavad-Gītā* could be regarded as determined by the nature of the text. In relation to the *Vedas*, he pointed to Brahman as the one reality and, in relation to the *Upaniṣads*, he pointed to the reconciliation of the impersonal absolute and the personal deity (Chinmoy 1996: 29, 41). However, reading through his commentaries on the *Vedas* and the *Upaniṣads*, a certain continuity of thought emerges. Indeed, as has been demonstrated, what he had to say about the *Bhagavad-Gītā* was representative of his teaching as a whole.

7 Rothstein identifies some of the complexities surrounding Maharishi's connection with the Advaitin tradition. It is related that he requested Swami Brahmananda Saraswati to accept him as a disciple but accounts differ as to whether he was ever initiated into the order and whether he succeeded his guru in the lineage of Śaṅkara. Rothstein points out that Maharishi did live a monastic lifestyle even after he left the monastery setting and, while the formal link with the Advaitin tradition may be contentious, it is evident that Transcendental Meditation has enjoyed some measure of acceptance from Advaitin authorities (Rothstein 1996: 26).

8 When Maharishi set out 'The Six Systems of Indian Philosophy' in an appendix to his commentary on the *Bhagavad-Gītā*, his account of Vedānta favoured Śaṅkara's Advaita as in the description of Īśvara as an appearance of Brahman and of Ātman as appearing in the form of individual selves (Maharishi 1990: 492). Furthermore, while insisting that complete knowledge required all six systems, he regarded five (Nyāya, Vaiśeṣika, Yoga, Sāṃkhya, Karma Mīmāṃsā) as offering analyses from the relative perspective whereas the sixth (Vedānta) revealed the absolute truth (Maharishi 1990: 473).

BIBLIOGRAPHY

Acharyya, B.K. (1914) *Codification in British India*, Calcutta: Thacker, Spink.

Almond, P.C. (1992) 'The end of "religious" pluralism?', in N. Habel (ed.), *Religion and Multiculturalism in Australia: Essays in Honour of Victor Hayes*, Special Studies in Religions Series No. 7, Adelaide: Australian Association for the Study of Religions, pp. 47–55.

Andrews, C.F. (1912) *The Renaissance in India: Its Missionary Aspect*, London: Church Missionary Society.

Anon. (1994) 'Shri Chinmoy: snapshots', *Hinduism Today* (February). Available at: http://www.hinduism-today.com/archives/1994/2/1994-2-03.shtml (accessed 9 July 2003).

Apffel-Marglin, F. and Simon, S.L. (1994) 'Feminist Orientalism and development', in W. Harcourt (ed.), *Feminist Perspectives on Sustainable Development*, London: Zed Books, pp. 26–45.

Appadurai, A. (1981) *Worship and Conflict under Colonial Rule: A South Indian Case*, Cambridge: Cambridge University Press.

Arnold, Sir E. (1989) 'Preface', in E. Arnold (trans.), *The Song Celestial or Bhagavad Gita (From the Mahabharata) Being a Discourse Between Arjuna, Prince of India, and the Supreme Being Under the Form of Krishna*, first published 1885, Los Angeles, CA: Self-Realization Fellowship, pp. vii–xi.

Asad, T. (1993) *Genealogies of Religion: Discipline and Reasons of Power in Christianity and Islam*, Baltimore, MD: Johns Hopkins University Press.

Bailey, A. and Khul, D. (1998a) 'Discipleship in the New Age I – Personal Instructions to Disciples – L.T.S.K.'. Available at: http://beaskund.helloyou.ws/netnews/bk/discipleship1/disc1328.html (accessed 18 August 2003).

——(1998b) 'Discipleship in the New Age I – Talks to Disciples – part V'. Available at: http://beaskund.helloyou.ws/netnews/bk/discipleship1/disc1025.html (accessed 18 August 2003).

Balagangadhara, S.N. (1994) *'The Heathen in His Blindness…': Asia, The West and the Dynamic of Religion*, Studies in the History of Religions Vol. LXIV, Leiden: E.J. Brill.

Belvalkar, S.K. (1947) 'Editorial note', in S.K. Belvalkar (ed.), *The Bhīṣhmaparvan: Being the Sixth Book of the Mahābhārata the Great Epic of India*, Poona: Bhandarkar Oriental Research Institute, pp. I–X.

Besant, A. (1897) *Four Great Religions: Four Lectures Delivered on the Twenty-First Anniversary of the Theosophical Society at Adyar, Madras*, London: Theosophical Publishing Society.

—— (1906) *Hints on the Study of the Bhagavad-Gita: Four Lectures Delivered at the Thirtieth Anniversary Meeting of the Theosophical Society at Adyar, Madras, December, 1905*, Benares: Theosophical Publishing Society.

——(1939) *The Ancient Wisdom: An Outline of Theosophical Teaching*, first published 1897, Adyar, Madras, India, Wheaton, IL: The Theosophical Publishing House.

——(1953) 'Preface', in A. Besant (trans.), *The Bhagavad Gītā*, first published 1895, Adyar, Madras, India, Wheaton, IL: Theosophical Publishing House, pp. 11–19.

Bharati, Swami Aghenanda (1971) 'Hinduism and modernization', in R.F. Spencer (ed.), *Religion and Change in Contemporary Asia*, Minneapolis, MN: University of Minnesota Press, pp. 67–104.

——(1980) *The Ochre Robe*, Santa Barbara, CA: Ross Erikson.

Bharucha, R. (1991) 'A view from India', in D. Williams (ed.), *Peter Brook and* The Mahabharata: *Critical Perspectives*, London: Routledge, pp. 228–32.

Bhatt, C. and Mukta, P. (2000) 'Hindutva in the West: mapping the antinomies of diaspora nationalism', *Ethnic and Racial Studies*, 23.3: 407–41.

Bhattacharya, A. (1998) 'Celluloid Guru', *Life Positive*. Available at: http://www.lifepositive.com/mind/arts/cinema/films.asp (accessed 26 January 2004).

Bowie, F. (2000) *The Anthropology of Religion*, Oxford: Blackwell.

Brerewood, E. (1614) *Enquiries Touching the Diversity of Languages, and Religions through the Chiefe Parts of the World*, London: no publisher. Early English Books Online. Available at: http://eebo.chadwyck.com (accessed 11 November 2003).

Brockington, J.L. (1989) 'Warren Hastings and Orientalism', in G. Carnall and C. Nicholson (eds), *The Impeachment of Warren Hastings: Papers from a Bicentenary Commemoration*, Edinburgh: Edinburgh University Press, pp. 91–108.

——(1998) *The Sanskrit Epics*, Leiden: Brill.

Brodbeck, S. (2003) 'Introduction', in J. Mascaró (trans.), *The Bhagavad Gita*, first published 1962, London: Penguin Books, pp. xi–xxix.

Brook, P. (1988) 'Foreword', in J.C. Carrière (and P. Brook trans.), *The Mahabharata*, London: Methuen, pp. xii–xvi.

——(1989) *The Mahabharata*, Channel 4 Television Co. Ltd, The Brooklyn Academy of Music Inc., Mahabharata Ltd, Les Productions du 3ème Etage.

Brown, C.M. (1986) 'Purāṇa as scripture: from sound to image of the holy word in the Hindu tradition', *History of Religions*, 26: 68–86.

——(1998) *The Devī Gītā: The Song of the Goddess A Translation, Annotation and Commentary*, Albany, NY: State University of New York Press.

Brown, D.M. (1958) 'The philosophy of Bal Gangadhar Tilak', *Journal of Asian Studies*, (February): 197–206.

Burroughs, K.C. (2001) 'About the translation and annotation', in Purohit Swami (trans.), *Bhagavad Gita: Annotated and Explained*, Woodstock, VT: SkyLight Paths Publishing, pp. xxi–xxii.

Caland, W. (ed.) (1926) *Ziegenbalg's Malabarische Heidenthum* Verhandelingen der Koninklijke Akacemie van Wetenschappen te Amsterdam Afdeeling Leterkunde. Nieuwe reeks 25.3, Amsterdam: Uitgave van Könenklijke Akademie.

Callewaert, W.M. and Hemraj, S. (1982) *BhagavadGītānuvāda: A Study in Transcultural Translation*, Ranchi: Satya Bharati Publication.

Carrière, J.C. (and Brook, P. trans.) (1988) *The Mahabharata*, London: Methuen.

Chatterji, P.C. (1984) *Secular Values for Secular India*, New Delhi: P.C. Chatterji.

Chinmayananda, Swami (1977) 'The Gita', in A. Pai and P. Mulik (eds), *The Gita* (*Amar Chitra Katha*: The Glorious Heritage of India Vol. 505), Mumbai: India Book House Limited.

Chinmoy, Sri (1973) *Commentary on the Bhagavad Gita: The Song of the Transcendental Soul*, New York: Rudolf Steiner Publication.

——(1994) 'Peace institute honors Chinmoy (interview with *Hinduism Today*)' (February). Available at: http://www.hinduism-today.com/archives/1994/2/1994-2-03.shtml (accessed 9 July 2003).

——(1996) *Commentaries on the Vedas, the Upanishads and the Bhagavad Gita: The Three Branches of India's Life-Tree*, New York: Aum Publications.

——(2002a) 'Aspects of the Supreme'. Available at: http://www.srichinmoy.org/html/spirituality/god_supreme/aspects_of_the_supreme.htm (accessed 9 July 2003).

——(2002b) 'The Guru: Your Private Tutor'. Available at: http://www.srichinmoy.org/html/spirituality/meditation/guru/1_guru_private_tutor.htm (accessed 9 July 2003).

——(2002c) 'Our Path'. Available at: http://www.srichinmoy.org/html/spirituality/our_path.html (accessed 9 July 2003).

——(2002d) 'The Personal Aspect of the Supreme'. Available at: http://www.srichinmoy.org/html/spirituality/god_supreme/aspects_god/personal_aspect_of_supreme.html (accessed 9 July 2003).

——(2002e) 'Religion and Spirituality'. Available at: http://www.srichinmoy.org/html/spirituality/god_supreme/communing_god/religion_spirituality.htm (accessed 9 July 2003).

Chopra, B.R. and Chopra, R. (2003) *Mahabharat* (15 hour DVD format containing the *Bhagavad-Gītā*), Arrow Films/Freemantle Media.

Christy, A. (1932) *The Orient in American Transcendentalism*, New York: Columbia University Press.

Clarke, J.J. (1997) *Oriental Enlightenment: The Encounter Between Asian and Western Thought*, London: Routledge.

Coburn, T.B. (1984) ' "Scripture" in India: towards a typology of the word in Hindu life', *Journal of the American Academy of Religion*, 52.3: 435–59.

Cohn, B. (1987) *An Anthropologist among the Historians and Other Essays*, Delhi: Oxford University Press.

——(1994) 'The command of language and the language of command', in R. Guha (ed.), *Subaltern Studies IV: Writings on South Asian History and Society*, first published 1985, Delhi: Oxford University Press, pp. 276–329.

Court Service (2004) 'CJS Online'. Available at: http://www.juror.cjsonline.org/ (accessed 12 February 2004).

Coward, H. (1988) *Sacred Word and Sacred Text: Scripture in World Religions*, Maryknoll, NY: Orbis Books.

Curzon, Lord G. (1909) (Contribution to Debate on Oriental Languages in the House of Lords, Monday 27 September), cols. *Hansard*, London: HMSO, pp. 375–83.

Dalmia, V. (1995) ' "The real religion of the Hindus": Vaiṣṇava self-representation in the nineteenth century', in V. Dalmia and H. von Stietencron (eds), *Representing Hinduism: The Construction of Religious Traditions and National Identity*, New Delhi: Sage Publications, pp. 176–210.

Dalmia, V. and von Stientencron, H. (1995) 'Introduction', in V. Dalmia and H. von Stietencron (eds), *Representing Hinduism: The Construction of Religious Traditions and National Identity*, New Delhi: Sage Publications, pp. 17–32.

Dandekar, R.N. (1971) 'Hinduism', in C.J. Bleeker and G. Widengren (eds), *Historia Religionum: Handbook for the History of Religions Vol. 2 Religions of the Present*, Leiden: E.J. Brill, pp. 237–43.

Das, G.K. (1979) 'E.M. Forster, T.S. Eliot, and the "Hymn Before Action"' in G.K. Das and J. Beer (eds), *E.M. Forster: A Human Exploration – Centenary Essays*, London: Macmillan Press, pp. 208–15, 300.

Dasgupta, D. (1991) 'Peter Brook's "Orientalism"', in D. Williams (ed.), *Peter Brook and* The Mahabharata: *Critical Perspectives*, London: Routledge, pp. 262–7.

Davis, R.H. (1995) 'Introduction: A brief history of religions in India', in D.S. Lopez (ed.), *Religions of India in Practice*, Princeton, NJ: Princeton University Press, pp. 3–52.

Deccan Herald (2003) 'G.V. Iyer no more', *Deccan Herald*. Available at: http://www.deccanherald.com/deccannerald/dec22/i6asp (accessed 15 January 2004).

de Humboldt, W. (1849) 'Essay on the episode of the Mahabharat, known by the name of Bhagvat-Geeta' (Lecture delivered in Berlin Academy of Science 1825–6; trans. Rev. G.H. Weigle), in J. Garrett (ed.), *The Bhagavat-Geeta or Dialogues of Krishna and Arjoon in Eighteen Lectures; Sanscrit, Canarese and English in Parallel Columns*, Bangalore: Wesleyan Missionary Press, pp. 121–47.

Derrett, J.D.M. (1968) *Religion, Law and the State In India*, London: Faber & Faber.

Deutsch, E. and Siegel, L. (1987) 'Bhagavadgīta', in M. Eliade (ed.), *The Encyclopedia of Religion*, New York: Macmillan, 2: 124–8.

Donoghue, D. (1969) 'T.S. Eliot's Quartets: a new reading', in B. Bergonzi (ed.), *T.S. Eliot* Four Quartets*: A Casebook*, London: Macmillan, pp. 212–36.

Duff, A. (1840) *India and India Missions: Including Sketches of the Gigantic System of Hinduism, Both in Theory and Practice; Also, Notices of Some of the Principal Agencies Employed in Conducting the Process of Indian Evangelization, & c., & c.*, second edition, Edinburgh: John Johnstone.

Dyer, W. (1992) *Real Magic: Creating Miracles in Everyday Life*, New York: HarperCollins.

Ebert, R. (2000) '[Review of] *The Legend of Bagger Vance*', *Chicago Sun Times*. Available at: http://www.suntimes.com/ebert/ebert_reviews/2000/11/110302.html (accessed 18 August 2003).

Eder, M. (2003) 'The Bhagavadgītā and Classical Hinduism: a sketch', in A. Sharma (ed.), *The Study of Hinduism*, Columbia, SC: University of South Carolina Press, pp. 169–99.

Edgerton, F. (trans.) (1972) *The Bhagavad Gītā*, first published 1944, Cambridge, MA: Harvard University Press.

Edwardes, M. (1967) *British India 1772–1947: A Survey of the Nature and Effects of Alien Rule*, London: Sidgwick and Jackson.

Eliot, T.S. (1974) *Collected Poems 1901–1962*, new edition, London: Faber & Faber.

Embree, A.T. (1990) *Utopias in Conflict: Religion and Nationalism in Modern India*, Berkeley, CA: University of California Press.

Encyclopaedia Britannica (1998) 'Bhagavadgītā', in *The New Encyclopaedia Britannica*, fifteenth edition, Chicago, IL: Encyclopaedia Britannica Inc., 2: 183.

Erndl, K.M. (1993) *Victory to the Mother: The Hindu Goddess of Northwest India in Myth, Ritual, and Symbol*, New York: Oxford University Press.

Ernst, Carl W. (1992) *Eternal Garden: Mysticism, History and Politics at a South Asian Sufi Center*, Albany, NY: State University of New York Press.

Farquhar, J.N. (1904) *The Age and Origin of the Gita*, London: The Christian Literature Society.

Farquhar, J.N. (1912) *Permanent Lessons of the Gita*, second edition, London: The Christian Literature Society for India.

——(1913) *The Crown of Hinduism*, London: Humphrey Milford/Oxford University Press.

——(1920) *An Outline of the Religious Literature of India*, London: Humphrey Milford/Oxford University Press.

——(1977) *Modern Religious Movements in India*, first published 1914, New Delhi: Munshiram Manoharlal.

Feiling, K. (1954) *Warren Hastings*, London: Macmillan.

Ferro-Luzzi, G.E. (1991) 'The polythetic-prototype approach to Hinduism', in G.D. Sontheimer and H. Kulke (eds), *Hinduism Reconsidered*, South Asian Studies No. XXIV, New Delhi: Manohar, pp. 187–95.

Feuerstein, G. (1983) *The Bhagavad Gita: Its Philosophy and Cultural Setting*, first published 1974, Madras: Theosophical Publishing House.

Firth, S. (1991) 'Changing patterns in Hindu death rituals in Britain', in D. Killingley, W. Menski and S. Firth (eds), *Hindu Ritual and Society*, Newcastle, NY: S.Y. Killingley, pp. 52–87.

Fitzgerald, T. (1990) 'Hinduism and the "World Religion" Fallacy', *Religion*, 20: 101–18.

——(2000) *The Ideology of Religious Studies*, Oxford: Oxford University Press.

Flood, G. (1996) *An Introduction to Hinduism*, Cambridge: Cambridge University Press.

——(2003) 'Introduction: establishing the boundaries', in G. Flood (ed.), *The Blackwell Companion to Hinduism*, Oxford: Blackwell Publishing, pp. 1–19.

Folkert, K.W. (1989) 'The "canons" of "scripture"', in M. Levering (ed.), *Rethinking Scripture: Essays from a Comparative Perspective*, Albany, NY: State University of New York Press, pp. 170–7.

Forster, E.M. (1940) 'Hymn Before Action', in E.M. Forster (ed.), *Abinger Harvest*, London: Edwin Arnold, pp. 328–30.

French, H.W. (1991) 'Swami Vivekananda's use of the *Bhagavadgita*', in R.N. Minor (ed.), *Modern Indian Interpreters of the Bhagavadgita*, Sri Garab Dass Oriental Series No. 127, Delhi: Sri Satguru Publications, pp. 131–46.

Frykenberg, R.E. (1991) 'The emergence of modern "Hinduism" as a concept and as an institution: a reappraisal with special reference to South India', in G.D. Sontheimer and H. Kulke (eds), *Hinduism Reconsidered*, South Asian Studies No. XXIV, New Delhi: Manohar, pp. 29–49.

——(2000) 'The construction of Hinduism as a "Public" religion: looking again at the religious roots of company Raj in South India', in K.E. Yandall and J.J. Paul (eds), *Religion and Public Culture: Encounters and Identities in Modern South India*, Richmond, VA: Curzon Press, pp. 3–26.

Gandhi, M.K. (1946) *The Gospel of Selfless Action or the Gita According to Gandhi*, M. Desai (trans.), Ahmedabad: Navajivan Publishing House.

——(1958) *All Men Are Brothers: Life and Thoughts of Mahatma Gandhi as Told in his own Words*, Paris: Unesco.

——(1960) *Discourses on the Gita*, V.G. Desai (trans.), Ahmedabad: Navajivan Publishing House.

——(1971) *The Writings of Gandhi*, R. Duncan (ed.), Oxford: Fontana Collins.

——(1978) *Hindu Dharma*, New Delhi: Orient Paperbacks.

——(1980) *The Bhagvadgita*, New Delhi: Orient Paperbacks.

——(1982) *An Autobiography or the Story of My Experiments with Truth*, first published in 2 volumes 1927–9, Harmondsworth: Penguin Books.

——(1988) *A Gandhi Reader*, K. Swaminathan and C.N. Patel (eds), Madras: Orient Longman.

Garbe, R. (1909) 'Bhagavad-Gita', in J. Hastings (ed.), *Encyclopaedia of Religion and Ethics*, Edinburgh: Edinburgh University Press, 2: 535–8.

Gardiner, H. (1978) *The Composition of* Four Quartets, London: Faber & Faber.

Garrett, J. (1849) 'Advertisment', in J. Garrett (ed.), *The Bhagavat-Geeta or Dialogues of Krishna and Arjoon in Eighteen Lectures: Sanscrit, Canarese, and English in Parallel Columns*, Bangalore: Wesleyan Missionary Press, pp. iii–iv.

Germann, W. (ed.) (1867) *Genealogie der Malabarishen Götter. Aus eigenen Schriften und Briefen der Heiden zusammengetragen und verfasst von Bartholomaeus Ziegenbalg, weil. Propst an der Jerusamels-Kirche in Trankebar*, Madras: Printed for the Editor at the Christian Knowledge Society's Press.

Ghose, A. (1964) *Sri Aurobindo and his Ashram*, Pondicherry: Sri Aurobindo Ashram.

——(1970) *Essays on the Gita*, Pondicherry: Sri Aurobindo Ashram.

——(1972a) *Bande Mataram – Early Political Writings I*, Pondicherry: Sri Aurobindo Ashram.

——(1972b) *Karmayogin – Early Political Writings II*, Pondicerry: Sri Aurobindo Ashram.

——(1972c) *Writings in Bengali*, Pondicherry: Sri Aurobindo Ashram.

——(1982) *The Life Divine*, Pondicherry: Sri Aurobindo Ashram.

——(1987) *The Essential Aurobindo*, R.A. McDermott (ed.), Great Barrington: The Lindisfarne Press.

Ginsburg, S. (2003) 'Interview: Sy Ginsburg, USA'. Available at: http://www.gurdjieff-internet.com/article_print.php?ID=24&W=9 (accessed 11 July 2003).

Gitā Press (2003a) 'Gita Press – An Introduction'. Available at: http://www.gitapress.org/english/epstat.html (accessed 12 June 2003).

——(2003b) 'Gita Press – Publication Overview'. Available at: http://www.gitapress.org/english/epstat.html (accessed 12 June 2003).

Gokhale, B.G. (1984) 'Hindu responses to the Muslim presence in Maharashtra', in Y. Friedmann (ed.), *Islam in Asia, Vol.1 South Asia*, Jerusalem: The Magnas Press and Boulder, CO: Westview Press, pp. 146–73.

Gokulsing, K.M. and Dissanayake, W. (1998) *Indian Popular Cinema: A Narrative of Cultural Change*, Stoke-on-Trent: Trentham Books.

Goody, J. (1986) *The Logic of Writing and the Organization of Society*, Cambridge: Cambridge University Press.

Graham, W.A. (1987) *Beyond the Written Word: Oral Aspects of Scripture in the History of Religion*, Cambridge: Cambridge University Press.

Griffith, R.D. (1849) 'An essay on the Bhagavat-Geeta', in J. Garrett (ed.), *The Bhagavat-Geeta or Dialogues of Krishna and Arjoon in Eighteen Lectures: Sanscrit, Canarese, and English in Parallel Columns*, Bangalore: Wesleyan Missionary Press, pp. xxxvii–lvii.

Griffiths, Bede (1966) *Christian Ashram: Essays Towards a Hindu-Christian Dialogue*, London: Darton, Longman and Todd.

——(1973) *Vedanta & Christian Faith*, Los Angeles, CA: The Dawn Horse Press.

——(1987) *River of Compassion*, Warwick, NY: Amity House.

Gupta, P., Gupta, M.D. and Vikram, N.K. (1977) *The Bhagwad-Gita*, New Delhi: Dreamland Publication.

Halbfass, W. (1988) *India and Europe: An Essay in Understanding*, translation of *Indien und Europe*, Albany, NY: State University of New York Press.

Halhed, N. (1777) 'The translator's preface', in N. Halhed (trans.), *A Code of Gentoo Laws, or, Ordinations of the Pundits*, London: no publisher, pp. ix–lxx.

Hardy, F. (1990) 'Hinduism', in U. King (ed.), *Turning Points in Religious Studies*, Edinburgh: T. & T. Clark, pp. 145–55.

Harrison, P. (1990) *'Religion' and the Religions in the English Enlightenment*, Cambridge: Cambridge University Press.

Harvey, A. (2001) 'Foreword', in Purohit Swami (trans.), *Bhagavad Gita: Annotated and Explained*, Woodstock, VT: SkyLight Paths Publishing, pp. ix–xiv.

Harvey, M.J. (1986) 'The secular as sacred? – the religio-political rationalization of B.G. Tilak', *Modern Asian Studies*, 20.2: 321–31.

Hastings, W. (1784) '[Letter to] Nathaniel Smith', in C. Wilkins (trans.), *The Bhăgvăt-Gēētā or Dialogues of Krēēshnă and Ărjŏŏn; In Eighteen Lectures; With Notes*, first published 1785 in London by C. Nourse, reprinted 1972 in New York by Scholars' Facsimiles and Reprints, pp. 5–16.

Hawley, J.S. (1991) 'Naming Hinduism', *Wilson Quarterly* (Summer): 20–34.

Heelas, P. (1997) 'Introduction: on differentiation and dedifferentiation', in P. Heelas (ed.), *Religion, Modernity and Postmodernity*, Oxford: Blackwell Publishers, pp. 1–18.

Heimsath, C.H. (1964) *Indian Nationalism and Hindu Social Reform*, Princeton, NJ: Princeton University Press.

Hiltebeitel, A. (1991) 'Of camphor and coconuts', *Wilson Quarterly* (Summer): 26–28 (Inset).

——(2003) 'India's epics: writing, orality and divinity', in A. Sharma (ed.), *The Study of Hinduism*, Columbia, SC: University of South Carolina Press, pp. 114–38.

Holmes, C.M. (1970) *Aldous Huxley and the Way to Reality*, Bloomington and London: Indiana University Press.

Horstmann, M. (1995) 'Towards a universal dharma: *Kalyāṇ* and the tracts of the Gītā Press', in V. Dalmia and H. von Stietencron (eds), *Representing Hinduism: The Construction of Religious Traditions and National Identity*, New Delhi: Sage Publications, pp. 294–305.

Huxley, A. (1965) *Ends and Means: An Enquiry into the Nature and Ideals and into the Methods Employed for their Realization*, first published 1937, London: Chatto & Windus.

——(1969) *The Perennial Philosophy*, first published 1946, London: Chatto & Windus.

——(1972) 'Introduction', in Swami Prabhavananda and C. Isherwood (trans.), *The Song of God: Bhagavad-Gita*, first published 1944, New York: Mentor Books, pp. 11–22.

Inden, R. (1990) *Imagining India*, Oxford: Blackwell.

International Gita Society (2003) 'Aims and Objectives of the American/International Gita Society'. Available at: http://www.gita-society.com/aboutus?O_aboutus.htm (accessed 18 August 2003).

ISKCON Educational Services (n.d. a) 'The Hare Krishna Movement' Fact Sheet no. 3.1.

——(n.d. b) 'Hinduism – A Brief Overview' Fact Sheet no. 4.1.

——(n.d. c) 'The Historical Development of ISKCON' Fact Sheet no. 3.2.

Jackson, R. (1996) 'The construction of "Hinduism" and its impact on Religious Education in England and Wales', *Panorama*, 8.2: 86–104.

Jacobs, A. (2003) 'Foreword' and 'Introduction', in A. Jacobs (trans.), *The Bhagavad-Gita: A Transcreation of The Song Celestial*, Winchester: O Books, pp. xiii–xiv, xv–xxii.

Jaffrelot, C. (1996) *The Hindu Nationalist Movement and Indian Politics: 1925 to the 1990s*, first published as *Les Nationalistes Hindoues* in 1993 by Presses de la Fondation Nationale de Sciences Politiques, Paris: C. Hurst & Co.

Johnson, W.J. (1994) 'Introduction', in W.J. Johnson (trans.), *The Bhagavad Gita*, Oxford: Oxford University Press, pp. vii–xix.

Johnston, E.H. (1937) *Early Sāmkhya*, London: Royal Asiatic Society.

Jones, K.W. (1981) 'Religious identity and the Indian census', in N.G. Barrier (ed.), *The Census in British India: New Perspectives*, New Delhi: Manohar, pp. 73–101.

——(1989) *Arya Dharm: Hindu Consciousness in 19th Century Punjab*, first published 1976, New Delhi: Manohar.

Kapoor, J.C. (1983) *Bhagavad-Gītā: An International Bibliography of 1785–1979 Imprints*, New York: Garland Publishing.

Kaul, N.N. (1980) *Writings of Sri Krishna Prem: An Introduction*, Bombay: Bharatiya Vidya Bhavan.

King, R. (1999) *Orientalism and Religion: Postcolonial Theory, India and 'The Mystic East'*, London: Routledge.

King, U. (1982) 'The Iconography of the Bhagavad Gītā', *Journal of Dharma*, 7.2: 147–63.

——(1987) 'Iconographic reflections on the religious and secular importance of the Bhagavad-Gītā within the image world of modern Hinduism', in A. Sharma (ed.), *New Essays in the Bhagavad-Gītā: Philosophical, Methodological and Cultural Approaches*, New Delhi: Books & Books, pp. 161–88.

Klostermaier, K.K. (1994) *A Survey of Hinduism*, second edition, Albany, NY: State University of New York Press.

Knott, K. (1982) *Hinduism in Leeds: A Study of Religious Practice in the Indian Hindu Community and in Hindu-Related Groups*, Leeds: University of Leeds.

——(1986) *My Sweet Lord: The Hare Krishna Movement*, Wellingborough: The Aquarian Press.

——(1998) *Hinduism: A Very Short Introduction*, Oxford: Oxford University Press.

Kopf, D. (1979) *The Brahmo Samaj and the Shaping of the Modern Indian Mind*, Princeton, NJ: Princeton University Press.

Krishna Prem, Sri (1976) *Initiation into Yoga: An Introduction to the Spiritual Life*, London: Rider & Co.

——(1988) *The Yoga of the Bhagavat Gita*, Shaftesbury: Element Books.

Laine, J. (1983) 'The notion of "Scripture" in modern Indian thought', *Annals of the Bhandarkar Oriental Research Institute*, 64: 165–79.

Larson, G.J. (1975) 'The *Bhagavad-Gītā* as cross-cultural process: toward an analysis of the social locations of a religious text', *Journal of the American Academy of Religion*, 43.4: 651–69.

——(1981) 'The Song Celestial: two centuries of the *Bhagavad-Gītā* in English', *Philosophy East and West*, 31.4: 513–41.

——(1993) 'Discourse about "religion" in colonial and postcolonial India', in N. Smart and S. Thakur (eds), *Ethical and Political Dilemmas of Modern India*, Basingstoke: Macmillan, pp. 181–93.

——(2000) 'Hinduism in India and in America', in J. Neusner (ed.), *World Religions in America*, Louisville, KY: Westminster John Knox Press, pp. 125–41.

Lawrence, B.B. (trans.) (1976) *Shahrastānī on the Indian Religions*, The Hague and Paris: Mouton.

Lawrenson, E. (2001) '[Review of] *The Legend of Bagger Vance*', *Sight and Sound*, 11.3: 53.

Levering, M. (1989) 'Introduction: rethinking scripture', in M. Levering (ed.), *Rethinking Scripture: Essays from a Comparative Perspective*, Albany, NY: State University of New York Press, pp. 1–17.

Levy, H. (1973) *Indian Modernization by Legislation: The Hindu Code Bill*, unpublished thesis, University of Chicago.

Lindop, G. (forthcoming) 'The Indian influence on Blake', manuscript of work in progress kindly supplied by author.

Lipner, J. (1994) *Hindus: Their Religious Beliefs and Practices*, London: Routledge.

Lopez, D.S. (2000) 'Pandit's revenge', *Journal of the American Academy of Religion*, 68.4: 831–5.

Lorenzen, D.N. (1999) 'Who invented Hinduism?', *Comparative Studies in Society and History*, 41.4: 630–59.

Losty, J.P. (1982) *The Art of the Book in India*, London: The British Library.

Lucas, B. (1907) *The Empire of Christ: Being a Study of the Missionary Enterprise in the Light of Modern Religious Thought*, London: Macmillan & Co.

Ludden, D. (1993) 'Orientalist empiricism: transformations of colonial knowledge', in C.A. Breckenridge and P. van der Veer (eds), *Orientalism and the Postcolonial Predicament: Perspectives on South Asia*, Philadelphia, PA: University of Pennsylvania Press, pp. 250–78.

McCutcheon, R.T. (1997) *Manufacturing Religion: The Discourse on Sui Generis Religion and the Politics of Nostalgia*, New York: Oxford University Press.

McLane, J. (ed.) (1970) *The Political Awakening in India*, Englewood Cliffs, NJ: Prentice-Hall.

Madhava Ashish, Sri (1976) 'Foreword', in Sri Krishna Prem (ed.), *Initiation into Yoga: An Introduction to the Spiritual Life*, London: Rider and Company, pp. 7–30.

Maharishi Mahesh Yogi (1966) *The Science of Being and the Art of Living*, New York: Maharishi International University Press.

——(1990) *Maharishi Mahesh Yogi on the Bhagavad-gita: A Translation and Commentary Chapters 1–6*, London: Arkana Books.

Malinar, A. (1995) 'The *Bhagavadgītā* in the *Mahābhārata* TV Serial: domestic drama and dharmic solutions', in V. Dalmia and H. von Stietencron (eds), *Representing Hinduism: The Construction of Religious Traditions and National Identity*, New Delhi: Sage Publications, pp. 442–67.

Mani, L. (1987) 'Contentious traditions: the debate on sati in colonial India', *Cultural Critique*, 7: 119–56.

Mascaró, J. (1961) 'Preface', in J. Mascaró (ed.), *Lamps of Fire: From the Scriptures and Wisdom of the World*, first published 1958, London: Methuen, pp. 9–11.

——(1962) 'Introduction' and 'Note on the translation', in J. Mascaró (trans.), *The Bhagavad Gita*, London: Penguin Books, pp. 9–36, 37–8.

Metcalf, T.R. (1995) *Ideologies of the Raj*, The New Cambridge History of India III.4, Cambridge: Cambridge University Press.

Miller, D.M. (1991) 'Swami Sivananda and the *Bhagavadgita*', in R.N. Minor (ed.), *Modern Indian Interpreters of the Bhagavadgita*, Sri Garab Dass Oriental Series No. 127, Delhi: Sri Satguru Publications, pp. 173–99.

Minor, R.N. (1991) 'Introduction', 'Sri Aurobindo as a *Gita*-yogin' and 'The *Bhagavadgita* in Radhakrishnan's apologetics', in R.N. Minor (ed.), *Modern Indian Interpreters of the Bhagavadgita*, Sri Garab Dass Oriental Series No. 127, Delhi: Sri Satguru Publications, pp. 1–10, 61–87, 147–72.

Mitchell, S. (2000) 'Introduction', in S. Mitchell (trans.), *The Bhagavad Gita*, London: Rider Books, pp. 13–30.

Monier-Williams, M. (1875) *Indian Wisdom or Examples of the Religious, Philosophical and Ethical Doctrines of the Hindus*, London: Wm H. Allen & Co.

——(1878) *Modern India and the Indians: Being a Series of Impressions, Notes, and Essays*, second edition, London: Trübner & Co.

——(1882) 'The Vaishṇava religion with special reference to the Śikshā-patrī of the modern sect called Svāmī-Nārāyaṇa', *Journal of the Royal Asiatic Society* (N.S.), 14: 289–316.

——(1883) *Religious Thought and Life in India*, London: John Murray.

——(1919) *Non-Christian Religious Systems: Hinduism*, London: Society for Promoting Christian Knowledge.

——(1976) 'Preface to the new edition', in M. Monier-Williams (comp.), *Sanskṛit–English Dictionary*, first published 1899, New Delhi: Munshiram Manoharlal, pp. v–x.

Muirhead, J.H. (1930) *Coleridge as Philosopher*, London: George Allen & Unwin, New York: Macmillan.

Müller, F.M. (1868) *Chips from a German Workshop Vol.1 Essays on the Science of Religion*, London: Longmans, Green & Co.

——(1873) *Introduction to the Science of Religion: Four Lectures Delivered at the Royal Institution with Two Essays on False Analogies, and the Philosophy of Mythology*, London: Longmans, Green & Co.

——(1875) *Chips from a German Workshop Vol. IV Essays Chiefly on the Science of Language*, London: Longmans, Green & Co.

——(1879) 'Preface to the Sacred Books of the East', in F.M. Müller (trans.), *The Sacred Books of the East Vol. I The Upanishads*, Oxford: Clarendon Press, pp. ix–lvi.

——(1883) *India: What Can it Teach Us? A Course of Lectures*, London: Longmans, Green & Co.

——(1891) *Lectures on the Origin and Growth of Religion as Illustrated by the Religions of India*, new edition, London: Longmans, Green & Co.

——(1899) *Auld Lang Syne Second Series: My Indian Friends*, London: Longmans, Green & Co.

Narayanan, V. (2000) 'Diglossic Hinduism: liberation and lentils', *Journal of the American Academy of Religion*, 68.4: 761–79.

——(2003) 'Hinduism', in A. Sharma and K.K. Young (eds), *Her Voice, Her Faith: Women Speak on World Religions*, Boulder, CO: Westview Press, pp. 11–57.

Nayak, R.S., Trivedi, P.K., Trivedi, C. and Vyas, R. (1984) *The Gita (The Song of the Supreme Being)*, Ahmedabad: Anada Book Depot.

Neufeldt, R.W. (1991) 'A lesson in allegory: Theosophical interpretations of the *Bhagavadgita*', in R. Minor (ed.), *Modern Indian Interpreters of the Bhagavadgita*, Delhi: Sri Satguru Publications, pp. 11–33.

Nikhilananda, Swami (trans.) (1942) *The Gospel of Sri Ramakrishna*, New York: Ramakrishna-Vivekananda Center.

Oberoi, H. (1997) *The Construction of Religious Boundaries: Culture, Identity and Diversity in the Sikh Tradition*, Delhi: Oxford University Press.

O'Connell, J.T. (1973) 'The word "Hindu" in Gauḍiya Vaiṣṇava texts', *Journal of the American Oriental Society*, 93.3: 340–4.

O'Connor, G. (1990) *The Mahabharata: Peter Brook's Epic in the Making*, San Francisco, CA: Mercury House.

Oddie, G.A. (2003) 'Constructing "Hinduism": the impact of the Protestant missionary movement on Hindu self-understanding', in R.E. Frykenberg (ed.), *Christians and Missionaries in India: Cross-Cultural Communication since 1500*, Grand Rapids: William B. Eeerdmans Publishing Company and London: RoutledgeCurzon, pp. 155–82.

O'Flaherty, W.D. (1979) 'Introduction', in W.D. O'Flaherty (ed.), *The Critical Study of Sacred Texts*, Berkeley, CA: Berkeley Religious Studies Series, pp. ix–xiii.

Omvedt, G. (1995) *Dalit Visions: Tracts for the Times/8*, London: Sangam Books.

Ong, W.J. (1982) *Orality and Literacy: The Technologizing of the Word*, London: Routledge.

Otto, R. (1930) *India's Religion of Grace and Christianity Compared and Contrasted*, F.H. Foster (trans.), London: Student Christian Movement Press.

——(1939) *The Original Gītā: The Song of the Supreme Exalted One*, J.E. Turner (trans.), first published in German in 1933, London: George Allen & Unwin.

——(1950) *The Idea of the Holy: An Inquiry into the Non-Rational Factor on the Idea of the Divine and its Relation to the Rational*, J.W. Harvey (trans.), second edition, Oxford: Oxford University Press.

——(1987) *Mysticism East and West: A Comparative Analysis of the Nature of Mysticism*, translation of *West-Östliche Mystik*, first published 1932, Wheaton: The Theosophical Publishing House.

Oxford World's Classics (2003) 'Homepage'. Available at: http://www1.oup.co.uk/WorldsClassics/ (accessed 6 January 2003).

Packer, B.L. (1985) 'The Curse of Kehama', in H. Bloom (ed.), *Ralph Waldo Emerson*, New York: Chelsea House Publishers, pp. 123–46.

Pai, A. and Mulik, P. (1977) *The Gita*, Amar Chitra Katha: The Glorious Heritage of India Vol. 505, Mumbai: India Book House Limited.

Parivrajak, B.V. Swami (1999) 'The first Western Vaishnava', *Vaishnava News* (17 October). Available at: http://www.vnn.org/editorials/ET9910?ET17-4959.html (accessed 11 July 2003).

Penguin Classics (2003) 'About Us'. Available at: http://uk.penguinclassics.com (accessed 6 July 2003).

Pennington, B.K. (2001) 'Constructing colonial dharma: a chronicle of emergent Hinduism, 1830–1831', *Journal of the American Academy of Religion*, 69.3: 577–603.

Pollock, S. (1993) 'Deep Orientalism? Notes on Sanskrit and power beyond the Raj', in C.A. Breckenridge and P. van der Veer (eds), *Orientalism and the Postcolonial Predicament: Perspectives on South Asia*, Philadelphia, PA: University of Pennsylvania Press, pp. 76–133.

Prabhavananda, Swami and Isherwood, C. (1972) 'Translator's preface', 'Gita and Mahabharata', 'The cosmology of the Gita' and 'The Gita and War', in Swami Prabhavananda and C. Isherwood (trans.), *The Song of God: Bhagavad-Gita*, first published 1944, New York: Mentor Books, pp. 9–11, 23–9, 131–7, 137–40.

Prabhupada, A.C. Bhaktivedanta Swami (1973) *Elevation to Kṛṣṇa Consciousness*, Boreham Wood: The Bhaktivedanta Book Trust.

——(1975) *Bhagavad-Gītā As It Is*, abridged edition, New York, Los Angeles, London: The Bhaktivedanta Book Trust.

——(1997) *The Quest for Enlightenment*, Los Angeles: The Bhaktivedanta Book Trust.

Pressfield, S. (1995) *The Legend of Bagger Vance: A Novel of Golf and the Game of Life*, London: Bantam Books.

Preus, J.S. (1987) *Explaining Religion: Criticism and Theory from Bodin to Freud*, New Haven, CT: Yale University Press.

Priolkar, A.K. (1958) *The Printing Press in India: Its Beginnings and Early Development*, Bombay: Marathi Samsodhana Mandala.

Pritchett, F.W. (1995) 'The world of *Amar Chitra Katha*', in L.A. Babb and S.S. Wadley (eds), *Media and the Transformation of Religion in South Asia*, Philadelphia, PA: University of Pennsylvania Press, pp. 76–106.

Purohit Swami (trans.) (2001) *Bhagavad Gita: Annotated and Explained*, Woodstock, VT: SkyLight Paths Publishing.

Radhakrishnan, S. (1927) *The Hindu View of Life*, London: George Allen and Unwin/ New York: The Macmillan Company.

——(1929) *Indian Philosophy*, Vol. 1, London: George Allen and Unwin/New York: Humanities Press.

——(1989a) *The Bhagavadgita: With an Introductory Essay, Sanskrit Text, English Translation and Notes*, first published 1948, London: Unwin Paperbacks.

——(1989b) *Eastern Religions and Western Thought*, first published 1939, Delhi: Oxford University Press.

Rajadhyaksha, A. and Willemen, P. (1999) *Encyclopaedia of Indian Cinema*, revised edition, London: British Film Institute/New Delhi: Oxford University Press.

Rashtriya Swayamsevak Sangh (RSS) (2003) 'The Mission of R.S.S.' Available at: http://www.rss.org/mission.htm (accessed 6 January 2003).

Rawlinson, A. (1997) *The Book of the Enlightened Masters: Western Teachers in Eastern Traditions*, Chicago, IL: Open Court.

Redford, R. (2000) *The Legend of Bagger Vance*. Twentieth Century Fox Film Corporation.

——(2002) *The Legend of Bagger Vance* (including 'Insight into The Legend of Bagger Vance' and 'Production notes' as DVD special features), Twentieth Century Fox Home Entertainment Inc.

Richards, G. (1982) *The Philosophy of Gandhi*, London: Curzon Press/Totowa, NJ: Barnes and Noble Books.

Richardson, R.D. (1986) *Henry Thoreau: A Life of the Mind*, Berkeley, LA: University of California Press.

Rocher, R. (1993) 'British Orientalism in the eighteenth century: the dialectics of knowledge and government', in C.A. Breckenridge and P. van der Veer (eds), *Orientalism and the Postcolonial Predicament: Perspectives on South Asia*, Philadelphia, PA: University of Pennsylvania Press, pp. 215–49.

Rosen, S. (2000) *Gita on the Green: The Mystical Tradition Behind Bagger Vance*, New York: Continuum.

Rothstein, M. (1996) *Belief Transformations: Some Aspects of the Relation Between Science and Religion in Transcendental Meditation (TM) and the International Society for Krishna Consciousness (ISKCON)*, Oakville, CT: Aarhus University Press.

Roy, D.K. (1968) *Yogi Sri Krishna Prem*, Chowpatty: Bharatiya Vidya Bhavan.

Roy, R.M. (1945) 'Translation of a conference between an advocate for and an opponent of the practice of burning widows alive' [1818], 'A second conference between an advocate for and an opponent of the practice of burning widows alive' [1820] and

'Abstract of the arguments regarding the burning of widows considered as a religious rite' [1830], in K. Nag and D. Burman (eds), *The English Works of Raja Rammohun Roy* Part I, Calcutta: Sadharan Brahmo Samaj, pp. 87–97, 101–27, 129–38.

Roy, S.C. (1941) *Interpretations of the Bhagavad-Gîtá Book 1: The Bhagavad-Gîtá and Modern Scholarship*, London: Luzac & Co.

Sachau, E.C. (trans.) (1989) *Alberuni's India*, Vols I and II, first published 1910, New Delhi: Low Price Publications.

Sai Baba, Sathya (1972) 'Lessons from the Gita'. Available at: http://beaskind.helloyou.ws/askbaba/discourses/d1972/d19720 (accessed 11 July 2003).

Said, E.W. (1995) *Orientalism: Western Conceptions of the Orient*, London: Penguin.

Sanderson, A. (forthcoming) *Śaivism: Development and Impact*, unpublished manuscript kindly supplied by author.

Saraswati, Swami Ambikananda (trans.) (2000) *The Uddhava Gita: The Final Teaching of Krishna*, London: Frances Lincoln.

School Curriculum and Assessment Authority (SCAA) (1994) *Model Syllabuses for Religious Education Model 1: Living Faiths Today*, London: School Curriculum and Assessment Authority.

Schwab, R. (1984) *The Oriental Renaissance: Europe's Rediscovery of India and the East, 1680–1880*, G. Patterson-Black and V. Reinking (trans.), New York: Columbia University Press.

Sharma, A. (1983) 'Introduction: the Gītārthasaṅgraha as a commentary on the Bhagavadgītā', in A. Sharma (trans.), *Abhinavagupta Gītārthasaṅgraha*, Leiden: E.J. Brill, pp. 3–98.

——(1986) *The Hindu Gītā: Ancient and Classical Interpretations of the Bhagavad Gītā*, London: Duckworth.

——(1993) 'Hinduism', in A. Sharma (ed.), *Our Religions*, New York: HarperCollins, pp. 1–67.

Sharpe, E.J. (1975) *Comparative Religion: A History*, London: Duckworth.

——(1977) *Faith Meets Faith: Some Christian Attitudes to Hinduism in the Nineteenth and Twentieth Centuries*, London: SCM Press Ltd.

——(1985) *The Universal Gītā: Western Images of the Bhagavadgītā*, London: Duckworth.

——(2003) 'The study of Hinduism: the setting', in A. Sharma (ed.), *The Study of Hinduism*, Columbia, SC: University of South Carolina Press, pp. 20–55.

Shevtsova, M. (1991) 'Interaction-Interpretation: *The Mahabharata* from a socio-cultural perspective', in D. Williams (ed.), *Peter Brook and* The Mahabharata: *Critical Perspectives*, London: Routledge, pp. 206–27.

Simpson, D.P. (comp.) (1966) *Cassell's New Latin–English English–Latin Dictionary*, fourth edition, London: Cassell.

Simpson, J.A. and Weiner, E.S.C. (comp.) (1989) *The Oxford English Dictionary*, second edition, Oxford: Clarendon Press.

Singer, M. (1972) *When a Great Tradition Modernizes: An Anthropological Approach to Indian Civilization*, Chicago, IL: University of Chicago Press.

Sivananda, Swami (1957) *Ethics of the Bhagavad Gita*, Rishikesh: The Yoga Vedanta University.

——(1961a) *All About Hinduism*, Sivanandanagar: The Divine Life Society.

——(1961b) *Gita Meditations*, Sivanandanagar: The Divine Life Society.

——(1969) *The Bhagavad Gita*, Sivanandanagar: The Divine Life Society.

——(1980) *Practice of Karma Yoga*, Tehri-Garhwal, India: The Divine Life Society.

Smith, B.K. (1989) *Reflections on Resemblance, Ritual and Religion*, Oxford: Oxford University Press.

——(1998) 'Questioning authority: constructions and deconstructions of Hinduism', *International Journal of Hindu Studies*, 2.3: 313–39.

Smith, D. (2003) *Hinduism and Modernity*, Oxford: Blackwell Publishing.

Smith, J.Z. (1982) *Imagining Religion: From Babylon to Jonestown*, Chicago, IL: University of Chicago Press.

——(1998) 'Religion, religions, religious', in M.C. Taylor (ed.), *Critical Terms for Religious Studies*, Chicago, IL: University of Chicago Press, pp. 269–84.

Smith, W.C. (1978) *The Meaning and End of Religion*, London: SPCK.

——(1993) *What is Scripture? A Comparative Approach*, Minneapolis, MN: Fortress Press.

Southey, R. (1844) *The Poetical Works of Robert Southey*, London: Longman, Brown, Green, and Longmans.

Srivastava, K.G. (2002) *Bhagavad-Gītā and the English Romantic Movement*, Delhi: Macmillan India.

Staal, F. (1979) 'Comments: the concept of scripture in the Indian tradition', in M. Juergensmeyer and N.G. Barrier (eds), *Sikh Studies: Comparative Perspectives on a Changing Tradition*, Berkeley Religious Studies Series, Berkeley, CA: Graduate Theological Union, pp. 121–4.

——(1989) *Rules Without Meaning: Rituals, Mantras and the Human Sciences*, Toronto Studies in Religion Vol. 4, New York: Peter Lang.

Subhananda dasa (1978) 'A request to the media: please don't lump us in' reprinted, in E. Bjorkan (ed.), *International Society for Krishna Consciousness*, New York: Garland Publishing 1990, pp. 355–72.

Sugirtharajah, S. (2003) *Imagining Hinduism: A Postcolonial Perspective*, London: Routledge.

Sweetman, W. (2001) 'Unity and plurality: Hinduism and the religions of India in early European scholarship', *Religion*, 31.3: 209–24.

——(2003) ' "Hinduism" and the history of "religion": Protestant presuppositions in the critique of the concept of Hinduism', *Method and Theory in the Study of Religion*, 15.5: 329–53.

Talbot, C. (1995) 'Inscribing the other, inscribing the self: Hindu–Muslim identities in pre-colonial India', *Comparative Studies in Society and History*, 37.4: 692–722.

Telang, K.T. (trans.) (1908) *The Bhagavadgîtâ with the Sanatsugâtîya and the Anugîtâ*, Oxford: Clarendon Press.

Thapar, R. (1985) 'Syndicated Moksha?', *Seminar*, 313 (September): 14–20.

——(1989) 'Imagined religious communities? Ancient history and the modern search for Hindu identity', *Modern Asian Studies*, 23.2: 209–31.

Thoreau, H.D. (1985) *A Week on the Concord and Merrimack Rivers; Walden; or, Life in the Woods; The Maine Woods; Cape Cod*, New York: Literary Classics of the United States.

Tiele, C.P. (1877) *Outlines of the History of Religion to the Spread of Universal Religions*, J.F. Carpenter (trans.), London: Trübner & Co.

——(1886) 'Religions', in *Encyclopaedia Britannica*, ninth edition, Edinburgh: A. & C. Black, 20: 358–71.

Tilak, B.G. (1922) *Bal Gangadhar Tilak: His Writings and Speeches*, third edition, Madras: Ganesh & Co.

Tilak, B.G. (1991) *Śrī Bhagavadgītā-Rahasya or Karma-Yoga-Śāstra*, BH A.S. Sukthankar (trans.), first published in Marathi 1915, seventh English edition, Poona: Tilak Brothers.

Timm, J.R. (1992) 'Introduction: texts in context', in J.R. Timm (ed.), *Texts in Context: Traditional Hermeneutics in South Asia*, Albany, NY: State University of New York Press, pp. 1–13.

Trapnell, J.B. (2001) *Bede Griffiths: A Life in Dialogue*, Albany, NY: State University of New York Press.

Travers, P. (2003) '[Review of] *The Legend of Bagger Vance*', *Rolling Stone*. Available at: http://www.rollingstone.com/reviews/movie/review.asp?mid=77512&afl=imbd (accessed 5 July 2003).

Tuck, A.P. (1990) *Comparative Philosophy and the Philosophy of Scholarship: On the Western Interpretation of Nāgārjuna*, New York: Oxford University Press.

Turan, K. (2000) '*The Legend of Bagger Vance*: Par for the Old Course', *Los Angeles Times*. Available at: http://www.calendarlive.com/templates/misc/printstory.jsp?slug=cl-movie001102–3&section=%2fmovies52Freviews (accessed 18 August 2003).

van Buitenen, J.A.B. (trans.) (1981) *The Bhagavadgītā in the Mahābhārata: A Bilingual Edition*, Chicago, IL: University of Chicago Press.

Vertovec, S. (2000) *The Hindu Diaspora: Comparative Patterns*, London: Routledge.

Vishva Hindu Parishad (VHP) (2003) 'The Origin and Growth of Vishva Hindu Parishad'. Available at: http://www.vhp.org/englishsite/a.origin_growth/origin.htm (accessed 6 January 2003).

Vivekananda, Swami (1985) *The Complete Works of Swami Vivekananda*, Vol. 4, Calcutta: Advaita Ashrama.

——(1992a) *The Complete Works of Swami Vivekananda*, Vol. 5, Calcutta: Advaita Ashrama.

——(1992b) *The Complete Works of Swami Vivekananda*, Vol. 7, Calcutta: Advaita Ashrama.

——(1994a) *The Complete Works of Swami Vivekananda*, Vol. 1, Calcutta: Advaita Ashrama.

——(1994b) *The Complete Works of Swami Vivekananda*, Vol. 8, Calcutta: Advaita Ashrama.

——(1995a) *The Complete Works of Swami Vivekananda*, Vol. 2, Calcutta: Advaita Ashrama.

——(1995b) *The Complete Works of Swami Vivekananda*, Vol. 3, Calcutta: Advaita Ashrama.

——(1995c) *The Complete Works of Swami Vivekananda*, Vol. 6, Calcutta: Advaita Ashrama.

von Stietencron, H. (1991) 'Hinduism: on the proper use of a deceptive term', in G.D. Sontheimer and H. Kulke (eds), *Hinduism Reconsidered*, South Asian Studies No. XXIV, New Delhi: Manohar, pp. 11–27.

——(1995) 'Religious configurations in pre-Muslim India and the modern concept of Hinduism', in V. Dalmia and H. von Stietencron (eds), *Representing Hinduism: The Construction of Religious Traditions and National Identity*, New Delhi: Sage Publications, pp. 51–81.

Weightman, S. (1997) 'Hinduism', in J.R. Hinnells (ed.), *A New Handbook of Living Religions*, Harmondsworth: Penguin, pp. 261–309.

Wilkins, C. (1785) 'The translator's preface' and 'The Bhăgvăt-Gēētā or dialogues of Krēēshnă and Ărjŏŏn', in C. Wilkins (trans.), *The Bhâgvât-Gēētā or Dialogues of Krēēshnă and Ărjŏŏn; In Eighteen Lectures; With Notes*, first published 1785 in London by C. Nourse, reprinted 1972 in New York by Scholars' Facsimiles and Reprints, pp. 23–135.

Williams, D. (1991) 'Theatre of innocence and of experience: Peter Brook's international centre an introduction', in D. Williams (ed.), *Peter Brook and* The Mahabharata: *Critical Perspectives*, London: Routledge, pp. 3–28.

Wilmshurst, W.L. (1906) *The Chief Scripture of India (The Bhagavad Gita) and its Relation to Present Events*, London: Philip Wellby.

Winternitz, M. (comp.) (1910) *A General Index to the Names and Subject Matter of the Sacred Books of the East*, Sacred Books of the East Vol. 50, Oxford: Clarendon Press.

Wollheim, R. (1963) *Hume on Religion*, The Fontana Library: Theology and Philosophy, London: Collins.

Woodcock, G. (1972) *Dawn and the Darkest Hour: A Study of Aldous Huxley*, London: Faber & Faber.

Young, K.K. (1993) 'The Indian secular state under Hindu attack: a new perspective on the crisis of legitimisation', in N. Smart and S. Thakur (eds), *Ethical and Political Dilemmas of Modern India*, Basingstoke: Macmillan, pp. 194–234.

Yule, H. and Burrell, A.C. (comp.) (1996) *Hobson-Jobson: The Anglo-Indian Dictionary*, first published 1886, Ware: Wordsworth Editions.

Zaehner, R.C. (1957) *Mysticism Sacred and Profane: An Inquiry into some Varieties of Praeternatural Experience*, Oxford: Clarendon Press.

——(1966a) *Hinduism*, second edition, Oxford: Oxford University Press.

——(trans.) (1966b) *Hindu Scriptures*, London: J.M. Dent.

——(1970) *Concordant Discord: The Interdependence of Faiths*, Oxford: Clarendon Press.

——(1973) *The Bhagavad-Gītā with a Commentary Based on the Original Sources*, First published 1969, Oxford: Oxford University Press.

Zavos, J. (2000) *The Emergence of Hindu Nationalism in India*, New Delhi: Oxford University Press.

——(2001) 'Defending Hindu tradition: Sanatana Dharma as a symbol of Orthodoxy in colonial India', *Religion*, 31: 109–23.

INDEX